YOUR GARDEN
MAKEOVER

YOUR GARDEN MAKEOVER

THE COMPLETE GUIDE TO GARDEN RENEWAL

LIZ DOBBS

AND

SARAH WOOD

MARSHALL PUBLISHING • LONDON

A Marshall Edition
Conceived, edited and designed by
Marshall Editions
The Orangery
161 New Bond Street
London W1Y 9PA

First published in the UK in 2000 by Marshall Publishing Ltd

Project Editor Stuart Cooper
Editor Gwen Rigby
Consultant Editor Catriona Tudor Erler
Proof Reader Lindsay McTeague
Art Editors Hugh Schermuly, Nick Buzzard
Design Assistant Sally Geeve
Photography Andrew Sydenham, Adrian Weinbrecht
Photography Stylist Frances de Rees
Illustrator Gill Tomblin
Picture Research Claire Taylor
Managing Editor Anne Yelland
Managing Art Editor Helen Spencer
Editorial Director Ellen Dupont
Art Director Dave Goodman
Editorial Coordinator Ros Highstead
Indexer Dorothy Frame
DTP Lesley Gilbert
Production Nikki Ingram, Amanda Mackie

Originated in Singapore by Chroma Graphics
Printed and bound in Dubai by Oriental Press

10 9 8 7 6 5 4 3 2 1

ISBN   1-84028-310-6

Note: Measurements are given in metric and in imperial.
Follow one set or the other, as they are not interchangeable.

CONTENTS

INTRODUCTION

The perfect garden will suit your needs and reflect your tastes – but since we are all individuals, what is perfect for one person is almost certain to be wrong for another. Finding out what is right for you, then making it happen, is both the key to great gardens and the idea behind this book.

When you look out of the window at your garden, do you feel cheered or irritated? Have you moved into the home of your dreams recently, only to find that the garden doesn't live up to your hopes? Or have you long thought that your garden isn't quite "you", or doesn't suit what may be changed circumstancess – a young family, for example, can make a once perfect retreat for a working couple wholly impractical.

YOU CAN MAKE CHANGES

The first step to having the perfect garden is to acknowledge that you are at liberty to make any changes you want. None of us by choice lives with wallpaper, furniture or curtains chosen by someone else – especially someone we don't know. Yet that is precisely what many of us do with the garden. If its lawns are neatly mown, roses clipped and flowerbeds waiting for annual bedding, we continue to mow, clip and plant, even if we don't particularly like a large lawn or rose bushes. Similarly, we don't decorate our houses and leave them alone – our homes change as we do, as colours move in and out of fashion, and as our families grow larger or smaller. So it should be with our gardens.

Often, the same people who enjoy sitting in the shade on a park bench, or relaxing in a beautiful paradise garden, or meditating in an austere courtyard garden don't feel able to re-create something similar at home. But with imagination and some work you can re-create almost any type of garden. Giving yourself permission to do what you want is the first step to achieving a garden that is right for you.

WHAT DO YOU LIKE?

The inital step to getting what you want is, of course, to work out what that is. The clearer you are about what your dream garden would be, and the more vividly you imagine yourself using it, the more likely you are to achieve it. There are two ways to work this out. The first is to decide what you don't like. You may, for example, not feel comfortable with the old-fashioned type of gardens, in which clipping, training and spraying are vital to maintain the look. Perhaps you prefer the minimalist, spare look, or have an easy-going personality that is not comfortable with the idea of bending nature to your will. Think about the type of person you are and your tastes and you will find that a rough image of the type of garden that would suit you starts to emerge.

Second, gather magazine pictures of gardens that inspire or move you. Don't be put off by thinking "I couldn't do that", or "I don't have the time or the money to re-create something like

▽ **COLOURFUL HERBS**
Herbs can be attractive as well as useful. Here a group of colourful herbs, in soft cool tones, is set against a pale grey stone wall. Decorative varieties, which are still good to cook with, are used. They include sage (Salvia officinalis 'Tricolor') and golden marjoram (Origanum vulgare 'Aureum').

▷ **FRESH FOODS**
There is nothing to beat the satisfaction of growing fine vegetables. Worthy of first prize at the village show, this cabbage epitomizes country life and the traditional cottage-garden dream.

△ **COLOUR AND TEXTURE**
In this quietly welcoming front garden, colours are restrained, with different tones of green and a flash of white variegation from the dogwood (Cornus alba 'Elegantissima'). Great depth and interest are added by the use of different textures, from the glossy leaves of the Mexican orange (Choisya ternata) and the fine fronds of the fern to the neat, clipped box edging the path.

that". At this stage what you are trying to get is an idea of themes, colors, styles and plants that may suit you. When you have a sheaf of cuttings, look long and hard at them and try to see if a pattern is emerging: are there several in which water forms an integral part of the design? Are all the plants that attract you tall, sculptural and monochromatic, or are the gardens you like best riots of spring and summer colour? Are there plenty of sheltered spots in which you can see yourself relaxing with a book, or are you more attracted to images of family barbecues while the kids play in a tree house?

Once you've decided what you want to do, remember that you don't need to do anything drastic right away. As people become more environmentally aware, they realize that it is possible to leave a garden alone and observe its wildlife for some time, without it going to rack and ruin. And if you find that you like a slightly tangled look, you can learn how to make a planned wilderness. Once you rid yourself of the feeling that you must "do something now", you can start to enjoy your garden, learn its real problems and undoubted assets, and make concrete plans for change.

WHERE DO I START?

This is a book to help and inspire you. It will work for you whether you've moved into a new house and can't face dealing with the garden yet

or are looking out of the window at your old, familiar garden and thinking: "I really must do something about this."

Chapter One shows you how to take stock of your garden, how to look more closely at it in order to analyse the problems and see the potential. You'll learn to assess what you have. Time spent establishing your garden's good and bad points is seldom wasted.

What sort of garden do you have now? Is it messy or extremely tidy? Is it too smart in style or too romantic for your taste? Maybe you have only an empty yard, or a small corner that is not really a garden at all. What are the good features – the sunny spots, the unexpected treasures? Are the problems serious ones that need sorting out fast? Or can they be ignored or transformed into assets? We also show you how to draw up a quick survey and make a plan for converting your garden.

If you're desperate, or simply impatient, Chapter Two offers plenty of "quick fixes" – easy

▽ **CHANGE OF USE**

An old outhouse has been converted into a studio. Even though there is no conventional garden as such, an enjoyable space, sheltered from the weather, has been created by means of a seat in the sun and a few flowering plants in pots.

solutions to common problems that won't compromise your long-term plans. You can import colour or instant maturity with plants in containers, revamp the lawn, add one or two key touches to make an immediate difference or create the atmosphere for an outdoor party.

LONG-TERM PROBLEM SOLVING

Chapter Three systematically offers you the widest options for creative solutions, both practical and visual, to any garden problem. The problem may be one of design – the garden is too big, too small, simply the wrong shape, dull, overlooked, or has no play space. Or it may be more fundamental – the type of soil or the microclimate is not appropriate for the plants you want to grow. Perhaps the plants themselves are the problem – roses and vegetables that you have no time to tend, overgrown shrubs, overpowering trees, unwieldy hedges or tangling climbers that have taken over. Finally, problems involving the

garden's structures are addressed – how to disguise a shed or garage, make steps or a pond safe and design a conservatory for plants or people. For every problem, practical, innovative solutions are offered.

Chapter Four presents the origins and key features of some of the best-known garden styles. Understanding the characteristics of each style will help you decide which elements will work best for you. This may help you to identify the influences that have shaped your garden, or inspire you to adopt a particular style when planning your new garden. Some types of gardens will be more appropriate for you than others, depending on the age and style of your house and the local landscape and climate.

PUTTING IT INTO PRACTICE

To help you implement your plans, Chapter Five explains basic gardening techniques. You'll learn how to clear the garden and carry out renovation tasks such as re-laying uneven paving or pointing brickwork. Planting and pruning; how to lay a new lawn or reshape the old one; what to do about weeds; and useful tools are all illustrated and described.

Gardens don't have to be an obligation or a concession to other people's expectations. They certainly shouldn't be all hard work and no fun. Your garden is probably one of the few areas of your life where you can express yourself. A garden that suits you is a successful garden. We hope that our book will help you find yourself in your garden.

Liz Dobbs

Liz Dobbs

Sarah Wood

Sarah Wood

◁ **BOLD STATEMENTS**
Emphasizing one colour in a bold way can create a charming effect, as this riot of pink shows. Flowering merrily together are bougainvillea, with deep rich tones, plump-flowered hydrangea and busy lizzies, tucked in below.

▽ **GREEN AND GREY**
In this arrangement in green and grey, the fierce shapes of yucca and agave, fescue grasses and fluffy pennisetum hold their own against the sharp lines of the concrete building and edges of the beds, mulched with slate and wood chips.

TAKING STOCK

△ **GRAVEL GARDEN**
Gravel forms an effective ground surface, giving a calming, flowing effect similar to water, but it needs raking regularly to avoid a buildup of weeds. Many sun-loving plants enjoy gravel as a growing medium and, if you let them, will grow out into it and seed themselves, creating a more natural effect.

◁ **RAMPANT ROSES**
The wooden bridge leads through a mass of flowers and fascinating foliage to a grassed area beyond, where a table and chairs stand invitingly in the shade of a tree. You might want to upgrade this lawn – or you could just leave it as it is and keep it as a wild area, mowing it once a month.

The most important thing to do before you can renew your garden is to look long and hard at it. Get to know it well and decide what you do and do not like about it. Does it match your tastes in design and planting? Are any elements missing? Does it suit your and your family's lifestyle? In this chapter we will show how to analyse the conditions and assess the problems. Once you know what you are dealing with and have a clear idea about what you want, the task of renewing your garden will become much easier. To make things easier still, we will also show you how to look at things slightly differently and turn what might appear to be problems into opportunities.

FIRST STEPS

Taking stock begins with learning about the growing conditions in your garden. This will help you to assess the existing plants and choose the right new plants. Along the way you will also have to make some difficult decisions about what to keep and what to remove.

The growing conditions in your garden include the physical characteristics of the soil as well as factors such as sun, wind and climate – all of which can vary even in a small garden.

SOIL TYPE

The first thing to do is to find out which type of soil you have. Pick up a handful and feel it between your fingers. Does it stick together in a lump, or is it hard-baked and bricklike, with deep cracks? Either quality indicates a clay soil, which can be hard and heavy to work, but rich and fertile once cultivated. Clay soil is a "cold" soil – it takes a long time to warm up in spring. If your soil is hard and cracked and pale orange-yellow in colour, the topsoil may have been removed altogether, leaving only subsoil. In this case, bringing in topsoil may be the only solution.

Sandy soil is gritty and does not lump together like clay. It is light and easy to work and warms up quickly in spring. However, sandy soils tend to be poor in nutrients and should be mulched with organic matter; extra fertilizer may be necessary too. Although chalky soils are similar to sandy soils in use, they are always alkaline.

The perfect soil is a loam – a mixture of sand and clay, with abundant humus, which gives it a crumbly texture and a dark, rich look.

Another important element is the soil's acidity. A soil-testing kit, available cheaply from garden centres, will quickly give you a pH reading, indicating whether you have acid soil (pH 4 to 6), which is good for lime-hating plants like rhododendrons, neutral soil (pH 7) or limy (alkaline) soil (pH 8). See also pages 92–97.

As well as assessing your own garden, look at the gardens next door and talk to your neighbours about what they grow. This will all help build up a picture of which plants suit the local soil.

MICROCLIMATE

The microclimate – the climate in each area of the garden – will affect what you choose to plant where and how you use the space.

Is it always windy in one part of the garden? There might be a wind-tunnel effect created by buildings, or you may be exposed to the prevailing wind of the area. In a large garden, some trees may have been bent by the wind, while others grow upright, indicating a more sheltered spot.

Note also the position of the garden in relation to the sun – known as its aspect – and the amount of sun or shade each area receives at different times of day. Snowdrops may flower a week earlier on sunny slopes than in cold, shady places.

WAIT A YEAR

The traditional advice when you inherit a garden is to wait for a year before doing anything, to see what plants come up. If you cannot wait that long, we have some suggestions for immediate changes that will not affect any long-term plans (see Chapter 2, Quick Fixes). However, knowing how your garden behaves through the year is important if you want to make major alterations such as adding a new border or a patio.

△ **SOIL SENSE**
Digging the soil will make it easier to plant. It also opens up the soil and lets more air into it, improving its structure and stimulating microorganisms to break down waste. After digging, cover the soil with compost or lawn clippings to prevent it from becoming compacted by people treading on it or by machinery.

Note which parts of the garden are in sun and shade at different times of the year; if there is a prevailing wind, what direction does it come from and does this change through the year; are there places that are particularly exposed or sheltered? Are there beds that dry out completely in summer; do you have a patch of lawn that becomes waterlogged in winter?

△ WINTER PLANNING

In winter it is easier to see what structural changes might be needed. In this case, clearing some of the plants away from the central path will re-emphasize the main axis of the garden.

◁ SPRING SURPRISE

A glorious display of yellow and white daffodils is an unexpected delight. It is always worth waiting to see what comes up in a garden before making changes.

ASK A PROFESSIONAL

A professional garden designer can provide invaluable advice about your existing conditions, and although you will have to pay for this, it could save you considerable time and possibly money spent on making the wrong decisions. Obtain a list of local designers from a professional gardening organization. When seeking quotes from a designer, ask how much they charge per hour, whether travelling time is included, and how long the consultation is likely to take.

PLANTS TO KEEP

Whether you consult a designer or not, you will need to decide what plants are worth keeping. This will of course depend on your tastes and also on your assessment of the whole garden, but there are some general guidelines that may help.

Plants with a long season Does the plant have more than one season of interest – for example, beautiful unfurling leaves in spring and a fine display of flowers in summer? Plants that look good in winter are useful, such as mahonia, which is evergreen and winter flowering.

Ground covers These are good for covering bare soil and preventing weeds. They are mainly smaller shrubs like hebes and herbaceous plants such as *Geranium* species, but large shrubs that cover the ground are also useful.

Plants for problem areas Plants that tolerate dry shade, such as *Prunus laurocerasus* 'Otto Luyken' and *Viburnum tinus* are valuable, as are those for hot, dry areas, like *Hebe pinguifolia* 'Pagei'.

PLANTS THAT CAN COME OUT

Again, this is largely a subjective decision: if you hate rhododendrons, no matter whether everyone else envies you, they will have to go. But there may be some plants in your garden that are just not earning their keep.

Plants with a short season If you are short on space, think about replacing plants that look good for a few weeks and boring for the rest of the year with plants that have good autumn colour or berries, as well as flowers. Lilacs, for example, are splendid in spring but otherwise rather dull.

Invasive plants Some plants can get out of control, such as bamboos, which spread quickly and may overwhelm slower-growing shrubs. Many herbaceous plants are invasive, but most are easy to dig up and can fill space until you need it.

▽ **WINTER TREAT**
A drift of cyclamen is a wonderful treasure to find in a newly acquired garden in winter. They have charming flowers and beautiful mottled foliage and are among the few plants that revel in the dry shade of tree roots.

Lady's mantle *(Alchemilla mollis)* is a case in point. It is a very pretty plant, but if it likes your garden you will never entirely get rid of it. Other plants are prolific self-seeders that might pop up anywhere, either effectively or not – sometimes the best results are created by chance. Self-seeding plants are not really a problem – they simply call for some creative weeding.

Bear in mind that if you remove a plant, weeds and surrounding plants will quickly colonize the space so wait until you have a replacement or are ready to redesign the whole area.

PLANT POSITION

The more difficult decisions relate to the position of a plant. Problems of plants casting shade are covered later, but if you have to remove a plant because of where it is rather than its appearance, consider moving it. Wait until autumn or late winter; or if this is not possible, wait for a spell of mild, damp weather. Plants with small rootballs and fibrous roots, like rhododendrons, generally move easily. Those with one main root, like a taproot, or fleshy potatolike roots, such as peonies, will not usually move happily (see page 207).

▽ **WELL-PLACED PLANTS**
These plants are happy in the hot sun and dry soil of British horticulturalist Beth Chatto's gravel garden in the UK. They need little maintenance, apart from keeping an eye on the yellow-spired verbascum, which could seed itself around too prolifically if allowed.

AN UNTIDY GARDEN

Tidiness is a state of mind: one person's mess is another's romantic tangle. The secret is to decide which view you take, then act accordingly. Left to nature, of course, every garden would tend towards disorder – even romantics must decide just how much tangle they can live with.

Some kinds of untidiness are the result of badly chosen and placed plants or poor initial construction of structures such as paths, patios, walls and fences. Infrequent maintenance of either plants or structures can also lead to problems. If these are serious enough to pose a threat to safety or security they must obviously be put right at once (see Chapter 3, Problem Solving).

Once you have fixed these serious problems you can work out what degree of visual untidiness you are able to tolerate.

▽ **WONDERFULLY WILD?**
Iris pseudacorus and oxeye daisies compete happily with the long grass beside an overgrown pond. This is a haven for wildlife – but does it appeal to you?

SELF-ANALYSIS

One way to assess your tolerance level is to ask yourself some questions about your home:

⊘ Do you keep it clean and tidy with everything in its place?

⊘ Does children's mess bother you, and do you have to clear it up straight away?

⊘ If you have visitors, does it make you anxious if your house looks untidy?

⊘ Do you like to plan events such as parties well ahead of time?

If the answer to all these questions is yes, then an untidy garden is not for you and drastic action is needed (see Chapter 5, Gardening Basics). You will still have to work out exactly what you want (see the checklist on page 39), and looking carefully at the elements of the mess is essential.

If, on the other hand, some of your answers are no, then with a little ingenuity your messy garden might easily be converted into an asset.

MAKING A JUNGLE GARDEN

An impenetrable tangle can easily form the basis of a jungle garden. All you need to do is make it look intentional: enclose or fence it and it becomes a wildlife sanctuary. If you want to play on the romantic theme, add sculptures and a trellised arbour with scented climbers and seating for two. Peer into the tangle and study it carefully – there may well be some hidden treasures in there, such as a rare plant or an antique statue. See also pages 106–107.

If there are lots of brambles and you do not want to make a wildlife garden, just clear them away and see what is left: you may be pleasantly surprised at the treasures you find.

There may be shrubs that have grown into each other, and you will need to decide which to keep (see pages 116–117). Make sure you remove the right plants and get the roots up; hire a shredder and you will have lots of useful mulch. Sometimes a suckering shrub, such as snowberry *(Symphoricarpos albus),* can take over, in which event you can either have a jungle garden or take it all out and replant one section with its roots in a buried container so it cannot spread.

An overgrown lawn is easy to deal with. You could simply treat it as a wildflower meadow. Mow a strip one mower wide around the edge of the lawn, and it will look intentional (see also pages 96–97) .

Alternatively, hire a heavy-duty lawn mower and mow the grass down. (You can use the hay to start off a compost heap.) Mow the grass once a week, and before long you will have created a usable patch of lawn.

◁ **DANGEROUS MESS**
Damaged structures such as patios should be cleared of debris and repaired as a matter of urgency to prevent accidents.

▽ **PROMISING PERGOLA**
With a little pruning and tying-in, this rose pergola will form the perfect centrepiece for a romantic garden. Place a table and chairs beneath, and it will be ready for a moonlit supper.

A JUNK-FILLED GARDEN

Neglected gardens often contain all kinds of rubbish, dumped by builders, uncaring owners or both. Do not despair – this usually looks a worse problem than it actually is, and most garden junk can be cleared quickly. Alternatively, with a little lateral thinking much of it can be put to good use.

△ **NOT JUST JUNK**
This may look unpromising, but there are some useful logs and wooden beams, and no doubt one or two potential plant containers under the debris.

Dealing with garden junk becomes much easier if it is put into some sort of order.

Builders' rubble Some gardens consist of builders' rubble covered with a thin layer of topsoil. If you don't want to go to the trouble and expense of replacing the subsoil, you can strip off the topsoil, leave the rubble and pave it over. Indeed, everything in this category can be used to form a foundation for patios and paths. Even if you do not want to pave over the rubble, a neighbour might want to use it. Otherwise, you could regard it as a specialized habitat for growing desert plants or other species that need good drainage, such as alpines.

Logs and bits of wood These form perfect wildlife habitats. If you have to move them, put them all together somewhere out of the way. They will be colonized by insects and small mammals, and eventually rot down to form good humus. Collections of tree branches make wonderful dens and hides for children. Three fairly straight branches can be tied together to make a tripod for climbers. Straight logs can be used to edge a raised bed or for growing vegetables or plants that require special soil, such as acid-lovers in an alkaline area. They also make good retaining edges for informal steps, which are filled with hardcore and surfaced with wood chippings.

Clay plant pots, chimney pots Use these to create a display of container plants on a patio or balcony. The tall, straight old-fashioned clay chimney pots provide a good contrast to the bushy shapes of geraniums in clay pots. Put the plants in plastic containers and wedge them in the chimney pots.

Old sinks, cast-iron bathtubs If you do not want to salvage these for your home or sell them, you can use them as containers for alpines or other specialist plants. They can also be used to make an instant water garden, complete with water lilies and goldfish.

Tin buckets, old watering cans Such items can just be cleaned up and artistically arranged on low walls or patios. If you want to plant in the buckets, remember to punch a hole in the base; or if they leak slowly, they might be good for moisture-loving plants.

Bedframes, chairs, old mattresses, old bicycles It is difficult to think of a use for an old mattress, otherwise, all these bits of junk can be used. Wooden chairs can sometimes be restored with a coat of paint or preservative and placed in odd corners in the garden. Metal chairs, old bicycles and bedframes can be used as idiosyncratic sculptures – good for growing plants over – or even as gates or fences, but this requires some imagination. Otherwise, they may have to be cleared away.

Ovens, refrigerators, an old car Ovens should be disposed of, but the metal grid shelves inside them can be reclaimed and used for barbecues.

SAFETY MATTERS

Old furniture Old mattresses can contain broken springs so do not let children jump on them; they are also fire hazards. Generally it is worth inspecting any piece of furniture before allowing children to use it for games and dens.

Refrigerators These have really dangerous doors, completely excluding air, and can suffocate a small child who might try to hide there. Older refrigerators also contain CFC gases and should be disposed of professionally. Your local authorities will advise. Children could also get trapped in old ovens.

Timber Most wood now used in the garden is impregnated with wood preservative. It is not good to burn this on a bonfire as it may give off noxious fumes.

Old cars These can contain many things that are irresistible and also dangerous to children, such as batteries full of highly corrosive acid, as well as more obvious dangers like doors with locks.

Old tools If you have young children, anything that is sharp or pointed, such as a scythe, should be either disposed of or put out of reach.

Sinks, bathtubs, buckets Anything that can hold water – no matter how shallow – could be a drowning hazard for a young child.

Bags of chemicals Many garden sheds have old and unreadable tins that may contain dangerous chemicals. These should not just be thrown away – again, telephone your local authorities for advice.

Broken glass Take care when poking around in the soil as there may be fragments of glass.

Refrigerators are dangerous and should be removed. Old cars take up a lot of valuable space in a garden and are potentially dangerous if you have young children. However, if you do not need this space and the garden is not used by children, you could leave a car to rust and grow ivy through it to make a modern romantic ruin.

Lawn roller If you don't think you will use it to roll your lawn or drive because it is so heavy, you can safely leave it to rust away quietly beside a shed or under an apple tree, as a reminder of days long gone. The same approach could be taken

with old, rusting tools such as mowers, wheelbarrows and spades, as long as they are placed where they will pose no danger.

Car tyres Secured with strong rope to a stout tree branch, these make wonderful swings, if you do not mind your children getting grubby. They make good dens, too – in fact kids just love to play with them, so you will not have to do very much. You may have seen them used as containers, possibly painted, although this is not to everyone's taste. They make good wormeries – somewhere to use up vegetable scraps if you do not have enough weeds or grass clippings to build up a substantial compost heap.

▽ **CREATIVE RECYCLING**
This old sink has been used to add another planting dimension to a small garden. Filled to the brim and stocked with water plants, it is surrounded by shade-lovers including foxgloves, Jacob's ladder, Primula vialii, pink and silver Lamium, meadow rue (Thalictrum) and ferns.

A BORING GARDEN

A garden can be the most thrilling place on earth – stimulating all the senses at once and evoking a range of moods from tranquillity to passion; gardens can inspire, tempt, even shock. If your own garden leaves you cold, you may need to make some fairly radical changes to the design and planting.

Many gardens are boring simply because they are empty, comprising a lawn and little else. In this case, you have a clean slate to work on and can start from scratch. Free your imagination and ask yourself what your ideal garden would look like. You may not be able to afford everything at once, but the cost and effort can be spread over several seasons or even years.

A wide range of garden styles and features is covered later in this book, but if it would help to consult a quick checklist of garden features now, see page 39. You can also find inspiration from other books and from television programmes, and by collecting tearsheets from magazines to create a mood board (see page 31).

DULL SHAPE

Is it the shape of your garden that makes it seem boring? If you have a long, thin garden, one option is to actually accentuate the shape – by narrowing the lawn, making it appear even longer, and putting a feature at the end so that the whole garden is about one visual statement. This takes confidence, but it is a simple idea that will not call for much upkeep. Another solution is to divide the garden with shrub plantings or trellis panels (see pages 60–61) to create several "rooms", each with a distinct mood, theme or function.

If your garden is much wider than it is long, you may be able to see all of it at once and it may lack any sense of surprise or mystery. This is more

▽ **THE PERFECT LAWN**
An expanse of lawn makes a good contrast to a more enclosed or densely planted area, as well as a useful surface, but a garden that is dominated by its lawn can look bleak and empty.

difficult to deal with, and calls for careful reshaping to enlarge the apparent length or to lead the eye in a different direction.

It is essential here to work out the various functions you want the garden to perform so that you can create different areas for each one, again separating them with planting or trellis. If you are lucky enough to have an attractive view beyond your boundary, use the Japanese technique of "borrowed landscape" – open up your boundary with a "window" of trellis and frame the view.

If the problem is that the "design" of your garden comprises just a central lawn with a straight border on either side, you could copy theatre designers, and bring out "wings" from the sides. This will give a sense of flow and create distinct spaces in the garden (see pages 78–79).

LACK OF DIRECTION

Some gardens just do not make sense – they offer no clues about where to go or where to sit. This is often the case with houses that sit in the centre of a plot: the front garden is sometimes large, with a few plants gathered in one place, and you can see around both sides of the house to the back, which looks very similar. The entire space merges into a dull sameness, with no sense of movement from one part to another.

In this case, you need to define each area of the garden, which again means deciding on the function of each part. Think about the working spaces that you need – for the rubbish bins, compost heap, dog kennel, lawn mower, greenhouse, toolshed, bike shed – and where they would most usefully be positioned. Then think about where you want to sit, and what you want to look at while you are sitting there – probably not the washing line and compost area. As you think about how you want to use the garden, a way of dividing the space will become clear.

Next think about screening one area from another. As well as trellis screens or planting, you could use buildings or structures such as a shed or pergola. Other areas, like a large, calm expanse of lawn, can be left open. Because these open spaces will contrast with smaller enclosed areas, the effect will be even more satisfying.

A NEW HOUSE

With a new house, developers generally put in a minimal amount of unimaginative landscape just to get the house sold. Because the developers are working to a building schedule, rather than a horticultural one, the landscaping is often done at a time of year when it is not ideal to plant.

If shrubs have been planted, or your lawn has been laid, in the heat of summer, they may not start to grow well until the damper, cooler weather of autumn arrives. Water a newly planted garden well, keeping it moist until the roots have had a chance to grow into the ground and the plants have become established.

If the lawn in a new house stays determinedly brown, or if dips and bumps appear after it has been watered in, then you may have a more serious problem.

△ **WELL FOCUSED**
A simple way of enlivening a dull layout is to create a focal point at the end of the garden. This seating area is a visual as well as a literal resting place; it also gives the garden a sense of direction.

It could be that the builders disposed of the rubble left from building the house by spreading it over the ground and laying turf or a thin layer of topsoil over it to make a "garden". One solution would be to remove the lawn and pave over most of the area, leaving pockets filled with good soil for the plants. But if you want a garden with shrub and flower borders and a lawn, you will have to remove the turf and dig out as much of the rubble as possible, before bringing in new topsoil. This is an expensive solution, however, and you may have to resort to some slow soil-building, while creating one or two areas of good soil for a few large plants.

Builders will often include a small, poured-concrete patio at the back of the house. To keep costs down, they don't worry about whether the patio is in scale with the house or garden, or even if it is big enough to hold a table and chairs for *al fresco* dining. To extend the living space of your house, one of your first projects might be to enlarge the patio, perhaps even resurfacing it with a more attractive material than plain concrete.

Developers often plant a narrow range of plants. Sometimes they are showy plants that are planted to flower at the time you move in. Alternatively, they may be what are known as landscapers' plants – serviceable evergreens, which are very tough but not usually very exciting. The one advantage of these is that they will be young plants and, therefore, easy to transplant if you want to move them around.

△ IN THE PUBLIC EYE
While a boring back garden can be kept as a guilty secret, a front garden is on permanent public display. This one could easily be improved by using tough evergreens in terracotta pots and adding a smartly painted gate at the side.

▷ LESS IS MORE?
A problem with some gardens is that the plants are confined to a narrow strip at the front of the house. Here the border is completely out of scale with the extensive lawn, a problem that is exacerbated by the thinness of the planting.

It is best not to throw them out, since many evergreens will grow in difficult places and they can be useful as screens and as foils to more colourful specimens.

PLANTING PROBLEMS

Some gardens have plenty of beautiful, well-grown plants, but the planting beds themselves do not quite work. Look at their position and shape. A common problem is that all the planting is bunched along the front of the house or down the side borders. If you want to create new beds or reshape existing ones (see pages 78–79), consider moving some of the present plants to new positions – you can try different effects without having to buy new plants. Once you are satisfied that the basic shape is right, you can then add to them (see also page 207).

FUNCTIONAL FRONT GARDENS

Sometimes it is the front garden that looks boring. A well-designed front garden can provide a frame for your house, give a welcoming impression to callers, and create a sense of privacy inside your home. A front garden also gives all sorts of messages about you – so "boring" is probably not the effect you want!

Again, analyse what is causing the problem. Is the space strictly functional – an oversized driveway with the plants, if any, squeezed around the edge? Is there nothing to frame the front door but a couple of empty pots? Perhaps you have a fussy little gate and a path that nobody uses because the most direct route is across the lawn, making a bare patch. Or maybe there is a little square of lawn that is a nuisance to mow because you have to bring the mower around from the back of the house. Perhaps the hedges are so high it looks as if you are a recluse – or you may have no privacy. There might be a wonderful display of bulbs in spring, and nothing else all year round.

All of these problems are easily remedied, once you have identified them (see pages 80–81).

△ **SHOWY SHED**
Sheds are often thought of as boring or unattractive and banished to the corner of the garden. However, there is no reason why a shed cannot be given a starring role by painting it attractively and adding some trellis and flowering creepers.

A TIME-CONSUMING GARDEN

The lawns are neat and tidy, the flowers are grown to perfection, and
there is not a weed in sight; the vegetables look as if they would win first
prize at a show. You have inherited a perfect garden, from someone who was
clearly a more devoted gardener than you. But what do you do now?

△ **HARD WORK**
Knot gardens may be charming
to look at, but the hedges
require extremely accurate
trimming to keep them level.
Furthermore, if the planting
involves different species these
may grow at different rates, so
you will not be able to trim
them all at the same time.

▷ **PROBLEM POTS**
A whole garden of containers is
extremely time-consuming.
These pots may need to be
watered twice a day in hot
weather and regularly checked
for slugs and snails that may be
lurking between them.

A perfect gardener is a hard act to follow. Even if you are a carefree sort of person, there is bound to be a nagging feeling of guilt at letting the garden go wild. Don't worry – it is possible to have a wonderful garden that does not require nearly so much maintenance and is a lot more relaxing.

What is more, the perfect garden may not be as good as it seems. If it is dependent on chemical treatments against pests such as aphids and slugs, an over-tidy garden can be a lifeless affair. It can become a minefield for birds, which may die from eating the poisoned slugs, and a starvation camp for helpful insects such as ladybirds and hoverflies, which would normally devour the aphids. A perfect lawn is wonderful to look at, but because it is composed exclusively of one plant – a situation never found in nature – it is non-sustainable and takes a lot of chemicals and precious water to keep it looking good. So you don't need to feel too bad if you let things go a bit.

Practically speaking, there are plenty of real advantages in inheriting this sort of garden: the hard work and clearing have been done, and you will have time, with just a few tasks, to allow it to sit for a year while you decide what to keep and what to change. The main thing that needs to be done, to lower the maintenance immediately, is to cover all the bare earth in sight with a 5-cm (2-in) layer of mulch. This will keep the weeds at bay while you think. Mow the lawn every two weeks, rather than weekly – if the grass is left a little longer it will withstand drought better. Then have a close look at the garden.

HIGH-MAINTENANCE ELEMENTS
It is worth examining the various elements of this sort of garden in some detail. You can then decide which you would like to keep and which to eliminate.

Hedges Formal hedges can be labour-intensive. Some, like privet, must be clipped several times a year. Others, such as box and yew, look their best when they are quite formally clipped, with good straight lines on top and at the sides. Less formal hedges or those with larger leaves, like beech or laurel, which can be allowed to bush out and make a softer outline, are easier to maintain, requiring just an annual trim. For lower maintenance, it is better to grow an irregular line of mixed evergreen shrubs, which will give a similar screening effect.

The most time-consuming features are patterns of low hedges, such as knots or parterres. You will either have to clip them frequently or take them out.

⊲ **PRODUCTIVE GARDEN**
The straw mulch around the strawberries in this potager will keep down weeds and reduce the need for watering, but a vegetable garden is by nature time-consuming, and one surrounded by clipped hedging is doubly hard work.

⊲**TRAINED FRUIT**
Training fruit trees requires dedication. An apple tree trained as a globe must be pruned both in summer and winter to keep its outline, otherwise it will grow out and become an unsightly bush.

Containers Displays of pots and other containers can look stunning, but this is very high-maintenance gardening. It is mostly the watering that takes time, but containers do need more care anyway. This is partly because they are so noticeable – any straggly plants have to be tended to or replaced immediately because they are not partially hidden by other more healthy specimens as they would be in a border. They must be clipped and flowers must be deadheaded.

Lawns Especially in a dry climate, where they are not a natural feature and will require constant watering, lawns can be one of the most time-consuming elements. If you want the "putting green" type of lawn, you will have to remove every weed and also any coarser grasses. Even an average-quality lawn will have to be edged and mowed regularly. A wildflower meadow is a much easier alternative. It will need mowing just once a month, except for paths, which need mowing once a week. In time, the meadow will bloom with daisies and other pretty flowers that are outlawed from lawns (see pages 108–109).

Small flowerbeds Flowerbeds that are small and surrounded by lawn are very time-consuming. Mowing around them is tricky, especially if the lawn paths are too narrow for a mower. Unless the edges are clipped, though, the grass will grow into the beds. Eliminating any small strips of grass will save time and labour.

Annual beds Annual bedding is extremely labour-intensive. Annuals grown in this way are bedded-out after all danger of frost is past, and at the end of summer they are either lifted and thrown away or put into a greenhouse to survive the frosts, and replaced by winter- or spring-flowering plants and bulbs. At each changeover, the soil must be cleared and prepared, and there is inevitably a period of a month or more before the new plants spread out and fill the space. Meanwhile the beds must be kept weed-free. To get the most out of your annuals in regions with a short growing season, make sure the soil is good quality and keep the plants well fertilized so they will grow vigorously when they're put in. Leave the beds empty during the winter, when they may be covered in snow. Again, mulch the soil thoroughly while you work out what to do in the long term.

Rose beds Although they look great in summer, rose beds are bare in winter, and the soil below the bushes is empty except for the weeds that emerge unless you keep hoeing. Since roses are a monoculture, diseases spread quickly from one plant to another. For insects that like roses, they are a feast, which means constant spraying. The minimum work required to keep a rose bed looking its best includes regular deadheading, weekly spraying for insects and diseases, and annual pruning. If you top-dress the bed with manure and add a weed-excluding mulch, it will help to keep weeds at bay, but rose beds are still labour-intensive. You can save work by growing roses among other plants, where their bare stems will be hidden and disease is less likely to spread (see pages 114–115).

Plants that need staking Any plant that has to be staked to stop it falling over is obviously extra work. The usual culprits are plants with heavy flower heads, such as some peonies, or plants that grow tall, like delphiniums. Nowadays there are shorter-growing varieties of many of these plants, or they can be planted sparingly between others that will hold them up.

Plants that do not suit the conditions Any plant that is not naturally adapted to the climate or soil of your garden will need special care. Acid-loving plants, such as camellias and azaleas, are the usual culprits. If your soil is alkaline, they can be grown only in beds or containers of lime-free soil. The same applies to blue hydrangeas – in chalky soil, the flowers will turn pink, and despite applications of iron, they will never recover the brilliance of their original colour.

Grey-leaved plants will not thrive in the shade, nor will shade-lovers in full sun on sandy soil because the microclimate is not right for them. In cool climates, tender plants such as dahlias and chrysanthemums need to be lifted every year and stored inside for the winter.

Overcrowding Sometimes shrubs are planted too close together, which means constant cutting back and often results in a poor shape. It is better to remove an overlarge shrub, or take out adjacent plants to give the shrub a chance to spread (see pages 116–117).

Vegetable gardens With the possible exception of annual bedding, vegetable gardening is far more laborious than any form of flower gardening. If you forget to sow seed in time or to thin out the seedlings, you will have to wait another year; in addition there are the pests and diseases to deal with, and in dry spells, vegetables need fairly constant watering. To remove at least some of the labour, you could try growing perennial vegetables (see page 139), or those that seed themselves and do the work for you – have a few globe artichokes standing like statues in the flowerbeds and rocket (*Eruca vesicaria sativa*) and spinach beet popping up in any bare soil they find.

For advice on dealing with these and other high-maintenance features, see pages 82–85.

△ **MEANS OF SUPPORT**
Herbaceous plants such as these delphiniums and centaureas sometimes need staking to prevent them from falling over. As well as remembering to put the stakes in early enough, it may be necessary to retie the plants after a storm or strong winds.

AN UNSUITABLE GARDEN

Some gardens are just not right for their owners, often for quite intangible reasons. It may be that the garden has all the elements you need, but it does not reflect your personal style. Conversely, it may look beautiful but does not work because of a practical, functional reason.

△ **NATURAL ORDER**
With its symmetrical layout, paved surfaces and square beds neatly edged in box, this small formal garden will appeal to those with a sense of order. Although the structure is strictly formal, it allows for looser planting around the edges and within the beds.

Deciding on the style and functions of a garden is the essence of design. It cannot be done instantly and requires both intimate knowledge of the plot and a clear recognition of your needs and tastes. Establishing what you do not like about your existing garden is a good way to begin.

GARDEN STYLE

The question of style is subjective, but there are basic distinctions, such as between formality and informality. Many variations are possible within these two categories. Gardens can be formal and tidy, with, say, a perfectly round bed surrounding a beautiful magnolia set in a sea of gravel, or with clipped hedges, topiary and paved surfaces.

Alternatively, they can be formal and overflowing, where the lines are basically straight, but the plants are allowed to froth over and blur the edges – the classic English style.

Some people say they do not like straight lines in a garden – "nature doesn't have straight lines" – when what they mean is they do not like the tidy and formal style. They may love cottage gardens without realizing that the key point of a cottage garden is usually its straight garden path. The overflowing beds on either side disguise the straight lines.

The confusion over straight lines and formality leads many people to add wiggles and curves to their lawns and flowerbeds, in the hope that they will look more "natural". You may have inherited one of these restless, fussy gardens. Simplifying it into gentle curves will make for a more peaceful effect (see pages 78–79).

Problems also occur when people mix very different styles within the same space. Styles should be strictly limited in a small garden; it is only possible to have several distinct styles in a larger plot that is divided into separate "rooms".

Styles are also sometimes adopted in a half-hearted or compromised way, something which often happens with so-called Japanese gardens. A true Japanese garden is beautiful and highly symbolic, with references to traditional customs, such as the tea ceremony, or Buddhist meditation. However, many interpretations of Japanese

gardens are simply pastiches, such as those 19th-century European gardens with bamboo fences, arched bridges and stone lanterns. They lack the clarity and integrity of a true Japanese garden.

SENSE OF BELONGING

Related to style is the way that a garden fits into its surroundings. It may be beautifully kept, but if it does not connect with the house it will never seem comfortable. A modernist house looks almost embarrassed with climbing roses draped over rustic archways; equally odd is a minimalist garden with a thatched cottage in a village.

The concept of sense of belonging leads to another problem of style – the way the garden connects to the local landscape.

▽ **ORGANIZED CHAOS**
Few styles are as cheerful and exuberant as the cottage garden. Despite its relaxed appearance, it still requires a fair amount of sowing, deadheading and trimming to maintain the prolific effect. This one is brimming with nasturtiums, marigolds and other annuals.

◁ **GEOMETRY LESSON**
This water garden is based on strong lines, both in the structure of the brick walling and the bold planting, which includes hostas, rodgersias, typhas and the tree Catalpa bignonioides 'Aurea'; the zigzag shape and the change of level give the composition a sense of movement. It will not appeal to those who prefer a softer, more restful effect.

▷ **SEPARATE STYLES**
It is advisable not to mix styles within the same space, especially in a small garden. Here, a low fence separates a formal parterre from a more informal seating area.

Failing to consider local influences can cause both visual and practical difficulties. The English garden style, for instance, is popular around the world, but it developed in a temperate climate with high rainfall and gentle landscapes that stay green all year round. Gardeners in arid climates struggle to grow old-fashioned border plants, and while their pale colours have an ethereal beauty under leaden English skies, they simply look miserable in Arizona. Equally, the brilliant reds of pelargoniums glare furiously under northern sunlight, but look absolutely right in the bright sun of an Italian window box.

Consider how your garden, particularly your front garden, relates to the gardens around you. In a quiet suburban street where every front garden has a neatly clipped hedge, an ultramodern work of sculpture may look wonderfully bold – if you know how to place it – or it could just look odd. In rural areas, the effects are even more drastic – a row of purple-leaved plums along a country lane is terribly jarring. Always consider the surrounding area before planting, particularly along boundaries. Planting within the garden is also important if you have a view and must complement it.

PLANTING STYLE

Particular groups of plants can have a strong influence on the look of a garden. For example, conifers are useful plants, but for many people they conjure up negative images of suburban gardens. Rhododendrons look out of place in a formal, sunny garden. Camellias, on the other hand, suit a formal setting.

▽ **COLOUR AND TEXTURE**
Green and gold dwarf conifers and purple Acer palmatum give a strong contrast of colour and texture that is enlivened by orange self-seeded poppies.

The effect of a rose in a rose bed is
formal – quite different from that of
a rambler growing around a doorway.

Look around the garden to see if
a particular plant or group of plants
is giving the wrong impression. It
may be the mood of a planting that
you do not like. If you prefer bright
colours, a serene white garden will
need lifting. Pastel shades of blue
and pink have a quieting effect,
while hot reds, oranges and bright
yellows are enlivening. Too many
variegated plants, or plants with
leaves other than green or grey, will
give a fussy, busy look – often the
addition of green-leaved plants with
white flowers will calm this down.

FINDING INSPIRATION

A simple way to find inspiration for
garden and planting styles is to
collect old gardening or lifestyle
magazines and tear out pictures of
gardens or views that appeal to you.
Lay them on the floor or paste them
on a board. Do they have elements in common,
such as bright colours, or deep shade, or a formal
layout? This will give you an idea of what your
preferred look is likely to be.

GARDEN FUNCTION

How you live in the garden – your lifestyle – will
dictate your functional needs. If you have
mountain bikes, then a place to keep them is a
functional need. If you have a dog, you may want
an enclosure to preserve the lawn. Often there is
nowhere to sit in a garden, or an existing seat is in
the wrong place for you. Some gardens are just
not made for children, with delicate flowers and
perfect lawns that are ruined by ball games. Or

there may be a large purpose-built
play area but nowhere to make a
den and hide from adults. Children
and adults do not always combine
well in gardens and may need
separating, with different areas for
each (see pages 88–89).

If you like fresh produce, you may
want a small kitchen garden in
which to grow special salad vegetables: a few
cherry tomato plants, rocket and sorrel – as well
as useful herbs. Or maybe you want a barbecue
and seating area for outdoor dining – elements
such as these can make all the difference to your
enjoyment of a garden.

A CONVERTED GARDEN

Nowadays, some of the most interesting homes started life as something quite different – a barn, an old church or school, or an industrial building such as a warehouse. They make unusual living spaces, but how do you deal with the outside, and create a garden where one has never existed?

These places have quite different problems from those of a "normal" garden, in that they are not really meant to be gardens at all. Sometimes there is a yard outside, used for storage, sometimes a cobbled space with a covered area for animals. In the case of a loft, there may be just a flat space on the roof, with a view of the city.

THE *GENIUS LOCI*

The important issue here is that of *genius loci,* or sense of place. This concept is useful when designing in "no-garden" situations, since it provides clues about what will feel right in the location. The idea originated in ancient Rome, where it was felt that every place had its *genius,* its guardian spirit, which determined its character. This may sound far-fetched, but it accounts for the sense of "rightness" we have when we see

▷ **CITY SPIRIT**
The essence of this roof garden is its magnificent view. Fussy details would detract from this. Simple pots of geraniums, all of one colour, indicate a garden while respecting the spirit of the place. Any pots should be securely fastened.

great architecture, and, conversely, the feeling of unease if a building or garden does not respect the location.

So what might the *genius loci* suggest for the garden of a converted building? In a farmhouse you could design the garden around something practical, such as a place to sit and eat – a big wooden table made from an old door, shaded with a pergola built of old beams, for instance. The roofs of city lofts lend themselves to inventiveness with industrial objects, such as a barbecue made from hubcaps or seats made from a bus stop bench.

Before you start to think about the *genius loci,* it is important to have a clear idea of what you want from the garden (see pages 31 and 39). Then find out as much as you can about the origins of your home. What was it used for; why are the walls so high or low; are there other buildings like it; is it typical of the area? In this way, you will begin to understand the meaning of the building and of the location. As you start to choose the elements of the garden – the seat, the paving, the gate – you will have a better idea of what "goes".

▽ **INDUSTRIAL SPACE**
This tiny yard is dominated by metal structures and an industrial landscape. What sort of garden will work here? Probably not rambling roses and a Victorian coach lamp; instead, try having pots of bright marigolds and scarlet runner beans.

△ BACKYARD JUNGLE

Any space can be greened, no matter how unpromising. This dark and dingy alleyway has been transformed into a jungle path simply by using pot-grown hostas, cyclamen, ferns, abutilon and climbers trained on trellis panels.

DESIGN DOS AND DON'TS

⌀ Look at similar buildings and how they fit into the landscape.

⌀ Keep it simple, so that the charm and originality of the building are not covered up and show through in your garden.

⌀ Use original and reclaimed materials, if possible, such as bricks or slate reclaimed from local buildings, or old pieces of wood from farm buildings.

⌀ If you want to introduce a garden building, try to respect the style of the original or another local building, but again, keep it simple.

⌀ Remember the view from the outside: take care when choosing trees and any structures that can be seen from the street.

⌀ Remember your own view of the outside and "borrow" the landscape if you can.

⌀ Don't bring in an outside style: an ornate Victorian iron chair will not accord well with a New England Dutch barn.

⌀ Don't "fake it". If you live in a converted 19th-century school, don't buy imitation 19th-century coach lamps for your lighting – they never look convincing.

AN UNATTRACTIVE VIEW

*Many people have to contend with a view that dominates the garden.
It may be outside the boundaries, such as a neighbour's garage, extension
or tree, or an ugly building. Or it may be within the garden – a garish piece of
play equipment that the children adore but which is rather too obvious.*

An eyesore dominates a garden both physically and mentally; just knowing it is there can be a constant source of irritation. If the eyesore is a neighbouring building you may also have the problem of lack of privacy and feel that prying eyes are watching you whenever you are in the garden, even if there is no one there.

CREATING DISTRACTIONS

Oddly enough, if you can disregard the unwanted view – whether it is internal or external – until you have dealt with any other garden problems you might have, the eyesore may mentally (if not literally) disappear. For example, with a dull-shaped garden, when you have defined the different areas within it, you may find that a shed that has been placed obtrusively halfway down the garden – perhaps with a trellised archway attached – becomes a useful screen for a children's play area.

Or if you realize the best place for a seat is not on the shady patio next to the house but at the end of the garden, it may be that the neighbours will not see you there, and that there is no immediate need for screening near the house.

GARDEN BUILDINGS

Buildings that are no longer useful can sometimes be converted – open up two sides of an old garage and you have created a shady arbour (see pages 158–159), or put some big windows into it to make a workshop or a children's playroom, where they can make as much noise as they like. If the building has to stay where it is, try putting simple trelliswork up the sides and planting climbers or wall shrubs. Be careful, however, not to fall into the trap of choosing very fast-growing varieties – after the first two years, you will spend all summer cutting the junglelike tendrils, or have to reinforce the building to support the climber!

You could even consider adding to the building and giving it a more central role in your garden. A paved space on one side, a shady pergola above with climbers growing over it, and a seat and table in front will completely change its appearance and turn it into a useful living space.

The problem of an intrusive building next door or at the end of the garden can sometimes be resolved by turning the garden in on itself and creating a meditative effect, rather like that of a courtyard. You could emphasize the sense of enclosure by bringing the planting in from the boundaries of the garden towards a small clearing in the centre, rather than having an open garden. Adding a strong focal point within the garden, such as a water feature, arbour, tree or sculpture, will further help to draw the attention inward.

Giving the garden a more interesting shape will have a similar effect – your eye will be distracted by the interest inside the garden (see pages 78–79). If there is nothing else to look at, your eyes inevitably will be drawn to the eyesore.

▽ **REFLECTIVE GARDEN**
This tiny garden is in a London suburb, but the dense jungle planting screens off the neighbouring buildings, leaving just the reflection of the house in the tranquil pool.

SCREENS

Screening structures can be useful for enclosing a particular area, such as a sitting place or a children's play space. Trellised

△ **CLIMBER COVER**

Vigorous wisteria can be used to cover any obtrusive garden structure and will create a charming effect with masses of sweet-smelling mauve flowers and attractive twining stems and foliage.

screens or openwork fences produce the lightest effect, allowing some glimpses beyond and so preserving the feeling of spaciousness (see pages 60–61).

Even something that is not primarily intended to act as a screen, such as a beautifully made wooden climbing frame or a planting of shrubs to catch the eye from the living room, can work effectively to partially hide an unwanted view.

A common way to screen an eyesore is to plant a tall, fast-growing, preferably evergreen tree. However, think carefully before you do so – the tree itself can soon cause problems by casting heavy shade; its roots will spread widely; and it will take up lots of water. A dark, gloomy hedge can't be screened off, but it can be used as a backdrop for the pale silhouette of a silver birch or a silver-leaved pear.

▷ **UPPER SANCTUM**

Surrounded by buildings, this roof garden has turned in on itself, with lush planting that draws attention away from the city into its calm greenness. A roof must be strong enough to support the weight of such luxuriant planting.

A TROUBLESOME GARDEN

Garden problems range in severity from the mildly irritating shade cast by a neighbour's tree to the extreme danger of an unprotected pond for small children. No garden can ever be entirely problem-free, but even the most serious difficulties can usually be dealt with fairly simply.

When you acquire a new garden, you also inherit the problems that go with it. Walk around it and inspect it with the critical eye of a surveyor. This may be a depressing experience, but at least there will be no nasty surprises later.

Problems can also develop in existing gardens. Plants grow, structures deteriorate, neighbours change, children are born. It is surprising how rapidly a paradise can turn into a battlefield, requiring you to be vigilant and flexible enough to adapt your garden as circumstances dictate.

BOUNDARIES

Many of the difficulties encountered involve neighbours, and boundaries are a common cause of dispute. Find out whose responsibility it is to keep the wall or fence in good repair. If it is yours,

▽ **TREE TROUBLE**
A magnificent oak tree is both a treasure and a liability. While it casts precious shade on hot days, if it is planted too close to a house, the roots will undermine the foundations, leading to subsidence, and old or rotten branches might fall on the roof and damage it.

and your neighbours seem anxious about it, make any repairs quickly. If they are likely to let their fence fall down, you will have to judge whether it is worth continually nagging them to maintain it or better to do it yourself. If you want to erect a screen, explain how high it will be and what you want to plant on it. You should also warn them about building work – people are less likely to complain if they are told about it beforehand.

BUILDINGS

Garden buildings are often neglected and should be inspected to make sure they are safe: check for rotten upright posts or floorboards in sheds, and replace roofing materials, if necessary (see pages 160–161). Greenhouses can present a problem either if they are positioned near play areas or if panes of glass become loose (see pages 162–163).

TREES

Within your garden trees often cause problems, both for you and your neighbours. They may cast too much shade, or the leaves may fall into ponds or swimming pools. It is possible to have a tree drastically thinned, while keeping the shape, but this is expensive; if your neighbours have complained, you could ask them to share the cost.

You may be legally entitled to remove any branch from a neighbour's tree that overhangs your property, but check local laws. The shape of the tree may be damaged by this, so discuss the problem before taking drastic action. If you are worried about a safety issue such as rotten branches, then consult a tree surgeon. If you suspect that roots are undermining your house, speak to a structural engineer – but remember

that removing an old tree can cause a sudden change in the uptake of water from the soil, which may itself bring problems.

OTHER PLANTS

There are other garden plants that can cause problems. Some climbers are strong growing, and an average fence or shed may not be sturdy enough to support them. They can often be cut back hard with little adverse reaction, making it possible to strengthen the structure. Self-clinging climbers like ivy can be a nuisance on house walls and near windows (see pages 128–129).

If you have young children, it is safer to get rid of any poisonous plants. Laburnum and foxgloves are well-known examples, but yew, oak and ivy are also poisonous. Although a child would have to eat a substantial amount of berries or leaves to suffer serious ill-effects, if you are worried, don't grow these plants.

PONDS

A frequent worry to parents of young children, ponds can be made safer with fencing surrounds or with a metal grid positioned just below water level (see page 153). Alternatively, you could alter the pond so there is no longer an open water surface. It could be filled with earth to make a bog garden, which can be planted with water-loving plants (see page 93). Water will collect on the top of the bog garden, and it will attract wildlife, but it will be less alluring for children.

Another option is to fill in the pond and make a pebble fountain (see page 144). This is a safer feature, which will still give you the sight and sound of running water. You could build it in the same place or perhaps in a more suitable location.

△ **PROBLEM POND**
With its beautiful planting and floating water lilies, this pond is enticing for young children and also potentially dangerous. If you feel that safety mesh would spoil the appearance of a pond, you could fence off that area of the garden.

△ **TOXIC EXOTIC**
Angels' trumpets (Datura) is a beautiful plant whose flowers have a sweet, heady aroma. It is also highly poisonous and so is best avoided if you have young children.

DRAWING PLANS

When taking stock of your garden, it is useful to draw some simple plans.
A site plan gives you a clear visual record of your existing plot – showing
the size and shape, and the good and bad points – and provides a framework for
planning major changes to the design and planting.

△ CASE STUDY GARDEN:
"BEFORE"

This steeply sloping garden was
originally so overgrown that
the hedges on each boundary
almost met in the middle. This
photograph was taken after the
initial cutting back and clearing
had been carried out – that is,
at the time the garden was
surveyed and measured for
the site plan (see opposite).

Drawing plans is not difficult, and you should not be put off by the precisely drafted and often highly artistic plans drawn by professional garden designers. These are intended to impress clients; for your purposes, basic plans will be fine.

MEASURING

Draw a rough outline of the garden and the house – it need not be accurate, but make it the right shape. Mark your measurements on this rough plan. You can measure with a piece of string marked in metres or feet, but it is easier to use a long tape measure – a 30-m (100-ft) measure can be hired from a tool hire shop. It will also be easier if you have a helper to hold the end of the tape while you measure. Start by measuring the length and width of the garden, then mark where the house walls are in relation to the boundaries. Measure all the dimensions, including the awkward angles.

DRAWING A PRECISE SITE PLAN

Using these measurements, draw the outline of the house and garden precisely on square-gridded paper, using one square to represent, say, one square metre or yard. The scale will depend on the garden's size – if it is very large, you may have to draw several areas separately. Draw the outline of the plan neatly, using a pencil and ruler. If your garden is an awkward shape, it may be easier to

get a copy of the plan from the house deeds or from the tax assessor's office. You will need to know what scale it is drawn to and may want to have it blown up to a larger scale at a copy shop.

ADDING FEATURES

Next measure the position of the house doors and windows, and any existing paving or paths. Draw these on the plan, together with features such as ponds, pergolas, lawns and beds. Mark the direction of the prevailing wind, if any, and the aspect – where the sun rises and sets, and which areas receive sun and shade. This changes through the day and it is worth recording the change – for example, if the evening sun falls at the end of the garden, this may be the best place for a patio. Sun and shade also vary with the seasons, and if you can wait long enough, this information is useful. Mark good or bad views and points where the garden is overlooked.

Next draw in the existing trees and shrubs, marking their positions, how widely they spread and where they cast shade. If you are unable to identify some of the plants, code them with a number and a descriptive note. As you gain knowledge of plants, you can add the names to your plan. At this stage, it is probably not worth marking smaller plants. If you find that drawing plans helps, however, you could draw separate sketch plans of beds later on, when you come to redesign planting schemes.

You now have a workable site plan. Make several copies as backups and for planning the redesign. Keep one on a noticeboard, so you can jot down any new details as soon as you discover them – the wind coming from the east and cutting through the rose bed, or the wet patch that forms on the lawn after heavy rain, for example.

If a knowledgeable friend visits you, ask if he or she can help to identify plants you are unsure about and provide any useful information about your plants in general, such as the speed of growth, flower colours and bloom times.

The site plan is a unique document. It contains a wealth of essential detail that is relevant to you, the user of the garden. Whether you want to build a new patio or simply add a new seat, the site plan will give you instant access to the information you need to make the right decision.

If surveying and planning seem too difficult, you can commission a garden designer to do it for you – contact a professional organization for a register of designers. The cost will depend on the amount of detail you want the plan to include.

WANTS AND NEEDS

The simple checklist (right) will enable you to clarify exactly what you want and need in your garden (mark your choices on a photocopy if you prefer). Check those elements that are essential or desirable to help you to narrow down your choice if you have limited space, funds or time. Your garden may contain some of them already, in which case, note whether they need changing in some way or replacing. If you are still not sure what you want at this stage, further details on most of the elements are given later in this book.

ADDING NEW IDEAS

Once you have drawn up your list of elements, take a fresh copy of your site plan, or lay a sheet of tracing paper over it, and start to add the new ideas. Blot out fussy little beds, draw the shed in a convenient place, and see if you need a pergola to shade the seating area. Experiment freely with several different options, then choose the best one.

▷ **CASE STUDY GARDEN: THE SITE PLAN**
The site plan shows the size and shape of the garden and how it relates to the house. The owners are keen gardeners and want to grow a wide range of plants. The amount of shade that falls over this narrow plot is considerable, and the soil is very chalky. Both these factors, together with the sloping site, will need to be taken into account before replanting.

Area shaded most of the day; low hedge to be removed and shade-tolerant bedding planted.

Hedge to be removed, since it takes up space on sunniest side of the garden.

Low retaining wall.

Flattest and sunniest part of the garden.

Low retaining wall.

Ground sloping steeply down to house.

All the concrete steps to be left because they are too difficult to remove.

CHECKLIST

Hard landscaping	Essential	Desirable
Walls	☐	☐
Fences	☐	☐
Paths	☐	☐
Steps	☐	☐
Living areas		
Patio or terrace	☐	☐
Barbecue	☐	☐
Other seating areas	☐	☐
Children's play area	☐	☐
Secret retreat	☐	☐
Features		
Pool	☐	☐
Pergola	☐	☐
Arbour	☐	☐
Summerhouse	☐	☐
Utilities		
Shed/storage area	☐	☐
Lighting	☐	☐
Compost heap	☐	☐
Potting/work area	☐	☐
Planting		
Trees and shrubs	☐	☐
Hedges	☐	☐
Borders	☐	☐
Island beds	☐	☐
Raised beds	☐	☐
Vegetable garden	☐	☐
Herb garden	☐	☐
Rockery	☐	☐

▷ **CASE STUDY GARDEN: THE NEW DESIGN**

The owners have a limited budget for hard landscaping work, so they want to make only straightforward improvements they can do themselves. They decide to concentrate on the middle section of the garden first (shown in the photographs and plans), since this is the area that receives the most sun and has the most potential for planting.

In the new design, most of the lawns and hedging have been removed to be replaced with a greater variety of plants. The end of the garden is heavily shaded by mature trees from protected woodland at the back. The owners decide to leave this as a wild garden, since many interesting chalk downland plants have become naturalized there.

Mature conifer left because it hides the garden beyond.

Rockery planted with lime-tolerant heathers and other lime-lovers such as rock rose (*Helianthemum*).

The hedge has been replaced with home-made trellis and a shrub border.

The sunniest part of the garden reserved for herbs, flowering perennials and bedding plants.

The low wall has been removed to open up more areas for planting.

This bed can be seen from the house and is at eye level when standing at the bottom of the steps. It has been planted with small, low-growing evergreens that look good viewed close-up.

▷ **CASE STUDY GARDEN: "AFTER"**

This shows the new planting and landscaping that has been carried out. The low rockery allows access to the rest of the site and is ideal for lime-tolerant plants. To make the most of the flat area, paving interplanted with herbs has replaced one lawn, and flowerbeds have been made on three sides. On the sunniest side, a shrub border has replaced the long hedge.

As with the site plan, if the redesign is difficult, consider calling in a professional designer. Give him or her the site plan and a good clear brief as to what you want.

PRIORITIZING AND TIMING

In setting priorities, there is a balance to be struck between urgency, importance and possibility. Make a list of tasks and indicate which category each falls into. Dangerous items and liabilities, such as a broken fence, are both urgent and important. There will be items on your list that

are expensive or time-consuming, or both. This is where the "quick fixes" in the next chapter can help. It is useful to create a schedule for all the tasks you need to carry out.

Think about the sequence of work – major hard landscaping, such as relaying paving, is best done in a mild spell in winter and should, ideally, precede replanting, both to provide hard surfaces for access and to minimize damage to planting beds. On the other hand, as long as you mulch to prevent weed growth, renovating a border can be done slowly, as time and weather allow.

QUICK FIXES

Here are some simple ideas for making your garden a better place. They will help you solve immediate problems without affecting any long-term plans that may have arisen from the taking stock exercise in the previous chapter. The quickest fix is container gardening: container plants can give instant impact. In addition to explaining techniques for renovating existing plants, many new plants are suggested that give rapid results without taking over your garden. There are ideas for quick screens of plants or wood, and ways to brighten up the garden with paint and decorative objects. Finally, you could turn your garden into an "outdoor room".

△ **FAST FLOWERS**
Annuals, such as the sunflower 'Pacino', reach flowering size quickly and give colour without commitment – by autumn they will be gone, leaving the way clear for a more long-term planting. However, sunflowers are so cheerful you may want to sow some every year.

◁ **INSTANT GARDEN**
You can create a mature effect within a single growing season by using simple structures and decorative objects softened with plants. Here trellis screens and an obelisk are clothed with a collection of attractive container plants.

CONTAINER GARDENING

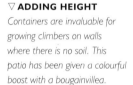

Using containers is a quick way of bringing the colours, shapes and scents of plants into a garden that is undergoing renovation. Containers also have valuable uses in established gardens, enabling you to change the look of an area in an instant and to liven up difficult spaces where there is no open soil.

If you are renovating a garden, container displays can be moved around the garden as the work is carried out to hide problems, to distract attention from eyesores or to fill gaps. But be realistic, one little pot of bedding is not going to distract anyone from an overgrown garden or a muddy building site. You will need to use large containers full of high-impact plants or a lot of smaller containers grouped together to create a cohesive display.

To maximize their impact, look for ways of getting height into container schemes – use steps, wall planters, plinths and display benches. Then fill them with tall-growing plants and climbers.

▽ **ADDING HEIGHT**
Containers are invaluable for growing climbers on walls where there is no soil. This patio has been given a colourful boost with a bougainvillea.

CONTAINER USES

Over the next six pages you will find suggestions for the best plants to grow in containers, starting with long-term plants such as shrubs, then the more tender fillers used for seasonal highlights, and finally perennials. First, here are some of the ways in which containers may be used to enhance a garden.

Brighten up a front door Use topiary in pots to frame a door; add seasonal touches with smaller pots of bulbs or bedding. Hanging baskets provide a cheerful welcome.

Soften hard landscaping Large expanses of wall or floor can be softened with container plantings. Use large containers or several small ones planted with the same plants.

Enhance seating areas Some plants help us to relax, such as scented plants or those that release a scent when the foliage is crushed. Flowers that hang down, such as hellebores and fuchsias, often have an intricate beauty that is hard to see when they are grown in the ground; container growing makes them much easier to appreciate.

Create a focal point A well-chosen container and planting can create an eye-catching display at the end of a vista, in the middle of a courtyard, in the corner of a patio, or wherever you want one.

Fill gaps Small containers with seasonal plants can be dropped into existing schemes; plunging a pot of lilies or cannas into a border is an easy way

△ **FOCAL POINT**
Large containers planted with shapely shrubs make strong focal points. Framed by an arch, this standard fuchsia marks the junction of two paths, where it can be seen from four different directions.

to fill a gap in summer. Later on, chrysanthemums or asters can be used. If you have gaps in spring, use pots full of small daffodils or tulips.

Hide eyesores If manhole covers, drainpipes and compost heaps offend your aesthetic sense, or if you have to live with a design eyesore for a while, containers are an effective means of disguise.

TYPES OF CONTAINER

If you have already decided on a garden style, use containers that will suit it. Otherwise, buy simple shapes in terracotta, plastic or wood, or make do with recycled containers such as old tin cans – they may inspire you to develop a distinctive style. Containers that will be left out in winter must be frost-proof.

▷ COLLECTABLE CACTI

Containers are useful for plant collectors who want to display their treasures to best effect. Ideally suited to container growing, these cacti have been cleverly arranged on steps so the sculptural form of each plant can be seen easily.

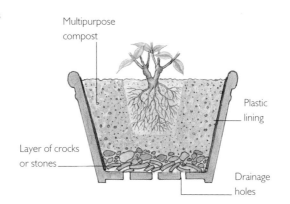

Multipurpose compost

Plastic lining

Layer of crocks or stones

Drainage holes

◁ GROWING TIPS

Cover the drainage holes with crocks or large stones. A layer of gravel on top of the crocks provides additional drainage and prevents the planting mix becoming waterlogged. Use compost or multipurpose mix, or acidic potting soil for acid-lovers. Leave a 2.5-cm (1-in) gap between the top of the compost and the rim of the pot to make watering easier.

WATERING

Containers may need watering once or twice a day in hot spells, but there are steps you can take to reduce the burden.

⌀ Do not use a lot of small containers; the larger the container, the less often it will require watering.

⌀ Choose a good-quality compost that holds the moisture without waterlogging. If needed, add water-retaining granules and use a mulch.

⌀ Line terracotta pots with plastic to reduce evaporation from the sides, but do not block the drainage holes.

⌀ Instal an irrigation system controlled by an automatic timer.

SHRUBS

Almost any shrub can be grown in a container, but a large collection of them can involve extra work in planting and maintenance, which you may not want if you are renovating your garden. Be selective: it is better to have a few attractive, healthy plants than many untidy, neglected ones.

Container-grown shrubs have several uses: both bare and messy gardens benefit from screening plants; a mature garden full of evergreens can be made more interesting with a shrub offering autumn colour or spring blossoms; and shrubs with impressive shapes make good focal points and also distract attention from untidy areas. Some of the shrubs that could improve your garden are listed opposite.

Containers can be used for favourite shrubs that need a particular soil. If a garden has no borders, group shrubs in containers to form a structural planting to set off small pots of perennials, bedding and bulbs.

Shrubs are long-term plants. Most should be potted in large containers, 45 cm (18 in) in diameter, so their roots will not become constricted. After a few years, vigorous plants should be repotted in even larger pots. Terracotta or stone pots look good, but large sizes can be expensive, and plastic, fibreglass or wooden containers work just as well.

When filled with compost, large containers are very heavy. If you need to move them, use a plant trolley or a wooden trolley fitted with heavy-duty casters. Small feet that raise pots off the ground will aid drainage. Soil-based compost lasts well and is good for long-term plants, but you can use soil-less mixtures based on bark or peat. Add a mulch of gravel, cocoa shells or bark chips to the surface of the compost and, throughout the year, check that it is moist by pushing your finger into it. Containers may need watering daily in summer. Add a

▽ **WHIMSICAL SHAPES**
A pair of topiary shapes in containers, like these box swans, can be moved around the garden as work progresses or as the seasons change.

△ **USEFUL EVERGREEN**
This camellia has been placed in a prominent position to make the most of the spring flowers. Later in the year, it could be moved so that the evergreen foliage can act as a screen or a foil for other plants.

▷ **POT HERB**
Although bay is a tree, it can be grown in a container, as a mophead standard. To maintain the size and shape it will need pruning each summer, but this will give you fresh leaves for cooking; they can also be dried.

slow-release fertilizer in spring or use a diluted liquid feed every time you water. In severe winters, even hardy plants can suffer if the roots become frozen, so protect containers that are too heavy to move by wrapping them in bubble wrap, straw or hessian.

CLIMBERS

Climbing plants can be grown in large containers either where there is no soil border or to create striking features. Attach wooden or plastic supports to the rim, then train the plant up and tie it in; even vigorous plants like golden hop (*Humulus lupulus* 'Aureus') can be trained into a small feature. Clematis are good for pots, especially those that flower on the lower shoots.

ROSES

Climbing roses can be grown in containers if they are under 3 m (10 ft), but they need large tubs. Combined planters and screens are good portable dividers (see page 61). Patio and miniature roses work well in pots, since most are no more than 45 cm (18 in) high; pink and peach-coloured varieties look good in terracotta pots. Standard roses about 1 m (3 ft) in height are also effective in containers, either on their own or underplanted with low-growing bedding. An innovative way of using roses in pots is to grow the modern ground-cover types, such as 'Flower Carpet' or the County Series, in hanging baskets.

SHRUBS FOR CONTAINERS

Acer japonicum and **A. palmatum** (Japanese maples) Valued for their overall form and their foliage shape and colour; some have coloured stems too.*

Buxus sempervirens (box) A neat evergreen that is easily clipped into all sorts of shapes and is invaluable for its ability to tolerate shade. Good for formal gardens.

Camellia japonica A glossy evergreen producing an impressive display of spring flowers. It prefers a sheltered, semi-shaded position and grows well against a wall.*

Choisya ternata (Mexican orange blossom) Has glossy evergreen foliage and bears scented white flowers in spring.

Fatsia japonica (Japanese aralia) Architectural evergreen with an impressive shape and large, glossy, lobed leaves. Tolerates sun or shade and makes a good screen.

Kalmia latifolia (mountain laurel) Evergreen that bears clusters of pink cup-shaped flowers in early summer.*

Pleioblastus humilis (bamboo) Excellent screening plant valued for its year-round, fresh green foliage. Container-growing controls its spread. Good for Japanese gardens.

Rhododendron (including azaleas) Evergreens available in a wide range of flower colours; flowers are borne in spring. Opt for the smaller-growing species, such as R. yakushimanum, or azaleas under 1 m (3 ft).*

Skimmia japonica Compact, trouble-free evergreen that is perfect for winter containers. The foliage is scented and small white flowers are borne in spring. If plants of both sexes are grown, female plants bear bright red fruits.*

Taxus baccata (yew) Long-lived plant with dense foliage and a neat habit. Either clip and train as topiary or grow a variety with a naturally attractive shape.

* requires acidic potting soil

SEASONAL FILLERS

Frost-tender plants such as annuals and tender perennials can be displayed outside only after frosts have passed (usually late spring or early summer). The perennials must be moved to a frost-free place or wrapped with insulation before cold weather sets in if they are to survive.

Annuals These are mostly small plants bred to give a good display of flowers, which in many species lasts all summer. You can raise your own plants from seed or buy young plants early in the year or more mature subjects later on. Plants raised indoors need to be acclimatized by exposing them to outdoor conditions for a few hours at a time before they are positioned outside; this normally takes 10–14 days. Plant young plants in small pots, which begin to get pot-bound before the danger of frost has passed, in display containers, and keep them in a light, frost-free place.

When planting a mixture of plants in a free-standing container that will be viewed from all sides, put the extra tall plants in the centre and underplant all the way around with low-growing ones. For containers that will be viewed from one side, such as a pot or tub against a wall, put in the main feature plants first, then add low-growing fillers and finish with trailing plants at the front only. Trailers work well in tall, thin containers, such as chimney pots.

Mixed hanging baskets are traditional but awkward to plant. It is easier and just as impressive to use a vigorous single subject like a trailing fuchsia, petunia (Surfinia type), geranium or tuberous begonia.

Tender perennials The best-known tender perennials for containers are geraniums and fuchsias. Today, though, many nurseries and garden centres offer a range of other perennials, as well as annuals. Some are sold when they are little more than small cuttings, for use in mixed plantings. They include interesting trailers such as bidens, diascia, lotus, scaevola, sutera and verbena. Others, such as marguerites, felicia, lantana and osteospermums, are also sold as larger single-subject pot plants to rival geraniums and fuchsias. Trained standard forms of tender perennials are more expensive, but they will provide instant, often dramatic, focal points. But unlike similar-sized hardy shrubs, they will die if they are left outside over the winter in colder climates.

▽ **SPRING CHEER**
Small spring bulbs such as dwarf narcissi and irises provide instant cheer when displayed in small pots near the house. Either pot the bulbs in autumn or buy them already potted in early spring.

Bulbs Although their flowering is brief, bulbs are good for seasonal highlights. Use the smaller spring bulbs such as dwarf narcissi wherever you can see them from your window – grow them on their own or use them to underplant evergreens in containers. Taller subjects, such as lilies and cannas, make effective summer focal points.

INSIDE OUT

If you have a house or conservatory full of plants, a quick fix for a dull patio is to bring them outside for the summer. They need to be acclimatized gradually, but it saves having to buy and plant out new plants, and they often do better outside if the conservatory becomes very hot.

FILLERS FOR WINTER/EARLY SPRING

Bellis perennis (double daisy) Perennial but sold in autumn and spring as a temporary filler for early spring colour.

Iris danfordiae and *I. reticulata* Dainty dwarf irises in yellow, purple or blue. Perfect for small containers, but leaves formed after flowering are unsightly.

Narcissus (daffodil) Small or dwarf daffodils fit into many types of container schemes, including massed plantings of single varieties and mixed displays.

Polyanthus (primula) Bear flowers in large umbels on stout stems. They are available in mixed colours and are good for cheering up an area in partial shade.

Viola (pansy) Winter-flowering types bloom on and off during mild spells and are available in many different colours.

▷ **MIXING SPECIES**
This terracotta pot, with rustic cladding, is filled with three different thymes: Thymus minus, 'Doone Valley' and 'Lady's Bedstraw'. As well as providing colour, aroma, and herbs for the kitchen in the short term, it is also a source of stock plants for the future.

▽ **TEMPORARY HOMES**
Young foliage perennials, such as these ferns and hostas, can be grown and enjoyed in pots before planting out in prepared borders. Alternatively, if the hostas are left in pots, with a layer of gravel spread on top of the potting mix, they may have a better chance of being ignored by snails and slugs.

HERBS

Tolerant of dry conditions, many herbs make good container plants, including most of the popular culinary species such as thyme, sage, rosemary and bay. Most herbs require full sun, but a few, including parsley, mint, fennel and chives, will tolerate shade. Tender perennial herbs such as tarragon and marjoram can be grown as annuals or brought under cover in winter.

Containers offer you the flexibility of growing herbs where they are needed, such as near the kitchen, beside the barbecue or on a table used for eating outdoors.

HARDY PERENNIALS

If it is going to take you some time to establish the flower borders, you can still enjoy your favourite perennials by growing them in containers. They can either be left in pots or planted out in the garden later when the borders are ready.

As container plants, most perennials will not provide the flowering impact of summer bedding or the year-round structure of shrubs. However, there are plenty with attractive foliage colour and form, seasonal flowering or an interesting shape that changes with the seasons. Some can also be

used to create unusual features, such as aquatic containers. Remember also that whereas bedding is temporary, perennials will last for many years.

There are hundreds of perennials available and it is important to choose the best types to grow in containers. Those that fit the following criteria are worth considering:

∅ Plants with a good shape and attractive foliage. These are best grown as single specimens.

∅ Low-growing foliage fillers that can be divided up easily. These make good permanent foils to bulbs and bedding that are introduced for seasonal highlights. Using perennial foliage saves having to buy foliage bedding each year.

∅ Plants that would be invasive in a border, such as mint, bee balm (*Monarda*), gooseneck, loosestrife and tansy.

∅ Perennials can be sown from seed or bought as plants. To save money, you could lift and divide border plants and plant them in pots. The best time to do this is in cool weather to minimize the stress on the plants, but you can get away with it at other times if you water well afterwards.

Most perennials are not fussy container subjects and, being hardy, they can be planted

outside before bedding plants. Most will grow in any type of compost, as long as it is well drained. If plants are to be kept in containers, they will need feeding; use a balanced feed for foliage plants and a tomato feed for flowering plants. Regular deadheading prolongs the display. Watch out for mildew and remove affected foliage as soon as you spot it so that it does not spread.

GRASSES

Ornamental grasses and the similar sedges are becoming very popular as container subjects, particularly in contemporary gardens. Their effects are more subtle and naturalistic than those of the usual bright summer-flowering perennials. The foliage provides the colour and also the texture, and the taller species add movement to a garden when they are caught by the breeze. Larger or more spreading types, such as the bamboolike *Hakonechloa macra* or the variegated sedge *Carex hachijoensis* 'Evergold', grow best one to a pot. To achieve a massed effect, group collections of pots.

Smaller grasses, such as the black-leaved lily turf (*Ophiopogon planiscapus* 'Nigrescens') and the tussock-forming blue fescue (*Festuca glauca*), work well in mixed plantings where their foliage acts as a foil for small flowering bulbs or bedding. Both are drought tolerant and can be divided and planted in the garden at a later date. Grasses are best suited to plain terracotta, wood or metal containers.

PERENNIALS FOR POTS

Agapanthus Excellent long-term single plants for late colour; move under cover in cold areas.

Dicentra spectabilis Well worth growing in a container to appreciate the sprays of heart-shaped flowers at close quarters. Dies back late in summer.

Euphorbia Good shapes, year-round interest and drought tolerant. The trailing stems of *E. myrsinites* are effective in tall pots.

Gunnera manicata Gigantic bog plant with enormous leaves and seed pods. Needs moist soil and a spacious, sheltered site. Suits a half-barrel.

Helleborus Sophisticated plant with a subtle beauty. Growing in pots in a cold greenhouse gives earlier flowers. Combines well with snowdrops or pulmonaria.

Hemerocallis (daylily) Select the more choice varieties with large flowers or with ruffled or bicoloured blooms.

Heuchera (coral bells) Produces large clumps of architectural leaves tinted bronze or purple. Graceful white, pink or scarlet flowers in summer.

Hosta Usually grown for the bold foliage, although the flower spikes are impressive too.

Sedum spectabile Drought-tolerant plant, with a long season of interest; looks good when grown alone in a stone urn.

Zantedeschia aethiopica 'Crowborough' (calla lily) Foliage and flowers have strong shapes; will grow in water but also tolerates drought. Very tender.

◁**BIG BLUE**
With their arching leaves, tall stems and striking blue flower heads, agapanthus are excellent container plants and make an impressive focal point on a patio. They are, however, very tender and in cooler regions should be moved under cover in winter.

BUYING A LARGE PLANT

A semi-mature tree or a few large shrubs will make an instant impact on your garden. Boring or flat gardens with no focal points can be transformed by a few careful purchases. If your garden is overlooked, a large screening plant will achieve in a moment what would normally take 10 years.

Not every tree or shrub is worth buying when semi-mature. Larger specimens of slow-growing plants are a good investment compared to smaller sizes, but smaller sizes of fast-growing plants will soon catch up to larger ones.

To justify the cost and the effort of planting, large plants must have something special to offer besides their stature. For example, evergreens should have a good shape and deciduous plants should possess beautiful blossoms, attractive or edible fruits, or wonderful autumn colour. Some examples of plants that are worth buying large are listed opposite.

It is increasingly common to see large trained plants on sale, such as fan-trained pyracanthas and espaliered apples, but these can be expensive when you consider how fast they grow – they are only saving you three to five years and in most instances it is easy to do the training yourself.

SOURCES

Garden centres may have a few semi-mature trees or shrubs, but you will find the widest choice at nurseries specializing in large specimens. You can send away for catalogues, but it is important to see the stock before buying. Take a reference book to check the hardiness, ultimate size, speed of growth and season of interest. Most nurseries quote a price per pot size in litres. As a guide, a 25-litre pot measures about 35 cm (14 in) in diameter and a 45-litre pot is 45 cm (18 in) in diameter. Some nurseries price plants by the girth or height. Many will deliver and plant large specimens for you.

PLANTING

Most semi-mature plants will be container grown and can be planted at any time as long as you water them well in dry spells. The best time to plant is from early to late autumn for hardy evergreens or early autumn to early winter for deciduous plants. This allows the roots to become established before winter sets in, helping the plant to withstand hot, dry spells the following summer.

You will need a large hole that is deep enough to accommodate the plant at the same level in the soil as it was in the pot. If the hole needs to go into the subsoil, this must be broken up and some topsoil imported (see also pages 202–203).

▽ **ETHEREAL WHITE**
Snowy mespilus (Amelanchier larmarckii) is a beautiful small tree or large shrub with profuse white blossoms in spring and brilliant red and orange foliage in autumn. It is easy to grow, but prefers a lime-free soil.

PLANTS TO BUY LARGE

Acer (maple) Trees and shrubs whose shape improves with age; many have good autumn colour.

Arbutus unedo (strawberry tree) Evergreen that grows in beauty as it matures.

Amelanchier Trees and shrubs with star-shaped flowers and good autumn colour.

Bamboo Useful as feature planting or screen.

Camellia Long-lived spring-flowering evergreen tree.

Cornus controversa 'Variegata' Slow-growing, with attractive horizontal branches.

Dicksonia antarctica (tree fern) Shape and foliage more impressive on mature plants.

Hamamelis (witch hazel) Slow-growing with winter flowers.

Ilex (holly) Slow-growing evergreen.

Magnolia Some are slow-growing; buy a large plant for the impact of the blossom.

Phormium Large specimens have a dramatic shape.

Pieris japonica Slow-growing evergreen with spring flowers.

Taxus baccata 'Fastigiata' (yew) Slow-growing, column-shaped evergreen.

Wisteria sinensis Older specimens flower more profusely.

◁ **INSTANT JUNGLE**
A single large specimen of the tree fern (Dicksonia antarctica) creates a subtropical feel. The trunk is actually part of the root system; water is supplied to the top of the plant where the fronds emerge. The growing point needs protection from frost.

SIMPLE QUICK PRUNING

Mature plants can become untidy or shapeless or they may stop flowering. If you have such plants, don't rush to take them out, since many can be rapidly rejuvenated at various times during the year just by pruning out old or sprawling stems or cutting back spent flower heads.

▷ **TIME TO TRIM**
Keep lavender looking neat by trimming it annually in spring. Old, sprawling plants are best removed and replaced with young plants, since shoots rarely sprout from old wood.

△ **SECOND SHOWING**
Lupins can look scruffy after flowering, but if you remove the flower spike promptly when it starts to fade, you might get a second one.

It can take two or three years for some plants to recover from major renovation, but there are others that respond more quickly. Many shrubs and perennials and some climbers show an improvement in flowering or growth habit in a single season, thanks to 10–15 minutes spent on pruning or trimming. For a plant to respond to pruning with renewed vigour, it must be healthy – not debilitated by pests or disease.

PERENNIALS

Trimming or deadheading perennials in summer can often produce new foliage or flowers. Hardy geraniums and alchemilla look good in early summer, but then the stems flop or the foliage dries. Shear them off, water well and new growth will appear. Delphiniums often produce a second flower spike if you remove the first when it fades.

SHRUBS

Many summer-flowering shrubs bloom on wood produced the same year. Cutting out the old wood in spring clears the way for new shoots. This gives a better framework for the flowers, which will be bigger and more numerous. Hardy fuchsias and tree mallow are two shrubs that respond well to pruning just as the buds begin to show.

Prune summer-flowering shrubs that no longer flower well just after blooming to improve the following year's display. There are two main techniques: cut back one stem in every three almost to the ground, or shorten all stems by two-thirds (see pages 210). The method to use depends on the shrub, so consult a pruning book.

CLIMBERS

Mature rambling or climbing roses that bloom in one flush are worth pruning when they finish flowering (see pages 210–211). Rambling roses that have produced strong stems growing from the base should have the same number of older ones cut down to ground level – don't spend time pruning all the old stems unless you are doing a complete renovation. With climbing roses, cut back any old, unproductive branches to just above a new shoot.

Vigorous climbers, such as wisteria and *Clematis montana,* soon become a tangled mass that needs frequent cutting back with hand pruners. A quick way to keep them within bounds after flowering is to prune back the whiplike summer growth – the woody framework can be tackled more easily in winter. Late-flowering clematis, such as 'Jackmanii' and the *viticella* types, flower on new growth, so remove old or weak top growth in late winter to early spring, cutting down to an active leaf bud.

WHEN PRUNING DOESN'T PAY

Old, short-lived plants are probably better replaced, and mature trees and hedges do not respond quickly. Trees need pruning only when a problem arises; for example, a branch breaks or dies back and the dead wood must be cut out (see pages 210–211). Tree renovation is not quick, though, and you may prefer to hire a tree surgeon. Hedges are dealt with on pages 212–213.

PREVENTING PROBLEMS

It is worth wandering around the garden once a week during the growing season with a pair of hand pruners so you can quickly snip away any potential problems. For example, variegated plants sometimes develop all-green shoots, which if left grow faster than the variegated shoots and swamp the parent plant. Cut out the all-green shoots as soon as you see them.

Unwanted suckering needs to be dealt with instantly, too. While the suckers are still young and soft, rub them off the parent plant or pull them out. Try to avoid cutting suckers off, since this can encourage them. If you do need to cut out a sucker, trace it back to where it grows from the parent plant. Among the plants worth checking for suckers are roses and grafted rhododendrons. Basic pruning and deadheading techniques are explained and illustrated on pages 210–213.

◁ **RAMPANT ROSE**
Climbing and rambling roses can be pruned quickly after flowering if they are in good condition. Old or top-heavy roses need a major renovation, which is best undertaken in winter, when plants are dormant, and followed by a mulch and feed in the spring.

LAWNS

A well-kept lawn can be a jewel in your garden. If you inherit a problem lawn that is more of an eyesore than an asset, don't despair. There is a lot you can do to rejuvenate a tired, sickly plot of grass, restoring it to full beauty. If a lawn is beyond restoration, your best option may be to tear it out and replant.

△ MINIMAL CARE
Inheriting a perfect lawn may seem daunting, but one weekend of maintenance in spring and regular mowing during the growing season will keep it in reasonable shape.

Even if you have long-term plans to do away with the lawn or change its position, there is a lot to be said for postponing this until work has been done on the rest of the garden. After all, there are few horizontal surfaces that are as cheap and easy to repair as a lawn. In addition, tearing up a lawn, then finding that the children have nowhere to play football can prove to be a costly mistake. What you can achieve in terms of quick fixes depends on the time of year, how long the grass is, the type of grass, and your long-term plans for that area.

A THREADBARE LAWN

A lawn that has been well used but not cared for can be restored quite easily. The best time to do this is in autumn or spring (see pages 216–217). There are a number of lawn kits available for quick lawn renovation. These contain grass seed in a dispenser and often come with a fertilizer to get the grass off to a good start. If you have broad, flat blades of grass, use a ryegrass mix; if the lawn contains mainly fine, needlelike grass use a mixture without ryegrass. A patching kit is ideal for the odd bald spot but where the entire lawn is thin you will need to scatter grass seed over all of it (a technique known as oversowing). The new seed will germinate and in time you will have a rejuvenated lawn.

AN IMMACULATE LAWN

The lawn you have inherited was the previous owner's pride, but your heart sinks at the thought of all the work involved in keeping it looking immaculate. Do not worry: just make sure you mow it little and often rather than leaving it and then taking a lot off at once. Extensive treatment with chemicals is unnecessary but any perennial weeds that appear should be dug out or treated with a spot weeder.

A perfect lawn is likely to be an ornamental grass mixture containing fine grasses and no ryegrass. These are more tolerant of close mowing than ryegrass mixtures but less tolerant of wear and tear. There are new varieties of ryegrass that look like fine grass but are harder wearing. It may be possible to oversow with these and mow little and often to a blade length of 2.5 cm (1 in), which would favour the ryegrass. If you cannot find a ryegrass variety that is suitable for your area, seek the advice of a groundsman or greenkeeper.

LONG GRASS

If the grass has been left to grow long, do not start cutting with a mower. Use a trimmer to cut it down to a height the mower can manage, let the grass recover, then use the mower on its highest

setting. A quick trick is to clear and maintain a small area, leaving the rest as a wildflower meadow. You could cut a path through to a feature or a small clearing to use for picnics. The path and clearing can be cut regularly to 2.5 cm (1 in). In time you could have other areas that are left to grow to 8–10 cm (3–4 in) and some parts can be meadow, which needs cutting only twice a year.

AN ILL-DEFINED LAWN

A neglected lawn will eventually drift into the borders or untidily lap the garden boundaries. If it is given a more definite shape such as a circle, square or rectangle, a lawn will enhance the overall garden design. Lawns that lack defiinition can be re-shaped quickly using a half-moon cutter to cut the turf along a line (see pages 216–217). If you know what size and shape you want the lawn to be, it is worth adding a mowing edge. This is an edging of brick or paving set just below the lawn surface, which allows you to mow right over, speeding up mowing and reducing the frequency with which you need to trim the edges.

△ **LONG AND SHORT**
If you have a large garden, maintenance will be easier if you leave some areas as meadow; it looks good, too.

△ **CUT TO SHAPE**
An imaginative way of dealing with long grass is to sculpt it into different shapes and patterns. Experimenting like this can provide ideas for long-term design solutions.

EASY BEDDING

Bedding plants are a quick way of brightening up existing borders. They are also useful for replacing old plants that have been removed or for filling spaces in new shrub borders. Being temporary, they are ideal for small spaces and for experimenting with different colours and styles of planting.

Most summer bedding plants are tender and are sold and planted in the spring after the last frosts have passed. They perform all summer, some flowering continuously for months on end, and are removed after the first frost. Cold-season annuals and short-lived perennials such as pansies should be planted in autumn as soon as the weather cools down, so they can establish good root systems before really cold weather sets in.

Traditional bedding schemes are time-consuming to design and plant, so opt for the following easy solutions. Choose a vigorous trailing plant such as one of the Surfinia petunias, *Helichrysum petiolare, Bidens ferulifolia, Verbena* 'Silver Anne', or *Scaevola aemula* 'Blue Wonder'. Plant a few and let them weave between established shrubs. When using more compact varieties to fill gaps, plant three to five plants to form a small drift. Alternatively, single specimens of large pot bedding plants, such as an argyranthemum, geranium or bush fuchsia, can be planted to fill a gap.

BEDDING HABIT

If space is limited or if you want a more formal look, plant dwarf bedding that is uniform and even in height and flowering time. Choose first generation (F_1) hybrids, which are bred for consistency. Elsewhere, larger, less uniform plants will be less work; for example, when filling summer gaps between perennials in a border, use taller plants such as cosmos or tobacco plant *(Nicotiana)*.

Bedding with daisylike flowers, such as marguerites and felicias, or those with flower spikes, such as antirrhinums or *Salvia farinacea* 'Victoria', often work well with perennials.

BEDDING IN NEW SHRUB BORDERS

Sweeps of bedding are ideal for filling gaps in a shrub border in its early years. Choose low-growing bedding, such as busy lizzies, gazanias or petunias, which will not smother the young shrubs. Since the shrubs will make a neutral background, there is no need to restrict your choice of colour, so use mixtures or single colours as you prefer.

SUCCESS WITH BEDDING

Since most bedding plants have just one season in which to perform, they need a good start. Plant them in a sunny site and water well to get a decent display. Most bedding plants prefer sun, but will tolerate partial shade. The best plants for shade are *Begonia semperflorens* and busy lizzies.

Bedding is available to suit both wet and dry conditions, and if your climate is unpredictable, buy some of each. Rain-tolerant plants include antirrhinum, tobacco plant, *Begonia semperflorens,* lobelias, pansies *(Viola wittrockiana)* and busy lizzies. Drought-tolerant bedding includes *Bidens ferulifolia,* cinerarias, diascias, felicias, gazanias, petunias, geraniums and zinnias.

Foliage bedding is useful, since the leaves are not as fleeting or weather dependent as flowers. *Cineraria* 'Silverdust' is a good standby – it will harmonize with anything. More unusual options include the striking foliage of scented geraniums like 'Lady Plymouth' and 'Chocolate Peppermint'.

▽ **SUMMER COLOUR**
Petunias now come in a wide range of single colours as well as mixtures. Here, a mixed planting of the variety 'Devon Cream' adds summer colour to a sunny, dry spot.

▷ **GAP FILLERS**

Bedding plants provide an easy way to fill gaps in a mature border of shrubs and perennials. Here, a neat edging of shade-tolerant Begonia semperflorens *adds a red highlight to the front of a mixed border.*

▽ **PLANTING PARTNERS**

The loose habit and daisylike flowers of osteospermums make them ideal companions for perennials such as the silver-leaved Stachys lanata. *Osteospermums are actually tender perennials, but most are sold as late summer bedding plants. Some, like* O. ecklonis *shown here, can overwinter in mild areas.*

SCREENS AND ARCHES

Screens make a garden more interesting and enable you to separate areas with different styles or colour schemes or different functions. They are also useful for hiding eyesores or renovation work. Arches between screens tempt exploration and can be used to frame ornamental features.

▽ **IN HARMONY**
When choosing or building garden structures, particularly large ones, make sure they fit in with other elements in the garden and with the house. This ornate trellis screen links closely to the conservatory.

Some of the garden structures described here, such as arches, are available in kit form, and all of them can be constructed in a weekend by a competent amateur handyman. Most involve fixing posts in the ground, and the quickest method is to use metal spikes that are simply hammered into the soil (see page 201).

TRELLIS SCREENS

Cheap trellis panels are often badly made and flimsy. In addition, the more unusual designs are expensive, so it is worth making them yourself or having them custom made. Roofing battens are inexpensive, readily available and just the right thickness for making trellis to fix between upright

supports. To make curved tops, use a jigsaw to cut out sections from sheets of exterior-grade plywood. Use galvanized nails or brass screws for outdoor woodwork.

QUICK SWAGS

Brick pillars supporting heavy rope swags that are bedecked with roses are often an impressive feature of large gardens. They divide up a plot, but create a more open feeling than a solid screen. To make a quicker version, use posts for the uprights topped with decorative post caps, and attach chains to brass hooks for the swags.

RUSTIC PANELS

Hurdles and panels made of willow or coppiced hazel have long been used for screening. They work well in cottage or wildlife gardens and even look good in modern gardens. Natural materials such as split canes and reeds are now sold in rolls, with the material held in place by plastic-coated wire. They will last three to five years.

ARCHES

A single arch marks an entrance from one area to another. Although an arch is quick to erect, you do need to position it carefully. Often it will contribute more to a garden if there is a screen or planting on either side. If you are putting an arch over a path or an entrance, there may already be a screen. For example, you can erect an arch over an entrance gate in the gap between the front wall or hedge. If you do not have an existing screen, it may be possible to extend borders to form one. If there is nothing, trellis panels can be quickly erected and an arch chosen in the same style.

Easy-to-assemble arches in kit form are made of plastic-coated metal or of rustic wooden poles, trellis or sawed timber.

COMBINED PLANTER AND SCREEN

Wooden planters backed by trellis screens can be bought or made. Best of all is that they do not need holes for uprights and can be used on sites with poor soil or none at all. They form good temporary screens in small areas, but make sure you match the climber to the space available.

PLANTS

It will take time for climbers to cover screens and arches. Quick-growers are not always the best option, since many are too vigorous for lightweight structures. For temporary screens, plant annual climbers or container plants. Use groups of containers in front of screens or beside arches; tall plants, such as lilies, will soften the screens. You can also fix small containers to the tops or sides of posts or the side panels of arches and fill them with fast-growing trailers (choose drought-tolerant species or use an automatic watering system).

Roses that reach 3 m (10 ft) or so and are of moderate vigour, such as many of the modern climbers, will give the best results on an arch. Since these are now sold as more mature plants in containers in summer, buy a couple and train them up the supports.

△ **ELEGANT ARCH**
Metal is extremely malleable, so intricate designs can be created even on small arches like this one. Metalwork can be painted if you wish or left to rust naturally.

▽ **DIVIDE AND LINK**
This wooden pergola also functions as an arch, both separating and connecting different areas of the garden.

QUICK CLIMBERS

Fast-growing climbers provide rapid vertical cover for walls, fences and plant supports. Many are annuals or tender perennials grown as annuals. Their temporary nature is an asset when you are getting to grips with a new garden, since permanent, vigorous plants need more thoughtful placing.

The growth produced by annuals in one year is copious, but not heavy, so they are ideal for lightweight or temporary supports. Annual climbers trained up posts or tripods are useful for filling gaps between permanent plantings; they fulfil the same temporary role as bedding plants, but provide greater height. Annuals need a warm, sheltered, sunny site; most prefer a moist but well-drained soil. If you cannot provide those conditions, or do not have time to raise annuals from seed, vigorous perennial climbers are an option (see box opposite).

PLANTING

Most annual climbers are bought as seed and are best started off indoors in early spring. Two exceptions that work well from outdoor sowings are nasturtiums and sweet peas. As the results with annuals depend very much on the growing season in that one year, it is worth sowing a few seeds each month in spring to get a succession of flowers. If you are too late to grow from seed, you may be able to buy small plants in garden centres later in the spring, or larger, ready-trained plants in summer.

EDIBLE CLIMBERS

It takes a while to get a kitchen garden organized, but runner beans and squashes are easy crops that can be grown in the garden proper. They are also very versatile, and you can grow them against a sunny wall or fence, up a wigwam in an empty

▽ **COLOUR AND SCENT**
Growing sweet peas is a quick way of bringing scent and a lovely range of colours into the garden. Sow seeds in autumn or spring. They are hardy, so once they have germinated, at 15°C (59°F), you can grow them on outside in a sheltered place.

TEMPORARY CLIMBERS

Asarina (climbing snapdragon) Small violet or red flowers on 2-m (6½- ft) plants.

Cobaea scandens (cup and saucer vine) Unusual flowers that open yellow-green and age to purple, borne on 4-m (13-ft) plants.

Codonopsis (climbing bell flower) Various species of twining climber ranging in height from 1–3 m (3–10 ft), usually with blue, bell-like flowers.

Cucurbita pepo (gourd) Scrambles up to 6½ ft (2 m) or more and bears a fascinating mixture of fruits that hang effectively when grown over an arch.

Eccremocarpus scaber (Chilean glory vine) Masses of red-orange flowers from summer through to autumn, on 2–3-m (6½–10-ft) plants.

Ipomoea (morning glory) Blue, mauve, or red trumpet-shaped flowers when grown in full sun. Can reach more than 3 m (10 ft).

Lathyrus odoratus (sweet pea) Grown as a cut flower for its wonderful scent and colour. Needs a fair amount of attention. Various sizes, from 2–3 m (6½–10 ft).

Thunbergia alata (black-eyed Susan) Flowers in orange, yellow or white. Not too vigorous, reaching only 1 m (3 ft). Often grown with success in containers.

Tropaeolum majus (nasturtium) Climbing forms in interesting mixtures of red, orange and yellow. Ideal for covering low walls, since they reach 1–1.2 m (3–4 ft). Does well in poor dry soils.

Tropaeolum peregrinum (canary creeper) Dense cover from figlike leaves; small yellow flowers. Reaches 2–3 m (6½–10 ft).

◁ **RAPID RUNNER**
One of the quickest-growing annuals is the runner bean. It is well suited to container growing, and a single plant will produce many beans. As well as having impressive cropping power, it offers rapid screening and attractive flowers.

MORE PERMANENT CLIMBERS

The following are more long-lasting plants for quick cover. They do not need the regular watering that annuals require, since they root deeply. However, they will need pruning if they encroach on other plants, and supports must be sturdy.

Ampelopsis and ***Parthenocissus*** Self-clinging deciduous climbers for large walls, with autumn colour and berries. *Ampelopsis* grow to 5–10 m (16–33 ft), *Parthenocissus* to 9–10 m (30–33 ft).

Clematis montana Rampant, spring-flowering clematis to grow over trees, pergolas and garages. All varieties are deciduous; some are scented. Reach 8–10 m (26–33 ft).

Fallopia baldschuanica (Russian vine) The fastest-growing climber, so needs careful siting, since it can swamp neighbours. Attractive summer flowers. Reaches 12 m (40 ft)

Hedera canariensis and ***H. colchica*** Large-leaved ivies for rapid cover; evergreen. Both plants grow to 6 m (20 ft).

Humulus lupulus 'Aureus' (golden hop) Hardy herbaceous climber offering golden yellow summer cover. Reaches 6 m (20 ft).

Lonicera japonica Several varieties of evergreen or semievergreen honeysuckles for quick cover. Grow to 6 m (20 ft).

border, on a temporary screen of canes, or on an arch. They need a sheltered spot and are often grown with sweet peas to encourage pollinating insects, and so ensure a good crop. Being fast growers, they need plenty of moisture in the soil.

The traditional way to grow runner beans is to dig a bean trench the previous autumn and fill it with garden waste, but you can get away with simply adding some well-rotted organic matter before planting and mulching well.

Squashes and runner beans can also be grown from seed in pots indoors; plant them out after the frosts. Grow runner beans on thin poles or canes, spaced 30 cm (1 ft) apart, with two plants on each cane. Train climbing squashes up arches, canes or trellis. They are vigorous plants, and growing them vertically is a good way to save space.

QUICK COLOUR

An effective way to introduce colour into a garden is to use the wide range of outdoor paints and stains that are available. This is quicker than using plants, and the colour will be there to cheer you up even in winter. And when you get bored with a colour or it becomes dated, you can quickly change it.

△ **FALSE WINDOW**
Use paint or a stain to give a new lease on life to a drab, but sound, wooden structure. Large structures can be used as a canvas for imaginative ideas, such as this false window on a garage wall.

Colour is subjective and fashion-based, but before you decide to go with the trend, bear in mind the effect of light on colour. Bright colours work well in strong sunlight, as in Mediterranean countries. Further north, cooler, softer colours, such as muted greens and greys, may work better. Colour can be used to link elements, such as a pot and a bench, but do not coordinate everything because this will look contrived.

Decide whether to use colours that either blend or contrast with existing hues from flowers, foliage, ornaments or structures. If you are undecided, buy sample pots of different colours and paint offcuts of wood. Leave them in position for a few days and view them at different times of day. Using two shades of a harmonious colour reduces the prominence of large structures such as sheds.

PAINTS

Outdoor paints are useful for adding a splash of colour, or for complementing a colour-themed planting scheme. Glossy paints give a shiny finish, so use them on structures that you want to stand out. A matt finish absorbs light, so will have a more subdued effect.

Most outdoor paints are solvent-based; some are water-based. Before painting onto bare wood, apply a primer or an undercoat. If you are painting over old paint, use a wire brush to remove any flakes, scrub the surface clean with hot, soapy water, allow it to dry and then rub it over with sandpaper.

STAINS

Wood stains change the colour of the wood while allowing the grain to show through. They are good for toning down the brightness of new pine furniture and structures such as pergolas and will help them to blend into naturalistic settings such as woodland and wildlife gardens.

Water-based stains are quick and pleasant to use and will not harm plants. Wood preservatives or treatments that claim to kill or discourage moulds, algae or fungi are less pleasant to use

(they are pesticides and most are solvent-based). If you want to use these products, take precautions to protect yourself and nearby plants.

QUICK PROJECTS

The following suggestions for decorating with paints or stains can all be carried out in a day. Water-based stains will be touch-dry in about three hours. The ideal time is on a warm, breezy day in spring before planting gets under way.

Seats These can be painted either to blend with the surroundings or to stand out. Slatted chairs and benches are difficult to paint, since there are so many surfaces, but being portable, they can be painted in winter under cover.

Trellis Painted trellis makes a big impact, especially early on before any plants are in place. This, too, can be difficult to paint because there are so many surfaces. Use a small brush that fits into the gaps and a larger one for tops and posts.

Plant supports These usually need to be in place before plants have grown up, so turn them into a feature. You could paint all the wooden stakes in a border the same colour. Bamboo canes will take paint if they are lightly sanded first. Formal pyramids look smart when painted.

Wooden edging Gravel boards used to edge beds can be painted in a colour to match a planting scheme, plant supports or nearby trellis. Paint them before adding mulch to the bed. You need only paint the wood that is visible.

Containers Change the colour of wooden tubs, planters and window boxes as often as you change the planting schemes. Stencils can be used to decorate window boxes or other containers that are viewed at eye level.

Sheds and greenhouses Instead of hiding sheds and wooden greenhouses behind screens, you can turn them into attractive garden features. A shed, in particular, offers great scope for creativity with paint and can be transformed into a beach hut, clubhouse, gypsy caravan or whatever your imagination suggests.

△ **RESTFUL HUES**
This arbour has been made more relaxing and inviting by the use of a restful green paint. The peaceful feeling is emphasized by the blue-checked cushions and pale-coloured flower arrangement.

◁ **INSTANT STYLE**
You don't need to spend a lot of money on ornaments and plants to create a garden style. A Mediterranean-style seating area has been created here simply by using appropriate warm-toned paint colours on the walls, windows and seat.

DECORATING WALLS

If a wall is sound and not in need of structural repair, it can make a great canvas for creative ideas, especially if ground space is limited. These simple decorative effects are also useful where there is no soil at the bottom of the wall in which to grow climbers or wall shrubs.

◁ GARDEN ART

A hand-painted mural will turn your wall into a work of art, but you need to be able to draw – or know someone who can! Choose a theme appropriate to the garden setting. This Provençal scene, with cypresses and lavender, is in keeping with the style of the wall.

A wide range of masonry paints exists for concrete, plastered surfaces and brickwork. Many are water-based and will dry within four hours, after minimal preparation. A shady site will benefit from white paint or pale colours to reflect as much light as possible. If you have a sunny wall, you could opt for a stronger colour such as ochre, and use this as a backdrop to suitable plants such as rock rose or lavender.

Wall planters filled with trailing plants are a quick way of getting plants high up the wall. For a sunny wall, use drought-tolerant plants, since they will be less vulnerable to drying out. Sun-lovers include geraniums, portulaca and variegated thymes. If the wall is shady, on the other hand, choose plants such as begonia, fuchsia, ivy or lesser periwinkle.

Where ground space is at a premium, look for semicircular planters that can be pushed right up against the wall. Triangular-shaped pots that fit into corners are also available.

A self-contained wall fountain makes an attractive feature near a seat. These fountains are available in kit form and can be set up quickly and run from an indoor power point. With more time, you could create an individual water feature incorporating tiles, pebbles or mosaics. Plant lush foliage plants around the feature to hide the cables.

TRICK THE EYE

Trompe l'oeil, where the viewer is tricked into thinking painted objects are real or that

real objects are larger than they actually are, has a long tradition dating back to ancient times. Modern materials can be used to create such effects quickly. The technique is most valuable for small gardens or enclosed areas where walls predominate and planting ground is limited.

Whatever form the trompe l'oeil takes, it will be most effective if you incorporate some type of frame or surround. A wooden surround or mock trellis arch is easiest to make, but brick or paint effects can also be used. If you are confident in the use of perspective, you could even paint a false door and frame – plenty of foliage plants grown at either side will help to make a believable setting.

Trellis panels Trellis panels can be purchased that give the illusion of a three-dimensional walkway when placed on a wall. There needs to be a clear contrast between the colour of the trellis and the wall for the effect to work.

Silhouettes For an evening illusion, buy or make large, wooden, black silhouettes of planters and attach these to the walls. Use paint and outdoor lighting to build on a sunset theme.

Mirrors An arched mirror can be used to enhance the impression of light, space and planting. Use an exterior-quality mirror, and try out several angles and tilts to get the most pleasing reflection before securely fixing it in place.

Murals A mural can be painted on the wall using exterior paint. Unless you are a skilled painter, stick to simple subjects or use stencils. If you don't want a wooden frame, you can paint a false frame.

CONCRETE WALLS

Cast-concrete is one of the cheapest walling materials, but it can look effective in a modern setting if the wall is well designed. Walls can be made less stark by the use of lush or spiky foliage, ivies or ferns for a shaded area, or grasses and yuccas for sunny spots. An alternative is to create patterns using shells, glass or pebbles, perhaps the "junk" found when clearing the garden.

NEW PLANTS

Climbers and wall shrubs make good use of the vertical space, but you may want to wait and do some research into which ones will suit the site and your style before planting permanent climbers. The direction the wall faces (the aspect) will dictate what plants will be successful. Often the soil at the base of the wall is dry and poor, so it may need to be improved. In some situations, there may be no soil at all, in which case you could use containers (see pages 46–47).

◁ **MIRROR TRICK**
You don't have to be a skilled painter to create a trompe l'oeil. *Here, perspective trellis and a mirror have been cleverly used to create the illusion that a small garden is larger than it is in reality.*

▽ **SHELL MOSAICS**
Simple shell patterns add a decorative touch to a painted wall. These effects work best in dry climates or on sunny walls, since shady or damp walls can become stained with algae.

GARDEN ORNAMENTS

The careful placing of an object such as a beautiful pot or sculpture is a quick, low-maintenance way to enhance your garden and establish a distinctive style. As well as the more conventional garden ornaments, many found and recycled objects can work well.

△ **HIDDEN STATUE**
Classical statuary adds a human touch to a mature garden. A stone bust does not have to be in a formal garden – it can be just as effective in an informal setting such as a shrubbery or woodland.

▷ **SMOTHERED SUNDIAL**
Completely overtaken by the summer flowers of French lavender and sea holly (Eryngium), this sundial will re-emerge to take centre stage when the plants die down in the autumn.

Ornaments have many uses in garden design, and since many of them are portable, it is possible to change the way you use them from time to time to give your garden a fresh look.

At the end of a path or an alleyway Objects placed here draw the eye and invite exploration. You could use an urn on a plinth or an upright figure.

In a border Some perennials, such as lady's mantle and fennel, create a frothy effect in summer. A large terracotta pot or an Ali Baba jar set among them will add impact to the planting.

To mark an entrance A pair of objects placed on either side of an entrance mark its importance as a transitional point. Guard dogs are a favourite, but you could also use obelisks or spheres.

As a centrepiece A formal area such as a courtyard, rose garden or herb bed often gains importance with an ornament in the centre. Choose something that can be viewed from all sides, such as a round pool with a circular tiered fountain, a sundial or a birdbath.

In a secluded area This can often be too shady for many types of plants, but you could add objects to create a sense of quiet mystery – perhaps bathing figures or animals near water.

CHOOSING THE RIGHT ORNAMENT

Personal taste will be the most important factor in choosing the style of an ornament, but it is not the only consideration. After all, some ornaments seem right in their setting and others do not, no matter how expensive they are. It is easier to choose an appropriate item if you have a clear idea of its destination. Study the intended site carefully. Note whether it receives the sun or is dark and gloomy, and whether it is open or secret. This is all part of the atmosphere of the place and will provide valuable clues as to what type of object is appropriate. For example, a "Green man" mask looks good in a woodland garden, partially hidden among plants, whereas a bold geometric piece such as a modern sculpture or an obelisk needs a more open position to make an impact.

A common mistake is to buy an item that is too small for the setting. To get the scale right, try out bamboo canes of different sizes in the space, viewing them from a distance, if relevant, and write down the dimensions. Take a tape measure when choosing ornaments to buy.

In a garden with a definite style, the type of ornament almost presents itself (see pages 170–195). Where a garden has no set style, aim to find something that reflects your personality and is in keeping with the sense of place.

◁ **KEEP IT SIMPLE**
Bold combinations work well if the design is kept simple. The obelisk and agapanthus flowers have contrasting architectural shapes, and they work well together because the setting is not cluttered with other design elements.

▽ **FALLEN URN**
Is this a remnant of a bygone age? Or a new addition, skilfully placed and coated with yogurt to encourage moss to grow? Either way, it forms an attractive addition to the woodland setting.

AGEING ORNAMENTS

Bronze, lead and terracotta age well on their own, but concrete or reconstituted stone needs a helping hand. Where the surface is porous and feels rough to the touch, moss will colonize in wet shady sites, although yogurt can speed up the greening. However, smooth concrete is a difficult surface for colonizing, so sandpaper it lightly before applying the yogurt. Lichen will thrive only in unpolluted air, so you will be lucky if your ornament becomes encrusted with lichen. These techniques can also be used for ageing containers.

DISPLAYING ORNAMENTS

Some objects, such as classical urns, busts or free-standing sundials, require a plinth to get the right effect. Even those that are more humble may need a level base for the best display.

With tall items viewed from one side, consider what will be behind them. Evergreens provide a year-round foil for permanent pieces and work well. Aim for the ornament to contrast with its background. For example, ivy or other small-leaved foliage sets off bold-shaped pieces with little detail. Intricate ornaments are best shown off by a background of large-leaved foliage such as vines. Solid shapes such as a large terracotta urn emerging from a cloud of small flowers in a border work well in summer, but will lose their impact the rest of the year. In this situation, perhaps look for an item that is easy to move indoors for part of the year.

CARING FOR ORNAMENTS

Ornaments should be secured in place if they are valuable or if children may tip them over. If you want to keep an ornament out all year round, you need to check when buying whether it is frost-resistant or whether glazes will crack. Many items from warmer climates are best moved into a conservatory over winter.

▷ **PERFECT FRAME**
Olive jars need no adornment. Their simple, rustic pedigree allows them to fit in with most styles of gardens even modern ones. Just find the right setting.

◁ **LARGE AS LIFE**
Work with what you have. In a large, mature garden just one impressive ornament may be all you need to create an impact. This realistic African antelope will give visitors to the garden quite a surprise.

▷ **PEACEFUL POSE**
It is not just the choice of sculpture but also the way it is used that can set the mood of a garden. These abstract doves are arranged in a pose that suggests peace and harmony.

ADDING A SEAT

Installing seating is one of the easiest quick fixes, giving you somewhere to relax and entertain, and adding instant style to your garden. Here are some ideas for movable or temporary seats you can use in the garden while you work out your long-term requirements.

A wide range of seating is available, especially if you look beyond traditional garden seats and include conservatory furniture, items from the home and secondhand items. Style will influence your decision, but should not override factors such as durability, comfort and ease of maintenance and storage.

You will also need to decide how and where you want to use seating: on the patio only, or are there other parts of the garden with attractive views? Do you want a suntrap or a shady retreat?

Do you prefer company, solitude or intimacy – or would you like to have all three in different places? The answers will soon become clear if you get into the garden in summer and relax in it.

SINGLE SEATS

Wooden folding chairs and wood and canvas director's chairs are stylish and easy to move around. They are good as a short-term measure in summer but are not durable. A more solid wooden or cast-metal chair will be stronger and make more of a feature. If well maintained with preservative or paint, it can be left out all year.

BENCHES

A bench is not as portable as a seat, but some can be shifted to follow the sun. Wood, cast metal and stone are the most common materials, and of these wood is the most popular. Cheaper benches are made from softwood such as pine, so are less durable than hardwoods such as teak. Try out several benches before you buy; even a cheap bench needs to be comfortable and should support your back.

Ornate cast-metal or stone benches score lower for comfort, but make more of a statement. Use them beside paths, and add cushions for comfort.

Benches can be incorporated into other structures, although this obviously involves more work and requires a handyman's skills. Ideas include a swinging seat under a pergola or strong arch, a wooden bench in a decking garden, or a stone seat as part of a brick-built raised bed. Makeshift items such as railway sleepers and wooden planks can be used, but beware of splinters and make sure the structure is stable.

▽ **FLEXIBLE FURNITURE**
Director's chairs are easy to move around the garden – doing so will help you to decide where to put permanent seating. In poor weather, bring the chairs indoors or cover them, to preserve the canvas.

ARBOURS

A traditional arbour was a seating area enclosed overhead with plants, but there are now many structures that give instant enclosure. The sizes, materials and styles of arbours vary greatly. To make a real impact with an arbour, you need to have settled on a garden style and design. If not, an arbour of woven branches or wicker hidden among mature trees is quick and in keeping. Add simple wooden stools or log sections for seats. In a more open area, trellis arbours can be bought as units and are quick to instal. Plant a scented climber such as a rose to complete the scene.

◁ **SIMPLE EFFECTS**
This wrought-iron bench and folding wooden table work well together, despite being made of different materials. Both have simple, clear lines and are pale coloured.

▽ **A PLACE TO RELAX**
Mature gardens usually score high for shade and privacy, so make sure you have the seating to enjoy their benefits, such as this lounger, designed for sitting or snoozing.

ENTERTAINING

Many people dream of a "room outside" to use for sophisticated al fresco dining or atmospheric night-time parties. Constructing patios and barbecues and installing lighting are long-term projects, but if you want to use your garden for entertaining in the meantime, here are some simple ideas to try.

To get a garden that is undergoing renovation into a fit state for entertaining, you need to adopt a two-pronged approach. First, concentrate on making the surfaces that guests will use clean and tidy, rather than worrying too much about small details and particular plants. Second, provide guests with a pleasant and comfortable seating area; apart from the main elements such as privacy, shade, shelter, good views or attractive planting, think about pleasing touches, such scented plants or temporary lighting.

QUICK SCENTS

Establishing scented shrubs and climbers such as roses and honeysuckle in your garden design takes time. The following are quick fillers for pots or spare ground near a patio or deck.

Heliotropium (cherry pie) Most produce purple or violet domes of flowers in late summer.

Hesperis matronalis (sweet rocket) Biennial with white or pale lilac flowers in early summer.

Lilium regale (regal lily) The easiest scented lily for borders or pots. White with pale purple flush.

Lobularia maritima (sweet alyssum) Low-growing with white, pink, apricot or purple flowers. The honey scent carries well.

Miribilis jalapa (four o'clock plant) Pink or red flowers that open in late afternoon and last until morning.

Nicotiana (tobacco plant) Tubular or trumpet-shaped flowers in white, lime green, pink or red. *N. alata* and *N. sylvestris* have the best scent.

Pelargonium (scented geraniums) Available in a range of scents including lemon, spicy, pine, apple and rose. 'Lemon Meringue' is pictured above.

Whatever stage of renovation your garden has reached, it will look much better if you tidy it before a function. Cut the grass, trim the lawn edges and remove the clippings; sweep paths and patios. New or bare beds and borders will look instantly better if a mulch is applied or topped up.

Position the furniture before guests arrive and make sure any parasols are correctly fitted. Arrange bold groups of container plants where they can be seen and smelled from the seats. If you have a wall-mounted fountain, turn it on.

A dining canopy is a quick and inexpensive way of providing shade, privacy and protection from summer showers. The fabric sides can be opened or closed and the tubular frame has feet that can be fitted to a hard surface or into a lawn.

THE GARDEN AT NIGHT

Outdoor lighting creates a magical atmosphere and can be used to direct attention to special features such as architectural plants or ornaments. Installing mains electricity in the garden is a job for a qualified electrician and takes time and planning because deep trenches need to be dug.

Quicker alternatives include low-voltage lighting, lanterns and candles. Low-voltage lighting kits run off a reduced voltage, thanks to a transformer, which is kept indoors where the unit is plugged in. The lights can be moved around easily, since the cables need only to be disguised, not buried deeply for safety. But there are drawbacks to low-voltage systems. Some are expensive for the amount of light they produce, so try to see several systems working before buying, and compare brands as the quality of the fittings vary in quality of finish.

Candles or flares provide natural light, and there is now a wide range available for garden use, along with various types of holders. Storm lanterns are attractive and protect candles from breezes. Citronella candles have the added benefit of keeping away insects. Make sure the route to the seating area is well lit, especially near steps and arches. Clear away any tools or debris from access areas. If paving is uneven, cover it with containers to prevent accidents.

Evening-fragrant plants, such as night-scented stock, sweet rocket and tobacco plant, are useful, and their pale colours are effective in the evening light (see box opposite).

BARBECUES

To make a temporary barbecue in under two hours, lay bricks without mortar, leaving small gaps between them to form a circular or square shape. About 100 bricks are needed to make a barbecue with a height of 75 cm (30 in). You will also need a stone or steel grate for the charcoal plus a grill. A stable work surface is useful for plates and utensils. Alternatively, obtain a hinged wooden chest or bench so the inside can be used for storage and the lid can be used as a table or seat. Site the barbecue with care: watch out for fire hazards such as overhanging branches and try to avoid smoking out your neighbours.

◁ **LOW-KEY LIGHTING**
To create the right atmosphere, lighting in an entertaining area is best kept subtle and low-key. It should provide sufficient illumination to eat by and perhaps highlight a few key plants and features.

▽ **CANDLE BASKET**
A group of candles nestling among pebbles in a wire basket is a quick way to add a touch of magic to an evening's entertaining.

PROBLEM SOLVING

Chapter Two suggested some quick-and-easy ways to give your garden a real lift. Here we look in depth at some of the more fundamental problems that occur all the time and offer a choice of clear and workable solutions.

The problems are tackled in a few broad categories: basic design and layout; soil type, climate and lie of the land; specific planting scenarios; and garden features and structures. Along the way we cover such diverse situations as dealing with a boringly shaped space, screening off a windy, exposed area, creating a lovely rose garden, and making the most of that knotty issue – the garden shed.

△ **WELL-PLANNED SPACE**
This tiny space has been cleverly designed to include a tiled living area enclosed with planting, a simple pool and a pergola.

◁ **TRANQUIL GARDEN**
The owners of this urban garden, with its air of seclusion and tranquillity, have taken full advantage of the shady site by planting woodland-edge species, such as grasses like wood rush (Luzula), and hart's-tongue fern (Asplenium scolopendrium).

A DULL SHAPE

A garden filled with the most wonderful plants and ornaments can still be let down badly by an unimaginative layout. One all-too-familiar example is the central rectangular lawn flanked by straight borders, leaving everything visible and no room for that essential element of mystery or surprise.

△ **TWISTS AND TURNS**
The lawn flows around this large shrub like a river – where does it lead to? Perhaps to a summerhouse, a secret garden, or a shaded seat. Erecting natural barriers like this can lend a sense of excitement to any garden.

The best way to break out of a dull lawn-and-border arrangement obviously depends on the size of your garden and on how you use it, but the pointers detailed below will apply in most cases, or can easily be adapted.

EXTENDING THE BORDERS

One solution is simply to extend your side borders into the lawn area at certain points, thereby altering your lawn shape at a stroke. As a first step, either mark this out on the ground, or draw a plan – see below and pages 38–41. On our plan, an imaginary line has been drawn from the right-hand boundary about a third of the way down. Another imaginary line extends from the left, two-thirds down the garden. Now bring your beds out in a swelling curve at these points and soften and curve them slightly around the rest of the border; there may be a conveniently placed large

tree or shrub around which your border can swell. Transfer your plan to the garden by marking out the shape with a garden hose and plants in pots. Leave the markers for a week or so while you consider the new design. When you are happy with it, make it permanent by using trellis, hedges or shrubs to define the new areas.

Making divisions in this way produces distinct areas that lend themselves to different roles – place a sheltered kitchen garden at the end, hide a seat around a newly created corner, or have a larger number of smaller divisions, simply to lend interest and flow to your garden.

CHANGING SHAPES

A common way of adding interest is to cut out differently shaped beds – circles or kidney shapes, for instance. While this may look effective viewed from an upstairs window, it has far less visual

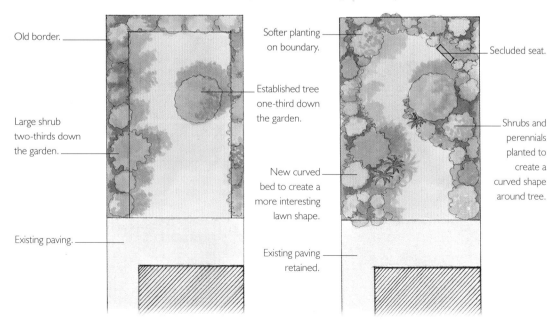

Old border.

Large shrub two-thirds down the garden.

Existing paving.

Established tree one-third down the garden.

Softer planting on boundary.

Secluded seat.

Shrubs and perennials planted to create a curved shape around tree.

New curved bed to create a more interesting lawn shape.

Existing paving retained.

◁ **STRONG FOCUS**
Two borders placed either side of a rectangular central lawn is the most common, and easily the least interesting, garden shape. Here, simply adding a seating area framed by a pergola has instantly lent the garden a strong sense of purpose and direction.

△ **BLURRED OUTLINE**
The rectangular shape of this lawn has been transformed by bringing the flowerbeds right out into the centre of the garden. Thick shrub-planting around the summerhouse has also worked extremely effectively, turning the space into something altogether more intriguing.

impact at ground level, where it really matters, than altering the actual lawn shape. In any case, changing the lawn also automatically changes the shape of the beds, and in a natural way.

Either plot a new lawn shape on the ground or sketch it out on a plan. A hose is ideal for marking curved shapes, while string stretched between sticks is better for rectangles or squares. To create a circular lawn, first work out the diameter (see pages 216–217). For irregular curved shapes, shrubs or trees provide useful starting points and anchors for the design.

ADDING A FOCUS

If your garden is an interesting shape, but there is still something missing, it may be that you lack a focal point to draw the eye and give the overall design a sense of direction. This might be something as simple as a bench, a boldly shaped plant or a piece of sculpture, but it must be carefully placed in order to make visual sense. Think about your main viewpoint. Do you want your eye to be drawn to the focal point when you look out of the living room window, or when you enter the garden? Do you need several focal points to link various parts of the garden visually? And be sensible – don't position a bench where you wouldn't want to sit. Once you have placed the focal point, stand back. It may need a little framing, with either plants or trelliswork.

Another technique, which might suit a more formal garden, is to place two large plants either side of the focal point and "echo" them with two similar plants nearer to the viewpoint.

FRONT GARDENS

Your back garden may be your private haven, but it is the front garden that gives the world a first impression of your home. It has several roles to play: not just reflecting who you are, but also fitting in with its surroundings and providing safe, easy access to the front door, plus perhaps space for a bike or car.

△ **RELAXED STYLE**
Exuberantly planted and charmingly messy, this front garden invites you to wander slowly up to the front door, pausing to admire a butterfly or smell a lily on the way.

▷ **CLASSIC PLANTING**
Twining through the railings and around the window, wisteria is the perfect plant to frame the front door of this classic town house. It does, however, need careful, hard pruning each winter, and some long whippy growths cut back in summer.

The basic function of a front garden area is to connect the house to the street, and your design should make this transition easy in a practical way and also make the link visually – especially if the house is a long way from the street. If, for example, a gateposted, tree-flanked entrance gives way to an empty drive up to the house, then your home could end up looking stranded and unwelcoming. A traditional way of anchoring the house in its surroundings and linking it to the entrance would be to hedge the drive or line it with an avenue of trees, but this is a rather formal solution. A more relaxed alternative is to line the drive with clumps of shrubs or trees – silver birches are delicately simple and attractive.

FORMAL AND INFORMAL PLANTING

Plant selection is crucial. To give a town house a neat and formal air, for example, your design should be crisp and well defined. You might choose a large specimen plant such as a magnolia as your centrepiece, and surround it with a circle of gravel, edged attractively with rope-topped tiles.

For those with more informal tastes, plant a group of shrubs based on a colour theme – red-leaved *Cotinus coggygria* threaded with pink clematis would be one such choice. As for shady spots, large-leaved ivy always creates a tranquil mood. Use it with care close to shrubs and trees, however, since it will twine around the trunks.

FRAMING YOUR FRONT DOOR

Draw the eye to the front door by framing it. For a smart effect, use tubs of evergreens clipped into simple balls, pyramids or topiary figures.

Climbers around the front door can look especially charming and welcoming. Fasten trellis up each side of the door, or in an arch over it, and make sure that it will hold your plants. Choose smaller-growing types as they are easy to control. Clematis is a favourite, but opt for a variety that is cut down each year; avoid the vigorous *C. montana,* which can become very untidy.

SURFACES AND DRIVEWAYS

Gravel provides a low-maintenance surface. Cobbles or pebbles are attractive but uneven, so do not use them in areas that are walked on.

Given a choice, most people prefer off-street parking, so a driveway often takes priority over planting. But all is not lost. You can plant the central strip of a driveway with tough species: aubretia or creeping thymes in a sunny spot, lesser periwinkle in a shady one. A large U-shaped or circular driveway needs bold planting if it is to have impact.

Gravel driveways can be treated with weedkiller, then topped up with fresh gravel raked into place. Use stones that are at least 2 cm (¾ in) across, to a depth of 20 cm (8 in). Make sure that the edge restraints are intact or the gravel will be dispersed into flowerbeds or the road.

Clean paved driveways with a high-pressure sprayer and re-point them if necessary. Any uneven or cracked paving slabs should be replaced, a job best done by a builder. A really cracked tarmac driveway should also be dug up and replaced – it creates a particularly bad

A HIGH-MAINTENANCE GARDEN

Most of us accept that even a minimal garden involves at least a little work, in order to create a pleasant, attractive space and to keep nature under control. However, if your patch seems to be making undue demands on your time, there are all kinds of steps you can take to ease the burden.

Perhaps you are new to gardening and have inherited a high-maintenance garden. Do not despair and do not take hasty, drastic action. You might surprise yourself and discover that, as your interest and skills increase, time-consuming chores actually become easy and enjoyable. What is certain, however, is that a few well-chosen, seemingly minor, changes can reduce the work load enormously.

ISLAND BEDS

One especially high-maintenance feature is a lawn with several flowerbeds positioned as islands in the centre or at the edges, leaving small areas that are awkward and time-consuming to mow and edge.

If the island beds are rectangular and run parallel to the side borders, the simplest solution is to remove the strip of lawn between bed and border. This enlarges the bed, but reduces mowing and edging.

△ **EASY MOWING**
A mowing edge or path laid at the side of a lawn makes mowing much easier. If you want to create a curved lawn, bear in mind that gentle curves like this one are much easier to mow than tight ones.

For beds set farther into the lawn, you might be able to remove the turf and create large beds that act as interesting garden dividers (see pages 78–79). Another option is to turf the beds over and incorporate them into your lawn. Keep the level even – your new grass may sink into the old beds. For the best results, tamp the soil down

firmly, and wait a month before laying turf. If you are using lawn seed, sow in early autumn or spring. Remember to prepare the surface in advance.

LAWN EDGES

Taking a lawn up to the garden wall or fence works well if you want to enlarge the space visually, but stop short by about 30 cm (1 ft) to allow room to mow or trim the lawn edges properly. Most lawn edges tend to grow out of shape after a while, either creeping into flowerbeds so that grass sprouts up among the plants, or growing away from a tree or shrub that is spreading out into the lawn. Edges really need trimming once a week with shears or a trimmer to keep them tidy, and cutting back into shape once or twice a season with a half-moon edger (see pages 216–217). Any seedling grasses that have strayed into the bed also need to be hoed back at least once a month.

One effective and attractive answer is to lay a permanent brick edging. This should be at least 20 cm (8 in) wide – a brick's length is ideal – to leave space for plants to flop over the edge, and for the grass to grow forward a little. The brick edge should be laid on a bed of mortar and placed so that its surface is just below that of the lawn surface, to avoid damaging the lawn-mower blade. Your lawn edge should now need trimming back only once or twice a year.

Concrete or stone slabs also make good edges for straight lawns; smaller units, such as bricks or small concrete blocks, are better for a curved lawn. If space allows, a wider lawn edge, or one merged with a garden path, looks stylish. It will also give bordering plants room to grow out and flop over.

HIGH-MAINTENANCE PLANTS

There is no escaping the fact that some plants are far more time-consuming to maintain than others. Classic bedding plants, for example, are highly labour-intensive and often very costly, since they have to be replaced each year – twice a year if you want a more continuous supply of flowers.

Some popular plants, such as asters, certain rudbeckias, helianthus, bee balm and heleniums, flower less prolifically unless they are divided once every two or three years. Standard roses are particularly high maintenance. Since they constantly strive to get back to nature by throwing out side shoots, they need careful staking, and those that are weeping in shape need regular cutting back to the framework on which they are

growing. Roses also need a good spraying regime to eradicate disease and pests. And if you plant hostas in a garden where snails and slugs are a problem, your plants will be riddled with holes unless you bait them frequently with slug pellets, or take some other regular action. As for vigorous or invasive trees, shrubs and climbers, such as bamboos and sumachs, these must be kept in constant check.

△ **GARDEN FEATURES**
A large herbaceous border or island bed needs an impressive planting scheme to make the time-consuming maintenance seem worthwhile!

◁ **PARTIALLY PAVED**
Mowing a large expanse of lawn can be a chore. As an alternative, you could simply pave over parts of it, as shown here. This will also create areas with distinct moods, lending more interest to your garden.

Also time-consuming are tall-growing plants that require staking, such as delphiniums, border carnations, dahlias, verbascums and peonies. You could try growing them without a stake, perhaps using surrounding plants to support them, but if this does not work, consider replacing them. There are plenty of tall flowering plants that do not need staking, including foxgloves, globe thistle (*Echinops bannaticus*) and *Verbena bonariensis*.

The key to dealing with high-maintenance plants is simply that you must be prepared to be a little ruthless at times. If you cannot give them the care they need, then take them out and replace them with plants that require less attention. Make sure that your replacement species are suited to the aspect and soil type.

▽ **CLIPPED YEW**
Add a simple elegance to tall, dark yew hedges with the sweeping curves of fragrant lavender bushes. Lavender is relatively low maintenance, but yew hedges must be carefully clipped back to their precise, straight lines if the effect is to be maintained.

FORMAL FEATURES

Formal garden features usually require a high degree of maintenance. However, for those who want to keep something of a formal air but reduce the work load drastically, there are ingenious solutions at hand. If your flowerbeds are edged with low-growing, clipped hedges such as cotton lavender (*Santolina*) or dwarf box, which take a lot of work to keep in shape, simply remove every other plant and replace it with one or two low-growing shrubs. Allow them to grow naturally, to give a softer, yet still neat, border of plants.

▷ **BOX HEDGING**
These low, carefully shaped box hedges need regular clipping to retain their formal effect, but this is compensated for by attractive paving – an easily maintained surface.

Use plants with a similar foliage colour: grey-leaved plants such as lavender or sage work well with *Santolina;* box is complemented by *Hebe rakaensis* or *Sarcococca humilis.*

Formal archways in hedges are attractive, but a ladder is needed to keep them in trim, and this can be awkward. Try removing the top of the arch, but leaving the hedge on either side. Doing this with a clipped archway over a front door won't necessarily spoil the framing effect – clipped "pillars" on each side of the door can be just as effective.

GROUND COVER

One thing that is guaranteed to increase your work load is bare soil between plants, quickly filling up with weeds and often drying out so much that your plants need very frequent watering. Adding a mulch reduces water-loss and weed-growth (see pages 208–209), but a longer-term, more creative solution is to put in ground-cover plants. Some form small hummocks, rooting as they spread – heathers are a good choice for acid soils, while *Cistus* species fare well in dry and sunny spots. "Carpeting" plants spread by throwing out shoots, which also root as they go. Popular examples include the periwinkles *(Vinca* species) and St John's wort *(Hypericum calycinum),* both of which thrive happily in the shade.

MATCHING PLANTS TO PLACES

Any plant growing in the wrong place automatically needs more work. If it is not happy, take it out. Perhaps you have a sun-worshipper in a shady spot or an acid-loving species in alkaline soil. Lime-haters such as rhododendrons, camellias, magnolias and heathers (*Erica* species) are often found struggling to grow in alkaline soil. If you have a dry, sunny garden, replace plants such as astilbe and dicentra, which like damp conditions, with Mediterranean-type plants such as *Cistus* species, which will thrive. Plants that are only just hardy in your area, such as *Agapanthus* species in Britain, need winter protection, whereas in their native South Africa they are prolific. *Crinum powellii,* dahlias and chrysanthemums need lifting in some areas and must be over-wintered indoors.

△ **EASY-CARE GRASSES**
Grasses are the perfect low-maintenance option, but must be chosen to suit the soil and aspect. Here, Stipa gigantea *and* Pennisetum villosum *revel in sunshine and a light soil.*

◁ **WELL COVERED**
The perennial Geranium macrorrhizum *and evergreen ivy provide good ground cover in a shady situation. Ivy planted at the foot of a tree or shrub will need regular cutting back to stop it from twining around the stem or trunk.*

SEATING

Well-designed, carefully placed permanent seating looks good and helps you to enjoy your garden much more. Seats need not be confined to a patio or terrace – use your imagination and dot them around the garden to encourage you to linger in different areas.

A sense of place is everything when it comes to siting permanent garden seating. Think long and hard about the right spot and perhaps try experimenting with a temporary seat (see pages 72–73).

Climate is a major consideration. Do you want your seat in sun or shade? This will depend on how hot your summers are, and on whether you, personally, are a sun-lover. A pergola or an arbour gives pleasant, dappled shade; on a patio or terrace, an awning attached to the house or a parasol fixed to a table can be used on hot days. Do you need shelter in order to admire the view and stay protected from a bitter wind? Or will your site bring a welcome breeze in summer?

EATING AREAS

You will need to do your sums when it comes to seating for an outdoor eating area. Your patio or terrace has to have enough room not just for a table and chairs, but also for people to move around them. As a rough guide, an area of 3.7 m x 3.7 m (12 ft x 12 ft) is large enough for six to eight people to sit comfortably around a table. More space is needed if you want a barbecue, which should ideally be placed downwind of the table.

RAISED-BED SEATING

Building raised beds around two or three sides of a space and topping them with a seat looks attractive and provides useful extra seating for garden parties. This kind of enclosure also has a special sense of privacy. Give your bed brick walls and wide coping to allow for a seat, or make it from railway sleepers as a cheaper option. Plant the bed with aromatic herbs, such as lavender, rosemary, mint, and thyme, or with trailers such as aubretia and alyssum. If you already have a raised bed, consider transforming it into a seat by topping it with coping slabs or sturdy, treated timber.

△ **TOPIARY SEAT**
This topiary armchair provides an amusing feature that suits its formal setting and also blends in well with the hedging on either side.

▷ **SCENTED SEAT**
Tucked to one side of a simple, paved area, this attractively curved wooden seat is the ideal place to sit and admire the view. Scented lilies and thyme planted nearby make it even harder to leave.

SECRET SEATS

It is always fun to tuck seats away in unexpected places – in a corner off a pathway, say, or behind a dividing trellis. A large, welcoming shrub arching over a border might have just enough space for a small seat or bench beneath it. If there is a gap in a border where nothing will grow, use a seat to fill the space and provide a focus.

Wooded areas are ideal spots for secluded seating. Use simple, rustic materials that are appropriate for the setting, such as roughly cut timber, but make sure you remove any splinters.

A perfect position for a hidden seat is beneath a pergola or an arch. If you are making an archway across an existing path, build it deeper and wider so that it spans the path and connects to the boundary, creating a quiet, shady spot for a seat. Allow enough height for flowers such as wisteria or bunches of grapes from a vine to hang without touching people's heads. A two-person seat is ideal for a hidden nook, providing space for quiet conversation or room for one person to stretch out.

BASES FOR SEATS

Giving your seating a base creates a dry surface for a permanent seat and prevents scuffed patches at your feet. The simplest option is to lay six concrete slabs. Make sure you've found the right spot by simply placing the base and using it for a few weeks. If you decide to go ahead, then level the area properly. If it is lawn, cut away the turf, spread sand over the area, and bed the slabs into the sand. Adjust until level. On either side of your seat, add large, beautifully scented shrubs such as roses or philadelphus, planted in the ground or in attractive pots. This gives a comfortable, enclosed feeling; but don't crowd yourself – position them at least 1 m (3 ft) away.

▽ **STUMP SEAT**
Hewn out of an old, ivy-clad tree stump, this woodland seat is a wonderful example of creative recycling.

▽▽ **HEDGE RECESS**
Carving a seating area out of a substantial hedge breaks up the plain green expanse and provides a shaded and secluded spot to relax in.

PLAY AREAS

If you have children, your garden can be a wonderful arena for all kinds of activities – from physical play on swings and climbing frames to fantasy play in tree houses and dens. But thought is needed if play areas are to be integrated successfully, in a way that keeps both adults and children happy.

A successful play area is created with a judicious mixture of caution and consultation. You need to think about both your children's safety and their enjoyment – and yours, too. When your children are babies or toddlers, you must make the decisions about what is right for them. Once they are older, however, find out what they want. There is no point buying an expensive playhouse if all they want to do is ride their bikes or kick a ball around – all you need here is a large, empty lawn, with no delicate border plants and a good level path all the way around.

Decide whether you can accept what your kids ask for, and think through long-term implications. The most elaborate play equipment may lose its appeal quickly, since children often prefer to make their own dens and hideaways. Let them do so, providing simple materials if necessary.

▽ **INTEGRATED PLAY**

In a small garden, play areas must be carefully integrated so that they blend in with their surroundings and allow adults and children to co-exist peacefully. Made of rustic timbers and clothed with climbers and the surrounding shrubs, this play-area scheme fits the bill perfectly.

▷ **FANTASY LAND**

This vividly coloured kids' garden, complete with silicone play surfaces, was designed for a flower show. In reality, the bright blooms might be short-lived, but the effect could be re-created with movable tubs.

PLAY SURFACES

Surfaces beneath play equipment must be soft. For movable structures, the lawn is ideal, but it will get worn and muddy if used regularly. A 20-cm (8-in) layer of bark is suitable, as are rubber safety surfaces, although these are expensive. None of these surfaces will prevent injuries but they will often reduce their severity.

YOUNG CHILDREN

It is nice to be able to let babies and toddlers play safely on their own for a short while without worrying. A patio provides a good level surface, but ensure that it drains freely and keep it free of moss and algae, which will make it slippery.

To prevent a young child from straying out of your view, enclose the play area with a low fence or screen, incorporating a gate through to the rest of the garden. It need only be about 1 m (3 ft) high – any higher and they will feel imprisoned. Make this space more attractive by planting in front of the fence or screen.

A simple but effective feature for toddlers is a series of stepping stones laid in a pattern across the lawn. It can either lead in a roundabout way to a playhouse, or, even more enticingly, weave in and out of shrubs or small trees.

OLDER CHILDREN

Older children generally prefer to play farther away from adults. The feeling is often mutual – somehow, no matter how large your garden, the ball or the chase always seems to locate itself precisely where the adults are trying to relax.

The obvious answer is to separate the areas. Children's needs usually take up more space than those of adults, so give them the larger share, as far away from the house as possible. Divide their space off with a structure such as a shed, perhaps attaching trellis in order to extend the partition.

One practical solution is to have a patio area near the house – with attractive planting and seating – that is kept totally out of bounds for ball games, and a large, rougher lawn farther back. This lawn can be edged with tough plants, such as kerria or bamboo, thereby screening the children and adults from each other.

△ **WIGWAM**
The simplest materials often make the best play structures. Here, twigs, branches and prunings from around the garden – plus an old blanket – have been used to create an instant wigwam.

WILLOW STRUCTURES

Willow stems can be used to create attractive and exciting structures, such as dens, tunnels, or animal sculptures, that will appeal to children of all ages. Simply insert the stems into the ground and they should sprout leaves and grow. Willow features grow with your children, enabling them to incorporate larger, more elaborate structures as the years pass.

Most forms of willow can be used, including those traditionally used for basket work, such as white willow (*Salix alba*) and the common osier (*Salix viminalis*). Willows prefer damp soil; in dry soil try red-stemmed dogwood (*Cornus sanguinea*).

Use thicker, two-year-old stems as supports, and flexible one-year-old stems for weaving. Experiment with different shapes by sticking uprights into the soil and weaving stems in and out. You'll be surprised at the effects you can achieve.

SAFE PLAY

There is a fine line between adventurous play and danger for children. It is important for them to have both physical and imaginative challenges and to learn their own limitations, but safety must be a prime consideration. If you want to create your own play spaces and equipment for children, always be alert to potential hazards you may be creating.

Alternatively, a wide range of equipment is now available from specialist suppliers. Ask for proof that it has been properly tested for safety. The suppliers may also advise on installation; some companies carry it out themselves.

All play equipment must be regularly checked for damage or weakness. Inspect wooden structures for splinters and make sure swings and ladders are intact and securely fastened. Keep sandpits covered when not in use to prevent fouling by cats and dogs.

▽ **TREE HOUSE**
This tree house was cleverly created from an old shed, raised on a wooden platform. With its blue gingham curtains and pots of flowers, it makes an idyllic playhouse.

CREATING PRIVACY

Most people value a little privacy in their garden. This may seem an impossible dream to urban-dwellers overlooked by all-too-close neighbours, and even those who are not overlooked may despair of ever escaping family eyes. However, creating a few hiding places is not as complex as it sounds.

▽ **SECRET ARBOUR**
Framed by shrubs and with a blackberry scrambling over the roof, this arbour provides a secluded place to sit or eat. Features such as this are invaluable in gardens that are open or overlooked.

Hedges, trellis and fences are the major options for screening large or small areas of a garden. Trellis and fencing also bring the added bonus of extra planting surfaces, but make sure that the climbers you choose are in keeping with the surroundings – look at the planting ideas for these surfaces on pages 62–63 and 128–129.

ENCLOSURES AND SCREENS

If you have a small garden, enclosing the whole thing is a fairly straightforward option. A fence of about 1.8 m (6 ft), or a lower fence, up to about 1.2 m (4 ft), with trellis above, will screen you from anyone at ground level next door. However, perhaps you don't like to be seen from upstairs windows, or don't want the bother of enclosing the whole garden. If either, or both, of these apply, then the answer is to create smaller screened areas.

First, identify the areas where it is essential to you to have privacy. You might simply place a trellis screen right across a whole section of the garden in which you like to read or sunbathe, perhaps with an archway placed in it. A popular area for privacy is the patio, and it is common to have higher fencing around this. It may be that your patio is just outside the house and is overlooked by neighbours at the back; or you may have sited it in a rather-too-sunny spot farther down the garden, where the seating needs some shading. Note that trellis placed on the side that gets strong sun may cast too much shade. In this event, it could be that planting is your best option.

USING PLANTS

For a patio, one substantial shrub, say 1.8–2.4 m (6–8 ft) high, with some smaller plants, will give partial

screening and a feeling of enclosure. Good deciduous shrubs include buddleias such as *B*. 'Lochinch', philadelphus and shrub roses like *R*. 'Frülinghsgold'. A sparsely planted pergola also works well in many paved eating areas, casting nicely dappled shade.

Elsewhere in the garden, shrubs make an attractive screen for small areas with a seat or work well in a larger space when planted in a line or gentle arc. Evergreens such as pittosporums, *Eleagnus ebbingei* or viburnums such as *V. tinus* can give effective year-round screening. A hedge also provides a permanent screen, but will take up much more space than one or two well-placed shrubs. Make sure your garden really can accommodate a hedge before planting.

CREATING PRIVATE AREAS

There are all kinds of ways of creating secluded private areas inside the garden. Trellis is useful as a partial screen for one side of a seat, for example, or to section off a quiet corner.

A pergola, covered arbour or gazebo can create a romantic hiding place for an intimate meeting or a quiet place to relax and read. Place these where they can only be glimpsed from elsewhere in the garden. Allow climbing roses or honeysuckle to scramble all over the structure, surround it with violets and forget-me-nots for their poetic associations, and escape to another world.

AN INNER SENSE OF SECLUSION

You may find that the sense of being overlooked diminishes naturally as you re-design your garden. When you define and separate off new areas, private places suddenly emerge, perhaps screened by a new large shrub or a garden shed.

And as the garden gains interest and variety through your replanning and replanting work, the distant view often becomes more hazy, especially if you add luxuriant plants growing out from the boundaries. This effect is enhanced by strong focal points placed within the garden – just a path leading to a seat, or an impressive tree or shrub, can hold the eye inside a garden. As the internal space gains emphasis, the outside area fades, often taking with it any feeling of being overlooked.

◁ **TRELLIS SCREEN**
Trellising has an immediate screening effect on the rear of this garden, and when the climbers have established themselves it will provide complete privacy. The pergola both frames the large pot and creates a sense of enclosure.

△ **INNER FOCUS**
This design instantly establishes a secluded, introverted mood, as the pool at its centre creates a meditative feel, and draws attention away from the boundaries. Clipped shrubs and formal paving accentuate the inward-looking atmosphere.

PLANNING PERMISSION

Before erecting large structures or making major changes, find out if there are any restrictions in your area on how you may use your garden or build in it. These are the items for which you may need planning permission:

∅ Fences that are more than 2 m (6½ ft) high, or more than 1 m (3 ft) high if they face a road used by cars.

∅ Garden buildings such as summerhouses or sheds, if they are more than 3 m (10 ft) high.

∅ Changes to the road access, such as a new entrance for a car.

∅ Buildings or structures in the front garden.

∅ Changed access for refuse collection.

Specially protected locations, such as conservation areas, may have much stricter rules, and there may also be health and safety issues to consider. It is worth checking with your local authority or city council for advice.

WET OR DRY CLAY SOIL

Well known for its fertility, clay soil offers perennials, trees and shrubs rich sustenance year after year. There are problems, however. In winter, a heavy, waterlogged clay soil can kill more plants than the cold; in summer, unimproved clay may bake dry and crack, putting great stress on plant roots.

It may be that you have clay soil and your plants seem fine – in which case, leave well alone and simply apply a mulch each spring. There are, however, various situations in which clay soil needs to be improved. Avoid doing this when the ground is very wet, since walking over wet clay or, worse, using heavy cultivating equipment, will compact the soil, making it dry hard.

IMPROVING CLAY SOIL

If your clay borders are compacted, dig over well before adding any new plants in spring – the best time of year if the soil is very wet during winter. Dig over the clay when it is slightly moist, but not too wet.

Most clay soils need mulching each spring. Spread organic material such as compost, well-rotted manure and peat moss on top of the bed and then mix it into the native soil by digging and turning over shovel-loads of earth, repeating until it is evenly incorporated. A good mulch will work its way into the soil and open up the structure, producing a soil that does not get waterlogged in winter and retains moisture better in summer. A very thick mulch may need an edging to contain it properly. Adding coarse grit also helps to loosen heavy clay.

PLANTING

Many shrubs perform well in clay soils – group them together in a large border to create a year-round feature (see box opposite for species

suggestions). After the initial effort of digging and planting, you will have a low-maintenance display that will last for 10 years or more. When planning a new shrub border, make it large enough to allow plants to be spaced correctly and add stepping stones at the back for easy access when pruning. Suitable perennials include firm favourites such as bugle *(Ajuga),* montbretia *(Crocosmia),* hellebores, daylilies *(Hemerocallis)* and peonies.

If a clay soil is moist (but not waterlogged) all year round and organic matter has been worked in to improve aeration, an option is to try turning part of your plot into a bog garden (see box opposite).

HARD LANDSCAPING OR RAISED BEDS

Where the soil quality is very poor, you may be unable to do much with it without a huge amount of work. Depending on the situation, and if a relatively small area is involved, it may be that paving over the area to create an attractive place to sit is a good option.

Another alternative is to build raised beds. These may be as simple as a mound of topsoil contained by stones, or as elaborate as a deep planter made of stone, brick, concrete or wood. The depth of the raised bed is obviously governed by what you want to plant. Small trees require

△ **SHRUB BORDER**
A shrub border offers an attractive, low-maintenance way of coping with wet clay. The many shrubs able to survive in cold and wet winter soils include the variegated dogwood (Cornus alba 'Elegantissima').

△ **WATERSIDE SCENE**
*Drifts of arum lilies
(Zantedeschia aethiopica)
thrive in muddy clay, either in
a sunny border or beside
water. The variety
'Crowborough' is the hardiest,
although it still requires winter
protection when young.*

◁ **BOG GARDEN**
*Choose the yellow spires of
Ligularia 'The Rocket' or the
creamy plumes of goatsbeard
(Aruncus dioicus) to create
impressive summer displays in
your bog garden. Yellow flag iris
(Iris pseudacorus) is another
good option.*

45–90 cm (1½–3 ft) of soil, whereas most annuals can get by with as little as 15–20 cm (6–8 in) of soil. If the bed has a solid enclosure, be sure to instal adequate drainage so that your plants will not drown.

SHRUBS FOR CLAY SOIL

Berberis (barberry) All are easy to grow, from spring-flowering evergreens such as *B. darwinii* to reddish purple-leaved deciduous *B. thunbergii*.

Chaenomeles (flowering quince) Reliable and versatile spring-flowering shrubs for borders, walls and fences or for use as hedging plants.

Cornus (dogwood) Choose variegated *C. alba* for its coloured winter stems and lovely foliage and *C. kousa* or *C. florida* for their shape and flowers.

Philadelphus (mock orange) Grown for its wonderfully scented summer flowers. Varieties range in size from 1–4 m (3–13 ft).

Rosa Roses thrive in the fertility of clay soil, but add organic matter each year to improve drainage.

Salix (willow) Most of the 300 or so species of willow thrive in wet conditions.

Viburnum This large, trouble-free group of plants offers winter or spring flowers, berries and a choice of evergreen or deciduous types.

PLANTS FOR BOG GARDENS

Aruncus dioicus (goatsbeard) Superb feature plant reaching 1.2 m (4 ft) high once plumes appear in early summer. Needs soil that is moist in summer.

Astilbe Colourful summer-flowering plants that need little attention if given moist or boggy ground; ideal in partially shaded sites.

Caltha palustris (marsh marigold) Large buttercup flowers in spring. Grows in wet soil or shallow water. Contrasts well with water irises.

Gunnera manicata Impressive feature plant with giant, rhubarblike leaves. Needs deep, rich, preferably wet soil, but the crown should not be waterlogged when plant is dormant.

Iris laevigata Has lavender-blue flowers in summer and will grow in shallow water.

Ligularia Impressive specimen plants with clumps of foliage and yellow summer flowers.

Primula japonica (candelabra primrose) Flowers are striking if it is planted in large drifts.

Rodgersia Many worthwhile species, all with beautiful foliage if given a moist, sheltered spot.

POOR, SANDY SOIL

Sandy soil consists of large mineral particles with lots of air in between. Water drains away freely, making this soil easy to work for much of the year, and it warms up quickly in spring, so the season starts early. On the minus side, nutrients may also drain away easily, and the soil can dry out in summer.

Dryness is one of the major problems with sandy soil. Each year, as the weather warms up, the soil starts to dry out and only the toughest plants survive – usually weeds. Even if a plant does survive, it might not perform well, with flowers dropping before they open or the foliage of large-leaved plants wilting and shrivelling. The topsoil may also be a very thin, giving trees and large shrubs little earth in which to anchor themselves. An additional problem is the free-draining nature of this soil – just as water drains away readily, so too does valuable soluble nitrogen.

If thin topsoil is your problem, try digging a planting pit down past the topsoil when planting shrubs and trees. Fill the bottom with soil mixed with well-rotted organic matter. Add fertilizer in spring to compensate for nutrients lost by leakage over winter.

▽ **GRAVEL PLANTING**
The well-drained soil of a gravel garden is the ideal site for sea hollies (Eryngium), with their metallic, teasel-like flowers, and rich, purple-leaved *Sedum telephium 'Atropurpureum'.*

IMPROVING SANDY SOIL

There are several ways of coping. You can either improve the soil so that it holds more moisture and nutrients, grow plants that tolerate drought and low nutrient levels (see list opposite), or provide irrigation.

Lost nutrients can easily be replaced by adding fertilizer, but it must be added at the right time or it will be leached away. Apply fertilizer to free-draining soils in spring, as growth gets underway. You may need to apply more in early summer. Well-rotted organic matter, such as compost and manure, will also bring about a huge improvement, holding water in the soil without letting it get waterlogged. Applied as a top dressing each spring, a rich mulch prevents evaporation from the surface initially, then breaks down to improve the soil structure.

USING DROUGHT-TOLERANT PLANTS

There are all kinds of plants that have evolved to tolerate hot, dry summers, so it makes sense to use them in dry or free-draining soils if the site is a sunny one (see list opposite). Once established, these will be much less work than plants that need regular watering.

HERB GARDENS

If you have a sunny site, a herb garden is another ideal option for sandy ground. Most culinary herbs thrive in a well-drained soil that is low in nutrients, and it tends to bring out the best flavour. Many other types of herb will also do well – lavender and hyssop are especially attractive choices.

IRRIGATION SYSTEMS

Extra water can be supplied to your soil, but choose a system that does not waste water. Leaky or seep hoses (see page 209) may be buried under mulches to supply water to new plantings, or a drip irrigation system can be set up.

This sophisticated dry garden planting has been created by using a limited colour palette, with a backbone of coloured foliage plants and flowering highlights such as alliums and lavender (Lavandula).

△ **SUNNY SCHEME**
Yellow-flowered Phlomis fruticosa and x Halimiocistus 'Merrist Wood Cream', with its saucer-shaped flowers, are easy-care shrubs for a sunny, well-drained site.

GRAVEL GARDENS

Making a gravel garden is a creative and highly attractive solution to the main problems that come with sandy soil. A gravel garden is not as densely planted as a traditional border, which, together with the lack of weeds, means that there is less competition for moisture. Make sure you have plenty of visual interest by using bold architectural plants and other natural objects such as large stones, boulders and interestingly shaped pieces of driftwood.

Gravel is much easier to use if it is laid on a heavy-duty landscape fabric (see pages 208–209) and the bed is edged to prevent the gravel from encroaching on other areas. The landscape fabric allows water to penetrate the soil, but prevents weeds coming through. Lay out the fabric, and then cut planting holes where they are needed. Choose drought-tolerant plants and use just a few dramatic species – such as mullein *(Verbascum)*, Scotch thistle *(Onopordum nervosum)* or a large ornamental grass – rather than lots of small fillers. Rake gravel into place to hide the fabric.

DROUGHT-TOLERANT PLANTS

Cistus (rock rose) Shrubs for early summer colour. Not fully hardy, they thrive in sunny, sheltered sites.

Eryngium (sea holly) Architectural plants with long-lasting flowers in metallic silver or blues.

Euphorbia Excellent group of plants grown for their shape, foliage and eye-catching bracts.

Kniphofia (red hot poker) Most modern varieties survive winter if the soil is well-drained. Impressive flower spikes in autumn.

Onopordum nervosum (Scotch thistle) Dramatic silver-green thistle-type plant that can exceed 2.5 m (8 ft) in height.

Perovskia (Russian sage) Grey-leaved shrub with powder-blue flower spikes in late summer.

Sedum Many species, most with succulent foliage and late summer to autumn flowers.

Verbascum Short-lived perennials. Architectural flower spikes work well in gravel gardens.

CHALKY AND ACID SOILS

*A huge range of superb plants flourishes in either chalky or acid ground,
so you should regard inheriting either of these soils as a wonderful
opportunity. Problems arise only if you choose types that are mismatched with
your soil – this may be the cause of any unhealthy-looking plants in your garden.*

△ **COLOURFUL CLIMBERS**
*Several popular climbing plants
thrive on chalky soil. Here,
Vitis vinifera (grapevine) and
Humulus lupulus 'Aureus'
(golden hop) grow alongside two
clematis – the red-flowered
C. 'Ernest Markham' and blue
C. 'Perle d'Azur'.*

Finding out whether your soil is acid, neutral or alkaline (chalky) is simply a question of using a shop-bought pH testing kit. This will help you decide which new plants to buy and may tell you why existing plants are failing. Make sure you test each bed – soils can vary within the same garden.

To find out the degree of acidity, you will need to send a sample to a soil laboratory. Most garden soils are between pH 5.5 and 7.5 (neutral soil is pH 7). A slightly acid soil (pH 6.5) is ideal for many plants, including lawns and fruit. Values outside the normal garden range may restrict your planting choices. Don't forget to match any new planting to the garden conditions as a whole, not just the pH.

CHALKY SOILS

Soil with a pH greater than 7 is alkaline. These soils usually have an underlying layer of chalk or limestone, and there is little that can be done to decrease the pH in the long term. Adding plenty of well-rotted organic matter will help to retain moisture and build up the layer of topsoil.

If you inherit a chalky garden, you may also inherit sickly, yellow-leaved plants with dark green veins. These are symptoms of lime-induced chlorosis, common in roses, hydrangeas and fruits, which are treatable with chelates of iron. Hydrangeas are prone to changes in flower colour caused by the soil's pH value. For blue varieties to be a true blue, they need acidic conditions. A blue that has faded cannot be recovered.

Lime-tolerant plants Clematis thrive on chalk, as do many bulbs. Small shrubs that like a well-drained site, such as *Cistus* and *Helianthemum*, also do well. Even among plants such as heathers, lilies and magnolias, which tend to hate lime, there are lime-tolerant exceptions, including *Lilium regale, Erica carnea* and *Magnolia grandiflora*.

Wildflower meadows The low fertility of chalky soil makes it ideal for creating meadows. A spring meadow – planted, say, with cowslips (*Primula veris*) and bulbs – should be left uncut until midsummer and then cut down to 8 cm (3 in). Do not cut it again until early autumn. A summer meadow, with plants such as greater knapweed (*Centaurea scabiosa*), can be left uncut until early autumn.

ACID SOILS

Woods and heaths are commonly associated with acid soil. In woodland, the soil is rich and moist from leaf mould, whereas in more open, sunny sites such as heathland, it is drier and often sandy.

Woodland gardens Woods of rhododendron and camellia dominate many mature gardens with acid soil. While these species are a glorious sight in spring, it is worth planting other acid-lovers to ensure visual interest all year round. As well as those plants listed (see box opposite), underplant with bulbs such as *Colchicum speciosum, Trillium grandiflorum* and *Narcissus cyclamineus*.

Heathland-type sites Many plants suited to this habitat are short-lived, so replanting with new stock is often better than renovating old plants. If your lawn is suffering because of poor fertility, try using heathers to turn all or part of it into a small heath. All this requires to maintain it is a single mowing each autumn.

◁ **THYME CARPET**
A mass planting of flowering thymes is a simple way to cover a large area of chalky soil. These sun-loving evergreens are trouble-free, since they just need clipping back lightly after flowering; they release a lovely scent when crushed.

PLANTS FOR CHALKY SOIL

Clematis Many different types, offering flowers all through the year. Wide range of colours and shapes.

Helianthemum (rock rose) Low-growing evergreens with early summer flowers in varied colours. Prefer sunny, well-drained sites.

Humulus lupulus 'Aureus' (golden hop) Hardy, deciduous climber, providing rapid cover of lush golden foliage. Attractive over blue or black trellis or in combination with clematis.

Thymus (thyme) Sun-loving aromatic evergreens. Impressive carpets of colour, and some varieties have variegated foliage.

Veronica Easy-to-grow flowering plants, ranging in height from 30–90 cm (1–3 ft). Blue, pink or white flowers, loved by bees.

Vitis vinifera (grape vine) Spectacular foliage climber for a large wall. Thrives in poor soil. Can reach 3.5 m (12 ft) in five years.

PLANTS FOR ACID SOIL

Woodland plants
Athyrium filix-femina (lady fern) and **Blechnum spicant** (hard fern) are among the many garden ferns that prefer acid/neutral soil.

Gaultheria procumbens (wintergreen) Creeping evergreen with red-tinged leaves and red berries in autumn.

Hydrangea Blue, pink or white blooms in late summer. Moist soil.

Kalmia latifolia (mountain laurel) Shrub with beautiful flowers in early summer.

Meconopsis betonicifolia (blue poppy) Needs light shade.

Pieris Shrubs with spectacular spring colour from flowers and leaves.

Skimmia Compact shrubs with flowers and berries, offering plenty of winter and spring interest thanks to evergreen foliage.

Heathland plants
Calluna vulgaris (Scotch heather) Evergreen ground-cover with summer flowers. Thrives on sandy soils.

Cytisus x praecox (broom) Spring flowers smother arching stems. Wide range of colours. Need sunny site.

Erica cinerea (bell heather) Named varieties offer colourful foliage and summer to autumn flowers.

◁ **FOREST FERNS**
Most ground-dwelling ferns prefer an acid or neutral soil, and they thrive in woodland-type conditions where there is plenty of leaf mould. Ferns make good partners for spring bulbs, since their unfurling fronds hide the fading bulb foliage.

SLOPES AND BANKS

Sloping gardens – and to a lesser degree banks within gardens – can present problems with drainage, accessibility and use. However, if you are prepared to put in the effort, these problems can be solved, and the topography can present exciting opportunities for design and planting.

Before embarking on landscaping work, think how the garden will be used and viewed. Consider the aspect of the slope and work out the best places for seating and structures such as sheds. Then decide on the position of steps and paths. If the garden slopes away from the house, a decking platform extending from the house will create a good viewing point. Upwards-sloping gardens are harder to make interesting from this perspective, since everything can be seen close to. Consider making the bottom of the slope more enclosed, with steps up to more open areas.

PLANTING ON SLOPES

When planting on a slope, take into account the soil (see pages 92–97) and the aspect. South- or west-facing slopes get more sun and, in cold areas, suffer less frost than the rest of the garden, but the soil will be drier and prone to leaching nutrients. North- or east-facing slopes will get less sun, so the soil may be damper than elsewhere in the garden.

A rockery is a low-maintenance feature for sunny or shady slopes. Place the rocks carefully to achieve the best effect. For a natural look, position the rocks so the strata are horizontal. For a more unusual rockery, try setting the rocks in patterns. All rocks on slopes need to be bedded in firmly for safety reasons. Plant alpines in sunny positions; ferns and spring bulbs in shady ones.

△ **CASCADES**
Building a series of water cascades on a shady slope and planting with shade-loving foliage plants, such as hostas, creates a lush, tranquil feature.

▷ **SUNNY SLOPE**
A south-facing slope is the ideal site for plants that like a sunny spot with good drainage, such as herbs and Mediterranean plants. In temperate climates, any tender plants, such as these spiky agaves, should be grown in pots so they can be kept frost-free in winter.

Another low-maintenance option is creative
ground-cover planting – regard the slope as a
canvas on which to paint bold blocks of colour.
Suitable plants include dark-leaved bugleweed
and yellow grasses, such as the sedge *Carex
hachijoensis* 'Evergold', for lightly shaded slopes;
foliage plants such as ferns, bergenias and hostas
on more heavily shaded slopes; or agapanthus and
red hot poker *(Kniphofia)* in sun. Foliage plants
for sunny slopes include *Ophiopogon planiscapus*
'Nigrescens' and blue fescue, perhaps interplanted
with pink busy lizzies and spring bulbs. Add some
taller shrubs or upright shapes, such as a tree fern
on a shady slope or dwarf conifers in sun.

A grass bank with a slope steeper than 1 in 3 is
difficult to mow. If you convert it to a wildflower
meadow, it will need just an annual cut with a
strimmer. On a large, steep slope, a stepped path
running diagonally from top to bottom, combined
with a retaining wall with planting pockets, will
hold the soil and create an impressive feature.

WATER FEATURES

If the slope in your garden has retaining walls, you
could incorporate a self-contained wall fountain.
A sloping rockery can be enhanced by a series of
cascades, while a waterfall will work if there is a
steep drop. Any complex water features are best
designed and built by a water garden specialist.

TERRACING

Terracing will enable you to create more flat spaces for seating, planting beds
or containers. It is an expensive option, but well-built terracing is a worthwhile
investment. If you plan to do it yourself, the cost and effort can be spread over
several years by doing a section at a time. The cut-and-fill method involves
moving earth from one area of the slope to another and building it up behind
retaining walls to create flat terraces (see illustration). This saves importing or
removing large quantities of soil. The terraces are linked by
steps. When excavating the earth, keep the
topsoil separate from the subsoil.

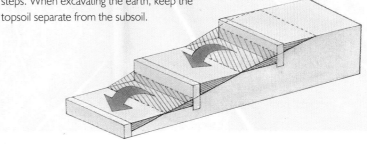

A HOT, SUNNY GARDEN

Plants need light for growth and many love the sun. Too much direct light and heat, however, may fade flowers, scorch and shrivel foliage, and dry out soil. Not all humans are sun-lovers either – your garden should be pleasantly comfortable for people to sit in.

The most common problems that come with excessive light and heat are easily overcome by appropriate, thoughtful design and planting. A good place to start is to try looking at how other countries cope with and use the sun in their outdoor living spaces – perhaps you can adapt these ideas creatively to suit your garden.

▽ **COOLING WATER**
This rill-fed pool takes centre-stage in a hot, dry garden. A nearby shaded seating area enables people to enjoy the refreshing effect of the water.

XERISCAPE

A xeriscape is a naturally dry landscape, such as a desert, where plants have evolved to survive with very little water. Re-creating such a landscape in a sunny garden requires minimal work and repays it with striking effects. Use gravel, stone and rock to set the scene and to cool the soil surface and retain moisture. Grow architectural plants (see opposite) or half-hardy species, such as agaves, aloes, echeverias and yuccas. Remember that these will need to be brought under cover for the winter in frost-prone regions.

MEDITERRANEAN-TYPE PLANTS

Pots of bold, drought-tolerant plants are evocative of hot, sunny places and in cool climates can simply be moved indoors for the winter. Citrus plants, small olives (*Olea europaea*) and sweet bay (*Laurus nobilis*) grow happily and attractively in terracotta pots. Herbs such as rosemary, thyme and lavender thrive in hot sun, as do silver- or grey-leaved plants – silverbush (*Convolvulus cneorum*) is a pretty alternative to bedding plants, as is the frost-tender trailer parrot's beak (*Lotus bertholetti*).

▷ **HOT COLOURS**
Hot, dry gardens are often home to a blaze of vividly coloured plants. Gardens such as this one in South Africa may inspire you to plant a sunny corner with bolder colours. Here, bright red aloes frame a planting that includes yellow-orange gazanias and white osteospermums.

PERGOLAS

A climber-covered pergola is a particularly attractive way to create a shaded walkway or seating area. Either specially built or bought in kit form, your pergola should fit in with your garden style and be sturdy enough to support its climbers. Vines or any large-leaved foliage climbers will

work well, as will vigorous flowering choices such as wisteria or *Clematis montana*. You can enjoy the flowers in late spring and sit beneath the shade of its foliage in the summer. A climbing rose is the perfect option if you want a summer-flowering climber. Advice on using pergolas and arbours to create havens of privacy is given on pages 90–91.

TREES FOR SHADE

Planting a semi-mature tree (see pages 52–53), either in the ground or in a large container, provides instant shade for a seating area. You are really spoilt for choice here, but opt for a species with a good canopy, such as the stag's-horn sumach *(Rhus typhina)* or the Indian bean tree *(Catalpa bignoniodes)*. An acacia will conjure up the south of France in a warm corner, while fruit trees such as *Malus* or *Prunus* species fare well in colder spots.

WATER FEATURES

A pond, rill, fountain, waterfall or a combination of different water features can be used to provide a cool oasis in the sunniest part of the garden.

To make the most of your water feature, construct a shaded seating area where you can sit and view it – an awning could be used if the seating is near the house. To emphasize the sense of shaded tranquillity, add lush plants, in large, decorative containers if necessary, in or around the seating area.

▽ **SHADY SEAT**
A seat beneath a rose-covered pergola provides a welcome, pleasantly scented break from the burning sun.

HARDY PLANTS FOR A HOT, DRY GARDEN

Acanthus (bear's breeches) Bold perennial with long-lasting flower spikes; forms a clump.

Bergenia Large evergreen leaves that cover the ground well, and pink or white spring flowers.

Cistus (rock rose) Some are hardy, grown on well-drained soil. Pink and white summer flowers go well with silver foliage plants.

Cynara cardunculus (cardoon) Large, dramatic, silver-grey leaves and thistlelike flowers.

Lavandula stoechas (French lavender) Distinctive, scented flowers in pink, white or purple.

Phormium (New Zealand flax) Swordlike, evergreen foliage in a range of colours.

Rosmarinus (rosemary) Many species, ranging from hedging plants to creeping types.

A SHADY GARDEN

Small or medium-sized gardens are all too often plunged into shade by the proximity of the house or boundaries, or by neighbours' houses or trees. This does not automatically spell disaster, however – although shade will certainly restrict your choice of planting, a shady garden need not be a dull one.

△ **AUTUMN COLOUR**
A tough climber such as Parthenocissus henryana grows happily against a shady wall and provides brilliant autumn colour.

▽ **WOODLAND PLANTS**
Moist shade provides an opportunity to grow all kinds of lush woodland plants.

The first step to making the most of a shady garden and deciding what to grow is to assess the depth of shade and the length of time the garden is affected each day – which may well vary at different times of year. It is also important to analyse the condition of the soil.

Numerous woodland plants thrive in light or moderate shade, particularly if the soil is moist. (Advice on planting in the shade under trees is given on page 125.) The range of plants that can tolerate permanent shade combined with dry soil is more limited. In this situation, consider other ways of adding interest apart from plants – such as paint effects, trellis and ornaments.

SHADE FROM WALLS AND FENCES

If a wall or fence is in shade for most of the day, the soil at the base may be either pleasantly damp or bone dry, hard and compacted. The more you can improve a dry soil the better. When planting a large permanent plant such as a climber or wall

shrub, it is worth planting it 20–60 cm (8–24 in) away from the wall, where the soil will usually be better, and training the plant back towards the wall (see page 205).

Climbers or wall shrubs can be grown on large, shady walls as long as the bricks and mortar are sound. As the range of flowering climbers that tolerate shade is limited, opt for foliage climbers with colourful leaves and avoid plants that will add to the gloom. Self-clingers such as parthenocissus and ivy do not need supporting, but others will need to be attached to horizontal wires or a trellis

WALL PLANTS FOR SHADE

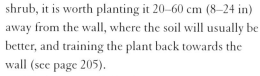

Akebia quinata (chocolate vine) Pretty, semi-evergreen climber with chocolate-scented purple-maroon flowers, borne in spring.

Decumaria barbara (climbing hydrangea) Semi-evergreen climber for sheltered positions.

Hedera (ivy) ***H. helix*** and ***H. colchica*** are popular choices. All are good in shade and tolerant of tough conditions. Variegated types can brighten up dark corners.

Hydrangea petiolaris A climbing hydrangea that looks impressive on a large wall, but requires rich, moist soil.

Jasminum nudiflorum (winter jasmine) Very hardy wall shrub that thrives anywhere. Produces yellow flowers on bare stems in winter. Although it can be allowed to sprawl, it is best tied in close to the wall and clipped hard after flowering.

Parthenocissus Climbers with beautifully shaped foliage that turns crimson in autumn. Tolerates dry shade and can be allowed to creep along the ground to cover a dry, shady slope.

◁ **SHADY CORNER**
Hostas thrive here in the shadiest spot, while violas, lupins and the rose 'Albéric Barbier' fare better in partial shade.

▽ **SHADED MEADOW**
Lawns seldom thrive in shade – one solution is to leave the area unmown and see what wild flowers emerge.

panel fixed to a thick batten. If they are grown on house walls, self-clinging climbers must be kept clear of window frames and gutters.

For a small wall, most of the less vigorous ivies *(Hedera helix)* are good options, but try to improve the soil, as they get going best in moist ground. For a springtime floral display, add *Clematis alpina* or *C. macropetala*. If the soil is moist, there are also many small, spring-flowering bulbs worth trying – for the best effect, grow them with ground cover.

Only a few plants will tolerate dry soil at the foot of a shady wall or fence. They include cuckoo pint *(Arum italicum* 'Pictum'*)*, with lovely foliage and flower spathes, and the autumn-flowering crocus *(Colchicum speciosum)* and *Cyclamen hederifolium*. If there is no soil, or very poor soil at the base of the wall, attach a painted trellis panel, plant a wall shrub such as a pyracantha in a large container, and train it up the trellis as an espalier.

SHADE FROM HEDGES

Hedges not only cast shade, but their roots also rob the soil of moisture and nutrients. In an informal area, try growing native plants or their relatives. Pale foxgloves *(Digitalis)* look stunning against dark hedges underplanted with violets, and honesty *(Lunaria)* is also attractive and shade-tolerant. If the hedge is deciduous, try spring bulbs such as bluebells. If you have a clipped hedge in a formal garden, cut a recess into it for a shady seat or to display an ornament or large pot.

A WINDY GARDEN

A strong prevailing wind can be a gardener's nightmare – harming plants and structures and making the space people-unfriendly. But such gardens often have hillside, coastal or rooftop settings with wonderful views, and you can use all kinds of strategies for shelter without walling yourself in.

Whatever its situation, a windy site must be sheltered in some way if you want to establish an interesting range of plants and create pleasant areas in which you can stroll or sit comfortably. If you are planting a new garden, research the best solution carefully and instal your windbreaks first – all future planting and enjoyment of the garden will depend largely on your success.

WINDBREAKS

A windbreak will shelter an area equivalent to about eight times its height. So, for most small or medium-sized gardens, a 2-m (6½-ft) windbreak is usually adequate. In a large garden, create an effective windbreak by including some trees, or by making a series of smaller windbreaks. A windbreak

△ **IRONWORK SCREEN**
The ironwork structure that surrounds this roof garden offers both a filter for the wind and support for climbing plants. At a lower level, troughs of the ornamental grass Calamagrostis x acutiflora *'Stricta' add tough, year-round privacy. This grass is long-flowering and remains upright, even in a windy site.*

PLANTS FOR WINDY GARDENS

Salt-tolerant windbreaks

Cotoneaster simonsii Upright, semi-evergreen shrub; bears berries. Good hedge; can be clipped.

***Elaeagnus pungens* 'Maculata'** Cheerful-looking variegated evergreen shrub that can be clipped as a hedge or used as an informal screen.

Escallonia Summer-flowering shrubs for mild areas. Look out for 'Crimson Spire' or 'Macrantha' (crimson flowers) and 'Iveyi' (white flowers).

Eunoymus japonicus Makes a dense hedge. Tolerates poor soil and pollution.

Rhamnus Deciduous species for tall windbreaks include common buckthorn (*R. cathartica*) and alder (*R. frangula*). Evergreen *R. alaternus* is a good hedging plant; *R.* 'Argenteovariegata', with grey and white foliage, is suitable for mild areas.

Perennials

Alchemilla mollis (lady's mantle) Soft mounds of foliage topped with a haze of yellow flowers. Thrives in a wide range of conditions.

Bergenia Glossy, leathery leaves can withstand harsh conditions and cover ground well all year. Pink, red or white flowers borne in spring.

Crocosmia (montbretia) Swordlike leaves and fiery flowers in red, orange or yellow. Not all fully hardy; red varieties such as 'Lucifer' are toughest.

Kniphofia (red hot poker) Flower spikes in orange, red, yellow or cream give impressive late summer colour. Need sun and well-drained soil.

Stachys lanata (lamb's ears) Provides a carpet of silver foliage. Hairy leaves help conserve moisture. Non-flowering types live longer.

◁ **COASTAL PLANTING**

If you have an exposed seaside garden and a windbreak would rob you of a stunning view, choose low-growing coastal plants. On this exposed slope, drifts of pink and white Lychnis coronaria *and the low-growing shrub* Phlomis fruticosa *thrive.*

PLANT CARE

⌀ Check that newly planted trees and shrubs are fixed firmly in the ground. Stake any trees (see pages 204–205).

⌀ Protect the tender shoots and foliage of hardy trees and shrubs, such as conifers or Japanese maples, from cold winds.

⌀ Climbers are very vulnerable, especially large-flowered ones, so secure them well. Use sturdy plant supports, firmly fixed in the ground.

⌀ Tall-stemmed, large-flowered herbaceous plants are easily blown over. Shield them with a hedge and stake them early in the season.

⌀ Avoid using hanging baskets.

⌀ Low bedding between shrubs should need no special care.

with holes or gaps in it is often preferable to a solid barrier such as a wall or fence. The former filters the wind, while a wall can force wind upwards and then downwards, creating damaging air turbulence.

The best long-term solution is to plant a living windbreak – either a hedge or a mix of trees and shrubs – but make sure that the plants you use are hardy in your area.

A living windbreak takes about five years to become fully effective, so you will need to instal a temporary, non-living one in the meantime.

△ **WILLOW SCREENS**

The gaps in these willow screens filter the wind, rather than blocking it as a solid wall or fence would do. Such screens make an effective windbreak while shrubs and hedging plants are young.

The wide selection of options available includes wooden trellis panels, plastic webbing, ironwork, wattle hurdles, rolls of bamboo and brushwood.

ROOF GARDENS

Roof gardens bring with them the added issue of safety, so choose a secure, non-living barrier, such as a strong metal fence, and use it also to support tough climbing plants such as ivies or vines. Alternatively, plant grasses or bamboos in large, heavy containers and place them within the fence as an attractive barrier to the wind.

COASTAL GARDENS

Coastal winds carry salt, so plants must be salt-tolerant (see box). A coastal site may also provide a milder climate and a chance to grow plants that would perish inland. If you opt for a non-living windbreak, bear in mind that wood withstands bleaching or salt corrosion better than metal.

A JUNGLE GARDEN

If your garden is very overgrown, and you have neither the time nor the money to clear it and start again, a jungle garden could be the perfect solution. Adored by children, and havens for wildlife, jungle gardens also provide an ideal opportunity to include some of the many dramatic exotics now available.

A den for children, and an escape from perpetual mowing and weeding, the jungle garden is also ideal if you want your garden to be a peaceful retreat – especially important in an urban setting. The slightly higher temperature in this dense, lush environment will also allow you to grow some of the many interesting less hardy plants.

CLEARING WORK

The simplest way to turn an overgrown tangle into a jungle garden is to cut a few paths through it and leave the rest alone. Looking down from an upstairs window, work out where the sunniest space would be if your thicket were cleared. Now go down and cut through the undergrowth until you reach it.

You will need a pair of sturdy shears, stout gloves and a scratch-proof jacket. When you reach your destination, clear a space around you until there is enough room to stand back and take a good look. You might decide to make several paths, radiating out from the clearing.

On a second trip, tackle the larger branches with a pruning saw. It is perfectly acceptable in this sort of garden to hide all your prunings out of the way under the bushes, in small piles. Known as "eco-piles", these will form new habitats for all sorts of wild creatures and will eventually rot down into the topsoil, providing nutrients for the plants just as they would in the wild.

If the cutting back has revealed long grass on the floor of your clearing and paths, you will need to reduce this to a more practical, manageable length. If necessary, cut it with a string trimmer to begin with, then use a rotary mower with the cutting edge set high. Mow every two weeks.

△ **HARDY EXOTIC**
Although it looks distinctly tropical, Fatsia japonica is, in fact, frost hardy in some areas, and is a useful evergreen shrub for temperate jungle gardens. With large, glossy, palmate leaves and a rounded growth habit, its mature height and spread is about 1.8 m (6 ft). The milky white flowers, borne in late autumn, attract bees and other insects.

PLANTS FOR A JUNGLE GARDEN

Aristolochia macrophylla (Dutchman's pipe) Vigorous, deciduous climber, up to 6 m (20 ft). Heart-shaped green leaves; greenish flowers in summer.

Arundinaria nitida (fountain bamboo) Evergreen bamboo, with dark purple canes and green leaves. Grows to 4.5 m (15 ft) high, with an indefinite spread.

Kerria japonica Vigorous, deciduous, graceful shrub with bamboolike stems and bright yellow spring flowers. Grows to 1.8 m (6 ft) high, with 1.5 m (5 ft) spread.

Sasa palmata Evergreen, fast-growing bamboo, forming dense clumps. Reaches 3 m (10 ft); spread indefinite. Enormous, vivid green leaves.

Symphoricarpos albus (snowberry) Deciduous shrub, bearing round white berries in late summer or autumn. Height and spread: 1.8 m (6 ft).

A TAMED JUNGLE

If you want a less impenetrable garden, take out the most invasive, junglelike plants. Wearing gloves, remove weeds such as brambles, which root from the tips of their shoots, as well as stinging plants such as nettles or poison ivy. Get rid of climbers that are hard to maintain, cutting back others that have run amok and training them over a fence or plant support.

As with the more extreme jungle garden, you could clear some paths through to a clearing and create a small woodland glade. If you want to turn your tangle into a proper woodland garden, see page 125 for planting ideas.

PLANTING

If you do not have enough of a jungle, or want to start one from scratch, there are plenty of plants that will create an authentic effect. Bamboo is one of the best jungle plants; other large specimens include the hardy palm *Trachycarpus fortunei* and the shrubs *Kerria japonica* and *Symphoricarpos*. Underplant these with ferns, hostas and other bold foliage plants (see box opposite).

PLAY AREAS

Jungle gardens make a wonderful playground for children of all ages. For older children, create exciting features like a tree house or a large climbing frame with a platform and rope swings; younger children will be happy with a playhouse or a den – sited where you can keep an eye on them. Further ideas for play structures are given on pages 88–89.

△ **TWIN SWINGS**
Overgrown with creepers, which give welcome shade from the hot sun, these twin swings in a California jungle garden appeal to adults and children alike.

◁ **EXPLORER'S GARDEN**
Jungle style is relatively easy to create – this urban garden uses a limited planting scheme of bamboos, palms and ferns, with a simple path for exploration.

LAWNS

Few of us have the time to achieve the neatly striped and weed-free "perfect lawn", but restoring a threadbare lawn to a respectable state and maintaining it is not difficult and will provide a wonderful natural surface. But if caring for a lawn is too onerous, there are several other good options.

△ **STRIPED LAWN**
If you can put in the time to maintain it, a close-cut, striped lawn is a strong design feature. This one plays a key role in defining a formal garden.

▽ **SUMMER MEADOW**
This vibrant wildflower meadow includes scabious (Knautia), cornflowers (Centaurea cyanus) and corn marigolds.

Quick fixes that can be used to improve lawns were discussed on pages 56–57. Here, we look at ways of making more long-term changes.

AN OVERSIZE LAWN

If your lawn is too large it can be easily reduced to a more manageable size. Decide whether you want to take this opportunity to change the shape of the lawn (see pages 216–217), and fit a mowing edge (see page 82). Stack any excess turf grass on grass and in time it will make excellent topsoil for use in large containers or raised beds.

CONVERTING TO A MEADOW

If lawn maintenance is too time-consuming or if you want a wildlife garden, consider converting all or part of it to a meadow, which is much easier to maintain. A sunny, sheltered site will be most beneficial to insects. In principle, conversion is easy: simply let the grass grow and do not apply feeds or weedkillers. The "weeds" will then reveal themselves as wildflowers, bloom, and set seed. Pot-grown native wildflowers can be planted to fill any bare patches.

The frequency of mowing necessary depends on the type of meadow. A spring-flowering meadow should be left uncut until early summer at least, so the nutrients in the foliage can return to the bulbs. It then needs cutting to 5–8 cm (2–3 in), and can either be kept to around 8 cm (3 in) or left to regrow and cut back in early autumn.

A summer-flowering meadow is not cut until early autumn. Alternatively, it can be mowed down to 8 cm (3 in) from spring until early summer, then left until a final mowing in early autumn.

With both spring and summer meadows, leave the grass cuttings to dry and then remove them to help reduce the fertility of the soil.

A WORN LAWN

If grass is worn in certain areas, a harder-wearing surface is required. This need not mean replacing the whole lawn: if it is level, you can lay stepping stones. Use paving slabs, a pace apart, bedded on sand so they are just below the lawn surface. If a grass slope is worn, consider building steps (see pages 146–149). Worn grass under children's play equipment should be replaced with bark, with a retaining edge, or another safety surface, such as rubber, although this is expensive.

◁ **STEPPING STONES**
An effective means of reducing the wear and tear on a lawn, stepping stones are also fun for children. They can be made very simply from single paving slabs bedded on sand, or from bricks or different types of stone, such as these flints.

▽ **CHAMOMILE LAWN**
The softness and rich green of a chamomile lawn make an effective contrast to hard landscaping, but it is only practical for small areas.

LAWN ALTERNATIVES

Alternatives to lawns are worth considering for areas where grass is growing poorly, such as shady or dry, sunny sites, or for filling in small gaps that are tricky to mow. However, no other plant is more resistant to wear than grass and most of the lawn alternatives cannot be walked on regularly.

Ajuga reptans (bugle) Creeping evergreen for sun or shade. Some varieties have colourful foliage, such as purple-bronze 'Braunhertz'.

***Chamaemelum nobile* 'Treneague'** (chamomile) Non-flowering. Needs a warm, sunny position and free-draining soil. Can be walked on and has a pleasant scent but often has to be replanted each year (you can take cuttings and replant small areas).

Hedera helix (ivy) Ideal for carpet effect in shade.

Lamium maculatum (dead nettle) Easy to grow in most sites and good in shade. Looks best from spring to autumn. 'Beacon Silver' has attractive silver variegation.

***Lysimachia nummularia* 'Aurea'** (creeping jenny) Yellow, evergreen, carpet-forming plant. Grows best on moist soil.

Mentha pulegium (pennyroyal) Low-growing aromatic mint for moist shade.

Origanum vulgare Aromatic; needs a warm site, and is good on chalky soil. Needs trimming.

Thymus serpyllum (wild thyme) Drought resistant, aromatic, with purple or mauve spring flowers. Needs trimming; can be walked on.

Vinca minor (lesser periwinkle) Tough ground cover with blue flowers from spring to early summer.

HEDGES

*A mature hedge is a valuable asset. As well as lending an established
look to a garden, it makes a much better windbreak than a solid barrier
like a wall or fence. An old hedge can become overgrown, untidy or gappy, but
there are several techniques for giving it a new lease of life.*

▽ **GREEN ARCHITECTURE**
*With its arch and windows, this
hedge makes a striking feature,
framing the table and offering
glimpses of the garden beyond.*

If you share a boundary hedge with next-door
neighbours and it requires renewal, you will need
to consult them about any major work, especially
if it involves replanting or renovating both sides
of the hedge. Usually you will be responsible for
maintaining your own side. If in doubt, consult
your house deeds or local authority regulations.

RENOVATING A HEDGE

To renovate an overgrown hedge, first clear out
any weeds that may have grown through it. Fill
any gaps by replanting in well-prepared soil, then
clip the hedge back hard (see page 212–213). With
an old hedge, you have the choice of cutting it
right down and letting it resprout and grow to the

desired height, or just reducing its height and/or width. Hedges tend to grow imperceptibly higher and wider every year, even when clipped regularly.

To lower a hedge, you will need loppers or a chainsaw. Cut it back to about 15 cm (6 in) lower than the desired height. The width can be dealt with over two years; one side each year. Cut it back almost to the main stem. It will look bare, but will sprout new growth after some months. Feed the hedge well after cutting it back by mulching with compost or well-rotted manure and sprinkling bone meal along its length.

This treatment cannot be used for most conifer hedges, since they will not grow back. Bare conifer hedges must usually be replaced. The best long-term hedges are yew, holly, box and beech. Privet and lonicera grow fast, which is useful at first, but once established they need frequent trimming.

RE-LAYING A HEDGE

If you have what was originally a country hedge, such as hawthorn, ash or hazel, the traditional way to renovate it is to re-lay it. Clear out and cut away all growth except the upright shoots. Cut these about three-quarters of the way through the wood at the base, so you can bend them down to an angle of 45 degrees. This will cause new shoots to sprout vertically from the bent layers. Hammer in wooden stakes, leaving about 1 m (3 ft) above ground. The wood need not be treated – by the time it rots, the hedge will be solid. Tie the angled shoots to the stakes and clip them neatly level with the tops of the stakes. The hedge will not need re-laying again for about another 20 years.

HEDGE WINDOWS

A novel way of dealing with a gappy hedge is to cut arches or windows in it. They can be shaped like Gothic arches, pointed at the top, or you could leave a stem in the centre like a casement window. This works especially well if you have a good view beyond, or if you want to break up the solid barrier of a dark hedge such as yew.

PLANTING WITH HEDGES

A mature hedge can form a good backdrop for a planting scheme. For example, the gold and green variegated foliage of *Elaeagnus pungens* 'Maculata' works well with the red and orange flowers of roses and broom *(Cytisus)*. Or you can train a climber through the hedge, using it as a support. Lime-green hop, or bright red climbing nasturtium stands out strongly against a dark yew hedge.

A TAPESTRY HEDGE

An attractive way both to renew and change the look of an old hedge is to replant a different type of hedging plant in any gaps. A hedge of green and copper beech is striking and their speed and habit of growth are similar. Green and variegated privet can be used, although the green will tend to grow a little faster. Tapestry hedges can also be comprised of quite different species – holly, privet and beech, for instance.

▽ **BEECH HEDGE**
It can be difficult to get plants to grow beneath a beech hedge, but this Euphorbia characias *is doing well. The euphorbia's steely blue foliage contrasts well with both the light summer green and russet autumn colours of the beech.*

◁**LIVING SUPPORT**
A flaming red garland of the climbing nasturtium (Tropaeolum speciosum) *lifts the sombre tone of dark yew foliage. The technique of growing climbers through a hedge can be used to great effect with both brightly coloured climbers and paler-flowered plants, such as* Clematis 'Marie Boisselot'.

USING COLOUR

Colour is entirely subjective. Some people say they have too little colour in their garden, while others complain of too much – or too many colours mixed together. If you are unhappy with the colour schemes in your own garden, it is often possible to make changes without extensive replanting.

△ COLOUR CONTRAST
Near-complementary colours are stylishly combined in this border. The gold-green leaves of the locust tree, Robinia pseudoacacia 'Frisia', make a pleasing contrast to the pinks and mauves below.

◁ BLUE SCHEME
Blue can be a difficult colour to use intensively. Here, shades of blue, mauve and purple are offset by the green of the box and a dash of gleaming white from the feverfew.

Colour in the garden is not provided by plants alone. As well as making full use of structures, containers and decorative objects to create satisfying effects with colour, it is important to consider plant colours in relation to these elements. It also helps if you bear in mind the effects of light when using colour (see pages 64–65).

NOT ENOUGH COLOUR

"People often forget that green is a colour", Gertrude Jekyll is said to have remarked. However, if you dislike unrelieved green in your garden, lightening it is simple. Green gardens often seem dull if they are shady. They can be brightened with variegated foliage – white- and yellow-variegated plants often grow well in shade. Mix them with plants that flower in shade. For a peaceful effect, use pale-coloured woodland plants, such as bluebells, primroses and wood anemones. White or blue hydrangeas or viburnums (which tolerate semi-shade) are equally lovely. For a brighter effect, add red, orange and yellow tints with Japanese quince, *Spiraea* 'Goldflame', and *Epimedium* × *warleyense* or *Euphorbia* 'Fireglow'.

White will lift and brighten almost any colour scheme. Use bedding plants, such as white busy lizzies for shady places and white geraniums or daisy bushes in sunny spots.

For a more long-term planting, train a clematis through a shrub or tree; a fairly large tree can take a white climbing rose such as 'Wedding Day'. Philadelphus and potentilla are good medium-sized, white-flowered shrubs. Plant phlox or Shasta daisy (*Leucanthemum maximum*) below; many herbaceous plants have white flowers.

A border of shrubs with light green, yellow and white foliage has a fresh, springlike effect. A good combination is *Pittosporum tenuifolium,* with wavy-edged leaves; tree peony *(Paeonia lutea ludlowii),* with serrated foliage and buttercuplike

THE COLOUR WHEEL

The wheel is based on the three primary colours of red, yellow and blue, with their secondary hues of violet, orange and green. Opposite colours, such as violet and yellow, are "complementaries"; they create the strongest contrasts. Adjacent colours, such as violet and blue, make colour harmonies. Hot colours range from egg-yolk yellow through to pure red. Cool colours range from pure yellow to deep purple. Hot colours appear to advance, while cool colours recede.

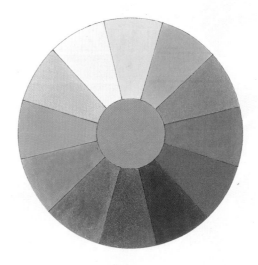

yellow flowers; and St John's wort (*Hypericum* 'Hidcote')*,* a rounded shrub with golden yellow blooms. Underplant with lady's mantle, comfrey and dainty bulbs such as *Narcissus* 'Tête-à-tête'.

The problem of too little colour does not occur only with green. Many plants have red or purple foliage, including copper beech, the bronze *Acer palmatum* 'Atropurpureum' and *Berberis* 'Dart's Purple'. Used well, they enhance flower colours and make them more brilliant, but an unrelieved display of red or purple leaves can look gloomy.

One option is to move such plants so they will be backlit by the sun, creating a lovely glow. Sombre colours can also be lifted by adding grey-foliaged plants: for instance, a base of *Stachys lanata* 'Silver Queen' planted at the foot of a wall covered in the grape vine *Vitis vinifera* 'Purpurea'. Another strategy for brightening red leaves is to use shocking pink. The climbing rose 'Pink Perpétue' growing over *Cotinus coggygria* 'Royal Purple' is a classic combination.

TOO MUCH COLOUR

The opposite problem – too much colour or too many colours mixed together – affects many gardens, especially those where the owner wants "a good show of colour". Examples include gardens with masses of different bedding plants and gardens with a wide range of rhododendrons and azaleas. The effect is very tiring to the eye. Cottage gardens are also jumbles of colour, but the individual plants are usually much less showy and vibrant, being mainly pastel coloured.

Colour can usually be toned down by adding plenty of green foliage plants – the forests where rhododendrons originate, for example, are full of deep green plants such as ferns, which enable the brilliant colours of the rhododendron flowers to glow softly without appearing harsh. Alternatively, try to harmonize the colours – if you have mainly blues and soft pinks, take out the bright orange and deep red. Keep these for a hot-coloured area, and add more warm tones to create a sunset border.

▽ **YELLOW BORDER**
In this bright yellow border, the flowers stand out brilliantly against the foliage. This has been restricted to green, since any other foliage colour would detract from the effect.

◁ **COLOUR FOIL**
The cool grey-green of lamb's ears (Stachys lanata) acts as a good foil for bright colours, such as pinks and oranges, and for green or purple foliage. In this garden it makes a neat, formal edging, echoing the grey of the gravel path.

A ROSE GARDEN

An old-fashioned rose garden may sound wonderfully romantic, but often the reality is disappointing. Except for a few months in summer, when it becomes a hodgepodge of colours, it can for much of the year be simply a collection of rather ugly bushes with bare, thorny stems, standing in barren earth.

△ **FORMAL BEDS**
These beds of Rosa 'Trumpeter' are moodily lit in autumn, but winter will bring bare stems and earth, and in this big garden the roses are hidden by a hedge.

▽ **BOX EDGING**
A box edge gives structure to a rose garden, and herbaceous plants such as salvias prolong the flowering season.

If you have inherited such a garden, it may be tempting to rip it out and turf it over or replant it with easy shrubs. With a little careful revision, though, and the introduction of suitable backup plants, a rose garden can become an outstanding feature that lives up to its romantic image.

SIMPLIFYING THE DESIGN

If your rose garden is overcrowded, the first step is to remove some plants. As well as roses you do not like, take out any that are old and unhealthy, with few leaves, lots of brown, dead wood, and little sign of healthy new growth. Look for strong, thick, light green stems, but if these are emerging from below ground, they are suckers from the original rootstock and must be removed.

The next step is to arrange the remaining roses according to a colour theme. Most roses are on the warm side of the colour wheel (see page 112) and range from red and orange, through apricot, peach and butter yellow, to cream. These colours all blend well, or you can choose just one or two, such as yellow and cream, or red and orange. Then there are the cool colours – many old-fashioned red roses have a hint of purple, which works well with cool pinks and whites. If you need to add any new roses, choose those that fit into these colour themes.

DEALING WITH BARE SOIL

Bare soil in a rose garden is easily dealt with. To retain a formal appearance, plant an edging of dwarf lavender, such as 'Hidcote', or the small, cushiony rock pinks, which look tidy when not in flower. Boxwood is also attractive; if it is planted as a hedge, you will need to keep it trimmed, or boxwood plants can be planted in the corners, and spaced out regularly along the edges. In this case, they can be allowed to grow more loosely, and be interplanted with other low-growing shrubs.

ADAPTING THE GARDEN

A more radical option is to convert part of the rose garden to another use. A formal layout is perfect for a kitchen garden. If, for example, the garden has four beds, two could be kept for roses and the other two used for vegetables. It is not essential either to underplant the roses or to edge the beds, but if you wish, you can try edging them with parsley or different coloured lettuces. Alternatively, the beds could be used for herbs. Some herbs repel pests with their strong odours – chives, for example, are said to deter aphids, a pest on roses.

EXTENDING THE SEASON

The introduction of other plants will extend the short season of a rose garden. Edging the beds with lavender or pinks will help, and you could replace some of the less attractive roses with other plants that flower at a different time of year. Bulbs are often planted beneath roses, and mixing some yellow daffodils with the pale green *Helleborus foetidus* will give a beautiful display as winter turns to spring. Spring-flowering shrubs, such as *Spiraea nipponica* 'Snowmound' and the lower-

growing *Viburnum carlesii,* can also be used. For a sumptuous effect, try exotic tulips, with stripes and frills, followed by voluptuous peonies, which will flower just before the roses. Good perennials for underplanting include geraniums such as *G. ibericum,* with soft blue flowers. Other shrubs that associate well with roses are the prostrate junipers – their soft blue-grey makes a perfect background, and they cover the ground effectively.

△ **UNDERPLANTING**
Here the climbing roses 'Kiftsgate' and 'Wedding Day' have been underplanted with rock pinks and cistus.

◁ **LAVENDER EDGING**
White roses with lavender is a classic pairing. In this example, Rosa 'Saunders White' is edged with Lavandula 'Hidcote'.

AN OVERGROWN SHRUBBERY

Gardens often have a collection of shrubs. In many old gardens, a shrub border that was originally meant to require minimal care may have grown to need major maintenance. If the shrubs were planted too close together, the scheme will have become congested and untidy.

Shrubberies became popular in the 19th century, when they were large affairs planted with newly discovered rhododendrons and camellias, as well as spotted laurel, euonymus and privet. They had walkways leading through them and were places for "taking a constitutional".

These are the forerunners of the shrub border, often planted as an easy-care option. The shrubs are frequently placed too close together to avoid gaps, and they soon become overcrowded, requiring constant pruning.

Whatever form the planting takes, the first step in renovating a border is to identify the plants. Use reference books and keep a note of what happens to each plant through the year. If there are plants that you cannot identify, try asking a knowledgeable gardening friend for help or take a leafy branch to your local garden centre.

△ **KEY PLANT**
In this border, a large bush of St John's wort forms the focus of a colour-themed planting of yellows and blues. Both flowers and foliage play their part in the scheme, which includes lavender, barberry and Spiraea japonica 'Goldflame'.

▷ **BALANCED SCHEME**
This dense but well-balanced shrub border comprises box, hydrangea, barberry, a profusely flowering clematis, and a ground-cover planting of geraniums. The tones are on the cool side, ranging from blues to purples and deep red.

▽ **ROOM TO GROW**
Corylopsis pauciflora *and* Magnolia stellata *are striking shrubs that need space, both to grow healthily and so you can appreciate their beauty. They prefer acid soil with plenty of leaf mould or humus.*

DECIDING WHAT TO KEEP

The general criteria for keeping or removing plants were outlined on pages 14–15, but it is worth focusing on the particular qualities that can make a shrub worth keeping.

Key plants A shrub can play a vital role in a planting scheme, providing an anchor for the whole bed. This is often because it is the tallest or most solid-looking plant. Assess it from different viewpoints in the garden and from the house, including

upstairs windows. This will also tell you whether it is screening an eyesore or preventing the garden from being overlooked. Any of these functions may be sufficient grounds for keeping it.

Plants with a long season Shrubs that flower over two seasons are useful, as are those that have different seasonal effects, such as skimmia, whose spring flowers are followed by attractive berries.

Winter-flowering plants Shrubs such as the scented wintersweet (*Chimonanthus praecox*) and witch hazels (*Hamamelis*), which flower or fruit in winter, are also valuable.

In this exciting planting, the tough, glossy leaves of loquat (Eriobotrya japonica) *contrast well with the feathery grass* Stipa gigantea *and the delicate* Buddleja alternifolia. *Colours are subtle, ranging from green through to creamy yellow, with just a hint of contrast in the pale violet buddleia blossoms.*

Choice plants Some shrubs have only one main season of interest, but their sheer impact earns them a place in the garden. Philadelphus, which produces an intense burst of deliciously scented white flowers in summer, is an example.

Evergreens These are essential for creating a balanced shrub border and providing year-round structure. Some, like the maligned spotted laurel *(Aucuba japonica),* can be attractive when they are given enough light and space. Evergreens seem dull when crowded together, since they can look quite similar. To avoid this, they should either be systematically repeated – for instance, planting *Mahonia × media* 'Charity' at 3-m (10-ft) intervals down a long border will give a striking rhythm to a planting – or interplanted with different colored foliage plants or deciduous species.

Healthy shrubs It is a pity to remove a really healthy plant. Once the bed has been cleared, consider keeping it for another season, when any virtues it may possess will become obvious.

Once you have decided what to keep, you can either dispose of the unwanted shrubs or move them (see pages 206–207). Prune the plants that remain (see pages 210–213) and give them a good feed of manure or compost and bone meal. Mulch over any bare earth (see pages 208–209).

PLANNING A NEW BORDER
You can now work out a scheme for a new border based on existing shrubs, shrubs that are moved from other parts of the garden and new ones. Having seen what happens when plants are too close together, always check the final height and spread before planting any new shrubs.

The main points to consider when combining plants are the overall habit or shape, the leaf shape, colour and texture, and the flower colour.

Start with the shapes of the shrubs you have kept. If you have repeating arched shapes, you could emphasize these by adding flat, spreading plants, such as the low-growing cotoneasters, to create a two-level bed. Alternatively, some of the arched shrubs could be replaced with those with contrasting rounded shapes, such as St John's wort and hebe. If the bed is unbalanced, with tall shrubs only at one end, you could either balance it with a small tree at the other end, or accept the irregularity and plant hummocky plants with a few arched shrubs, such as deutzia or weigela.

When looking at colour, begin with the foliage, since this will be with you far longer than flowers. Use one of your evergreens for the background colour. If you have a variegated shrub, use it, since it will have a strong impact. All shades of green foliage can be combined with yellow-variegated shrubs. Against these background colors, flower colors can either tone (yellows to reds) or contrast (blues and purples). White variegation gives more options, since it works with both warm and cool colours. Try to coordinate seasonal flower and foliage colours.

Your border may lack any lower-growing and ground-cover plants because the taller shrubs have crowded out the smaller plants. Choose these in the same way, thinking about background foliage colour first, then flower colour.

Leaf textures are also important. They can be combined or contrasted depending on the effect you want to create. The use of predominantly matt or shiny leaves will create plantings with very different moods.

Herbaceous plants are useful for extending the flowering season, since many flower in late summer when few shrubs are in bloom.

CREATING A HEDGE

If a shrubbery consists mainly of evergreens, and you need to keep them as a screen, consider using some of them in a tapestry hedge. Take out the shrubs at the front of the border, leaving those at the back. If you don't have much space, leave only the plants that form a fairly straight line. You can cut all the shrubs back hard and low, and let them grow back together. For a gentler line, hard prune each shrub, removing branches that stick out too far. This will give a softer grouping, which will not need to be clipped each year. If the shrub planting divides your garden, you could train two neighbouring shrubs to form an arch in the hedge.

△ **REPETITIVE SHAPES**
This border contains mainly deciduous plants with rounded shapes. Replacing some of them with horizontal evergreen shrubs and adding ground cover would give it visual variety and year-round interest.

▽ **VIBRANT COLOURS**
The strong colours of these rhododendrons ('Cynthia' and 'Lavender Girl') are echoed by candelabra primroses and irises, but they need to be offset by plenty of cool green foliage, preferably provided by large trees, if they are not to become overwhelming.

RHODODENDRONS

Many old shrubberies contain rhododendrons. In an appropriate woodland setting, and with plenty of space so they can be fully appreciated, they are majestic plants. Rhododendrons that are spindly, with yellowing leaves, may be suffering from a lack of iron because the soil is not acidic – test it with a pH kit (see page 96). You can apply chelates of iron, but this is expensive and not always successful. Alternatively, the soil may be too dry. Although rhododendrons will grow in full sun, they like shade and damp at their roots, which should ideally be provided by applications of leaf mould. They also appreciate a feed of well-rotted manure. If you have space, the light shade cast by silver birches (*Betula pendula*) is ideal for rhododendrons, and their brilliant flower colors will glow in the soft light. Rhododendrons associate best with other acid-loving plants, such as mountain laurel (*Kalmia*), strawberry tree (*Arbutus*), pieris, gaultheria and evergreen azaleas (see pages 96–97).

CONIFERS

Conifers are found in many gardens – sometimes they fill whole borders, island beds or front gardens. Being dense and often bulky, evergreens can become overbearing if they are poorly used or overused. This is a fault of many conifer plantings, and it has given these plants an undeserved bad name.

△ **IMPOSING FORMS**
In this shrubbery there is just about enough space for these majestic conifers, which include a golden Lawson cypress and a yew. If they were thought to be too dominant, however, one could be removed without sacrificing the air of solidity that is attractive in this garden.

▷ **SPIRE SHAPES**
This dramatic composition uses the pale, ethereal spires of the foxgloves to echo and lighten the deep green conifer. The pale green locust tree (Robinia pseudoacacia 'Frisia') stands out strongly against the tall, shady forest trees.

If you have inherited conifers that dominate your garden, consider these ways of integrating them and making good use of their distinctive forms and evergreen foliage.

SIMPLIFYING THE PLANTING
The first thing to do is simplify, if you have too many different varieties of conifer. Remove any you do not like or that are casting unwanted shade, keeping the healthiest plants and those with a strong shape. If any of these has a colour you particularly like, remove others that clash with it. You can now try the following suggestions.

PLANTING PARTNERS
One way of integrating conifers is to find good flowering and foliage partners for them. Grey spreading junipers work well with pale pink roses; the little white cedar, *Thuja* 'Rheingold', is effective in a bed of bright autumn or golden-variegated foliage; and the blue tones of many conifers can be echoed with blue or purple crocus.

Azaleas combine well with a background of larger conifers, which have the visual weight to set off their brilliant flower colours. The traditional acid-soil plantings of conifers with azaleas and rhododendrons, with blue hydrangeas for later interest and maples for autumn glory, make a grand garden spectacle.

JAPANESE-STYLE PLANTINGS
The Japanese use conifers to make gardens of spiritual beauty that are anything but suburban. The essence of this treatment is restraint, which

means removing plants that will look out of place and using a restricted colour palette. Leaf tones must be soft, so remove any golden and variegated plants; grey- and red-tinged leaves are fine. Take out roses and herbaceous plants. For flowers, use Japanese cherries, camellias or azaleas, alone or in a group. Such gardens work best if there is only one floral effect at a time, and all blossoms must be balanced by at least three times as much foliage, mostly plain green (see also pages 188–189).

CONIFERS IN ISLAND BEDS

An island bed that is filled with conifers can be connected to the main garden (see pages 78–79), and interplanted with other shrubs and suitable herbaceous plants to make the conifers seem less intrusive. This will probably mean removing some of them, and perhaps reshaping the bed to make the connection look more natural. All but the largest conifers are shallow rooted and easy to transplant.

▽ **JAPANESE STYLE**
The cool, reflecting surface of the water and the glimpsed view of the house help to calm this rather hectic garden scene, but it would be much improved by the removal of either the red- or the gold-foliaged shrub.

◁ **RESTLESS PLANTING**
The plants in this heather and conifer garden include blue Atlas cedar, white cedar and Cornish heath. While it will provide colour all year round, the planting is visually restless and could be calmed by opting for either golden or green conifers, rather than growing both together.

A CONGESTED BORDER

A herbaceous border that has become overcrowded is not an attractive sight. Whether it was overplanted in the first place, or has not been regularly thinned, or a rampant self-seeding plant has taken over, some careful "editing" will be required to keep it looking good.

▽ **3-D SCHEME**
Although it is densely planted, the layering and variation of forms in this border create a pleasing composition. The tall yellow spires are those of Verbascum bombyciferum 'Silver Lining'.

The best time to renew a border is autumn, when the cooler weather makes it easy for the disturbed roots to regenerate. In climates where perennials disappear underground in winter, do the job while they are above ground so you can see what is there.

RENEWING A BORDER

The most thorough way to tackle an old and overcrowded herbaceous border is to dig up all the plants and divide them, throwing away the woody inner stems and replanting the vigorous young shoots emerging around the outside of the clump (see page 206). Dispose of any plants that do not appear to be thriving, and any that have become inextricably intertwined. Dig the border over thoroughly, removing weeds, and incorporate humus or well-rotted manure. Assess the gaps in the border's season of interest – does it come to life only in the middle of summer; or fade around the end of summer? Now is the time to improve the structure of the border or the colour scheme.

ADDING SHRUBS AND CLIMBERS

Flowering shrubs and climbers can be pleasing additions to a herbaceous border. They provide height and substance, and many flower in spring and early summer, whereas the main herbaceous season is late summer.

Choose new shrubs carefully: large evergreens are too heavy for the soft leaves of perennials. Deciduous shrubs, such as deutzia and weigela, are easier to incorporate. The smaller evergreens are good for winter interest: hebes and the variegated pieris are worth considering, being smaller and softly coloured. Strongly coloured shrubs, such as *Hypericum* 'Hidcote', are better

suited to shrub borders, where herbaceous plants usually form the understorey rather than the main partners. Small shrub roses are excellent for these areas, especially the smaller-flowered varieties such as 'Ballerina' and 'Yesterday'. Climbing roses create a good floral background, as do clematis species. The foliage of the Virginia creeper (*Parthenocissus tricuspidata* 'Veitchii') is delicately attractive. As with the shrubs, evergreen climbers

GRASSES

Ornamental grasses have much to offer as border plants and are beautiful even in winter. There are species to suit all conditions. *Carex buchananii* has fine, russet-coloured foliage, grows to about 60 cm (2 ft), and is happy in a hot, dry position, as is the small, blue-grey *Festuca glauca* and the steely grey *Leymus arenarius* (which can be invasive, especially in sandy soil). Wood rushes *(Luzula)* like shady places, and *L. sylvatica* 'Marginata' forms good ground cover in difficult sites. The graceful miscanthus needs sun and prefers a moist position.

△ **GOOD COMPANIONS**
Grasses are natural companions for herbaceous plants such as campanulas and salvias. Many herbaceous species evolved in grassland and compete well with the grasses.

such as ivy can appear heavy, and variegated types are too strident for most herbaceous borders, although a colour scheme of yellow, orange and red flowers can be echoed with such a background.

CONVERTING TO A MEADOW

If a border is in a central position, or surrounded by lawn, then a radical but effective option is simply to let it go to grass. Generally, the flowers will be less abundant, but the effect will be wild and romantic – a sort of exotic meadow – and it will be easier to maintain than a border. You will need to establish an area of long grass around the meadow, otherwise it will betray its origins as a border. Decide whether you want it to be early or late flowering, and mow accordingly (see pages 108–109). Use peony, geranium, columbine, campanula and bulbs for an early-flowering meadow, and plant asters, golden rod, montbretia, phlox and masterwort *(Astrantia)* for a late one.

▽ **FIXED POINT**
The clipped box ball in this scheme acts as a visual anchor, around which the perennials, including phlox, daylilies and deep red Knautia macedonica, weave airy patterns.

AN OLD TREE

*Old trees are great survivors. Some even predate the gardens they stand in –
the presence of old apple trees in your and your neighbours' gardens may
show that the land was once an orchard. As well as being a dominant feature in
a garden, an old tree is also part of the landscape, and many are protected.*

Unless it is in a dangerous condition, an old tree
is best acknowledged as a long-term inhabitant.
You may, however, need to carry out renovation
work and adjust the garden to accommodate it.

RENOVATION
Whether it involves felling a tree or reducing the
crown, renovation work on large trees is a job for
tree surgeons. They have the special equipment

necessary and can advise on legal precautions –
make sure they have proper insurance so they will
be liable if the work causes any damage. Renovation
is best carried out in the dormant season.

The crown can be thinned to allow more light
to reach the ground beneath. Some of the lower
branches can be removed (crown lifting) or the
whole of the crown can be reduced by removing
the weaker branches (crown thinning).

> **▷ UNDERSTOREY**
> *There are many perennials
> suitable for planting under
> trees. A large euphorbia, such
> as E. characias wulfenii, makes
> an impressive clump even in
> dry soil, but it needs some sun
> for at least part of the day.*

Once a large tree has been removed, you may notice smaller trees nearby whose growth is stunted or which have been neglected. If these are small enough for you to tend to from the ground, they can be tackled easily. Spread the task over several years to allow the tree to recover. For example, in the first dormant season remove any dead or diseased branches, and in the second, thin out branches to reduce overcrowding.

SEVERE PRUNING

Some trees and large shrubs respond well to drastic pruning. It is possible, for instance, to prolong the life of an old oak or yew by hard pruning during dormancy (autumn to early spring for oaks; early spring for yews). This is best tackled by an expert.

The dogwood *Cornus alba* and willow *Salix alba* 'Britzensis' can be cut back hard in early spring to stimulate the growth of attractive winter stems; this also restricts the size. If you inherit a plant that has been pruned this way, it is worth keeping up the practice.

Coppicing as a method of managing trees has a long tradition. Instead of letting a tree grow one thick trunk, it is cut back to the ground each year, which causes the tree to send up many thin shoots, which can be harvested and used for plant supports and hurdles. Only a few plants can cope with hard cutting back; hazel is the best-known example.

UNDERPLANTING

Any tree renovation should be carried out before underplanting. If you want to plant under a tree, consider both the amount of shade, which is determined by the tree's shape, and when the shade is cast. Evergreens cast shade all-year round, although the position of this will vary in different seasons. Deciduous trees offer some relief from shade, allowing light through in the dormant season. Woodland spring bulbs have evolved to make use of this opportunity, but they will struggle under a large evergreen. Consider thinning the crown to reduce the amount of shade.

Planting under a tree may be further hindered by the root system, which is often as extensive as the mass of foliage above ground. This not only makes digging holes for new plants difficult, but competition from the tree's roots will prevent new plants from establishing. One solution is to plant farther away from the tree, where the roots are not so dense, and train the growth back towards the tree. Ground-cover plants such as ivy and vinca can be used in this way.

If it is not possible to reduce the crown, plant tough perennials or shrubs that can cope with dry shade (see box right). Even these will need help to get started, so add soil improvers before planting, mulch well and water regularly for the first couple of years until the roots are firmly established.

If you are underplanting a large area, consider setting up an automatic watering system using a seep hose. Where the tree roots make digging planting holes impossible, build a raised bed around the tree and fill it with topsoil or compost. Grass is unlikely to thrive under a mature tree, but ivy pegged to the ground makes an acceptable substitute.

UNDERPLANTING

Perennials

Digitalis (foxglove) Copes well with dry shade. Pink, red, purple, white or yellow flowers.

Euphorbia Prefers sun but can tolerate partial shade and dry soil. *E. amygdaloides* 'Robbiae' is reliable.

Geranium (cranesbill) Tough; long-flowering. Best for dry shade are *G. macrorrhizum* 'Ingwersen's Variety' and *G. nodosum*.

Physalis alkekengi (Chinese lantern) Unusual orange-red seed heads in autumn; can be cut and dried. Good for dry shade.

Tiarella Weed-supressing evergreen with creamy white flowers in early summer.

Shrubs

Aucuba japonica (spotted laurel) Tolerates poor conditions. Yellow splashes on variegated types.

Mahonia aquifolium Low-growing suckering shrub with yellow spring flowers.

Vinca (periwinkle) Vigorous, fast-growing, evergreen ground cover with blue or white flowers. In a single season *V. minor* covers 45 sq cm (7 sq in).

◁ **TEMPTING HAMMOCK**
If you are fortunate enough to have two mature trees the right distance apart, it is hard to resist the temptation to hang a hammock between them.

A HOST FOR CLIMBERS

Climbers have the advantage that they can be planted as much as 2 m (6½ ft) away from the tree, so avoiding the area most densely filled with roots; train the climber along a rope or chain to the tree. Honeysuckle *(Lonicera periclymenum)*, clematis *(C. montana)* and wisteria are excellent used in this way. If the tree is large and sturdy enough, it could play host to a vigorous rose such as 'Rambling Rector' or 'Kiftsgate'. Foliage climbers, such as Virginia creeper and crimson glory vine *(Vitis coignetiae)*, have fiery autumn colour; use them to add seasonal interest to evergreens.

TREE SEATS

If the ground at the base of a tree is level and firm, consider making a tree seat to create a shady retreat. The seat can be hexagonal, octagonal or circular in shape and will allow you to enjoy several different views of your garden. Tree seats are usually made of metal or wood and are easy to construct, either from your own design or from a kit. It is worth putting a waterproof cover over the seat at the end of the summer to make cleaning easier the following year.

ASSESSING A TREE

If a tree poses a safety risk, all or part of it will have to be removed. Seek professional advice when dealing with large trees. If a tree is near a house, an insurance company may ask you to arrange for a tree surgeon to assess the risk of subsidence, particularly if the garden is on clay soil. If a tree is safe and poses no threat, decide if it is serving a useful purpose. Is it a valuable source of shade in the garden? Does it cover up an eyesore or provide a windbreak? Does it have seasonal highlights, such as autumn colour, or bear edible fruit? Consider every aspect carefully before taking the decision to remove a tree. A mature tree is a valuable asset, giving a sense of history and permanence to your garden.

A TREE HOUSE

An exciting way of using a large tree within the garden is to build a tree house. At its most basic, a tree house is a wooden platform between the branches that is reached by a ladder or a rope. However, it is also possible to build a complete house with walls, windows, a door and a roof.

Because each tree has a different arrangement of branches, a tree house has to be made to measure. You can make your own or get one specially designed – whatever you opt for, the safety of the users and the tree is paramount.

The best designs have a platform that encloses the trunk but does not press on it, the platform being supported by posts sunk into the ground. Guard rails or a wooden wall around the platform make it safer; the ladder or rope should be securely fastened.

Quicker additions to mature trees include climbing ropes, rope swings and hammocks. The attachments must be securely fixed and regularly checked for wear. Cover the ground beneath with hardwood chips.

SURPLUS WOOD

Try to use surplus wood around the garden rather than disposing of it or burning it. A shredder will convert prunings into wood chips, which can be composted or used as mulch (see pages 208–209). Branches that are too thick for the shredder can be used as firewood. Tree stumps are best removed from the ground, since they encourage honey fungus, which spreads through the soil and kills garden plants. If you employ a tree surgeon to remove a large tree, he or she should deal with the stump for you, either grinding it out or pulling it out with a winch. If it is not possible to use these machines, a chemical stump killer can be applied. This must be done as soon as the tree has been felled; cover the stump with thick polythene.

ATTRACTING BIRDS

A mature tree will provide food and cover for a large number of bird species. It also supports a vast army of insects and smaller creatures, which help to attract the birds and add to the diversity of the garden fauna. The tree might offer the ideal site for some birdhouses. They should be sited away from direct sun in a sheltered position, and securely fixed well above the ground to protect the birds from interference from other animals or humans. Different birds prefer different types of birdhouse, so consult a local ornithological or wildlife society.

△ **PLAY HOUSE**
A tree house such as this sentry box will keep older children entertained without cluttering up the garden. Tree houses must be safe and secure, with no risk to people or to the tree.

◁ **FEEDING BIRDS**
This attractively painted birdhouse is attached to an elder, a fast-growing, large shrub or small tree that can exceed 4 m (14 ft). It provides food for birds in the form of juicy, purple-black berries, which appear at the end of summer.

CLIMBERS

Most gardens have some climbing plants, used to adorn pergolas and other structures or to cover house or garden walls. Neglected climbers soon become a tangled mass, often growing out of reach or bearing down on collapsing supports. Fortunately, most can be brought under control by pruning.

△▽ USEFUL IVY

With its shapely evergreen foliage and ability to tolerate dry shade, ivy is one of the most useful garden plants. It needs to be planted with care as it clings tightly to walls by its aerial roots and is hard to remove. Leave ivy where it is not in the way, but cut back stems growing towards windows, gutters or loose mortar. Mature ivy, with bushy adult growth and berries, should be left where possible, since it provides shelter and food for birds.

There are many types of climbing plants – the following are the ones you are most likely to find in a newly acquired garden. Climbing and rambling roses are discussed on pages 130–131. Techniques for planting new climbers are outlined on pages 204–205.

IVY

Overgrown gardens often have ivy, clothing tree trunks, spreading up walls or entangled in hedging. Ivy on house walls is best restrained, since it can block gutters and penetrate gaps left by loose mortar. Cut it off at waist height and pull the stems off the wall. The ivy will regrow and can then be kept in check. To keep ivy away from windows, trim it back to 45 cm (18 in) from the frame in late spring or early summer.

Ivy that is used to clothe a trellis screen or a fence should be be kept neat by cutting out excess shoots that are growing outwards.

If large-leaved ivy is swamping a structure such as a pergola, gazebo, arbour or arch, cut back one stem in every three close to the ground but do not try to remove them immediately. After a week or so the stems will have wilted, and it will be much easier to trace and remove them. Take out an ivy that is encroaching on young trees and hedges promptly, since it will prevent them from becoming established.

CLEMATIS

A clematis that has not been pruned tends to grow into a "bird's nest" shape at the top, and any flowers will be concentrated there. The late-flowering clematis that bloom on the current season's growth, such as *Clematis* 'Jackmannii', can be cut back hard to within 30 cm (1 ft) of the ground any time from late winter to early spring. *C. montana* is particularly vigorous. Either cut back the thin young growth after flowering or cut the whole plant back to the base after flowering. Cutting back to the base should not be done every year, but once every five years or so to bring the plant under control. If a clematis is too vigorous for the site, it is better removed rather than being repeatedly chopped back to the base.

HONEYSUCKLE

You can usually renovate climbing honeysuckles *(Lonicera)* if they become tangled or grow too large. Cut back all the stems to within 60 cm (2 ft) of the base in late winter or early spring (check there are no nesting birds); if the stems are thick or entwined you may have to cut higher up. New shoots will sprout in the spring. These need to be tied in to the support. Renovating a honeysuckle often means you will lose the flowers that year, but it will flower subsequently and renovation gives you a chance to repair the support.

ORNAMENTAL VINES

These foliage climbers have beautiful autumn colour, but they can soon engulf their supports, so hard pruning is needed. Prune crimson glory vine *(Vitis coignetiae)* in midwinter before the sap rises or cutting could cause the sap to bleed, which might weaken the plant. Prune *Ampelopsis* species in late winter or early spring. With both plants, shorten all side branches to within two or three buds of the main branches. Old plants can be cut to the ground and will usually resprout from the base. Cut back Virginia creeper to within 1 m (3 ft) of the base in autumn or early winter. Keep plants growing on house walls away from windows and gutters; the small, suckering pads are very difficult to remove from plaster, bricks or glass.

WISTERIA

The older wisterias produce spectacular displays of flowers and have attractively gnarled trunks. If renovation is needed, spread it over several winters, removing one or two main branches at a time and tying in a replacement shoot. If the plant is on a wall that requires maintenance, it can be cut back almost to the base and should resprout, but could take a few years to flower again. Summer pruning is needed to control the whippy leaf growth.

△ **WALL OF COLOUR**
Often found in warmer regions, bougainvilleas are among the most colourful climbers. Once the plant has developed a strong framework, it needs light pruning in early spring and deadheading in summer. Old plants should respond to hard pruning.

◁ **DRAMATIC VINE**
An ornamental vine such as this Virginia creeper makes a dramatic feature trained over an arbour. Although extremely vigorous, it responds well to being cut back hard.

CLIMBING ROSES

A mature climbing or rambling rose can be either an impressive feature of the garden in summer or a weakly growing eyesore. If you have a rose that has been neglected, there are several steps you can take to give it a new lease of life and restore it to its full flowering potential.

Whether or not to keep a rose will depend on your tastes, but consider also how well it performs. Some roses flower in short bursts, while others will keep going all summer. Some resist rust, blackspot and powdery mildew, but others succumb easily and spraying climbers is difficult. Varieties with large, full blooms are beautiful, but become sodden after a downpour; roses with smaller blooms or stronger stems are more tolerant of wet weather.

ROSE SUPPORTS

Decide also whether the rose is too vigorous for its support. Metal arches are often planted with over-vigorous types, making the structure unstable. Such varieties are best grown on strong supports such as walls and pergolas. Wooden posts that are in contact with the soil will eventually rot, but if you catch the problem early, it is possible to fit concrete spurs to hold them (see page 201).

RESTORATIVE PRUNING

Pruning a rose will improve the display of flowers. First establish if it is a climber or a rambler, since they differ in their growth, which affects how they are pruned. Ramblers throw up shoots from the base each year, whereas true climbers make less growth, not from the base but higher up, from the old wood. A rose book will tell you what type a variety is, but if you do not know the variety, look at the growth at the base. Another clue is that ramblers have more flexible stems than climbers.

To deal with an overgrown rambler, cut all growth down to the ground in late summer. New shoots should come up from the base and these can then be trained in to the support. In future years, cut out one stem in every three during the dormant season. Choose the oldest stems and cut them to the base. Pruning techniques for climbing and rambling roses are shown on pages 210–213.

Old climbing roses become bare near the base, with the new growth emerging from the top of the plant. To improve flowering, cut back a few of the main stems to within 30 cm (1 ft) of the ground. Spread the hard pruning over several years. Leave the young wood and feed the plant in spring.

Renovation work should be carried out in the dormant season, even if you might lose a year's flowers. Once the rose has been cut back, take the opportunity to repair or maintain its supports.

Roses must be fed with a rose fertilizer the first spring after hard pruning, when they should also be given a generous mulch of organic matter.

TRAINING

Ensure climbing roses are trained and tied in correctly (see pages 206–207). For flowers lower down, bend the young growth horizontally and tie it in. If the support is upright, wind the shoots in a spiral to obtain the most flowers.

If you inherit a trained rose that appears to be straining against its ties, undo and retie them.

AVOIDING DISEASE

If you decide to remove a rose, do not plant another one in the same place, since it could be vulnerable to rose replant disease. Either choose a different climber or, if you want to plant a rose again, dig the hole at least 75 cm (30 in) deep and fill it with topsoil from another part of the garden.

△ **ROSE PERGOLA**
Made of rustic poles and with an underplanting of lady's mantle (Alchemilla mollis), this pergola makes an ideal support for a climbing rose that is rather bare at the base. The rose 'Parkdirektor Riggers' has been trained horizontally to stimulate a copious display of flowers, which should repeat well through the summer.

▷ **TOUGH ROSE**
The rose 'New Dawn' has a strong constitution and will grow even on a partially shaded wall. Here it thrives among self-seeded valerian (Centranthus rubra) and fleabane (Erigeron karvinskianus).

FRUIT GARDENS

Inheriting an established fruit garden from a keen gardener can be a daunting prospect. However, if the plants are thriving, this is actually a fortunate position to be in, since most of the hard work of planting, establishing and training will already have been done in the early years.

Once they are established, most fruit plants are less labour-intensive than vegetables, many of which have to be grown from scratch each year. So there is a lot to be said for simply enjoying the fruit, or making a few small changes to suit your needs.

SIMPLIFYING THE GARDEN

If the fruit garden is particularly large, consider removing or reducing some elements to make it easier to manage. If there is a fruit cage, it is worth leaving this, since crops will be more plentiful, not only because they are protected from birds but also because of the shelter from wind. Fruit enthusiasts often grow early, mid and late varieties of the same crop, such as strawberries. If this is too much to cope with, you could keep the early ones and take out the rest. Likewise, there might be a cooking and a dessert gooseberry, and you may not need both. A glut of fruit can make harvesting a chore, so you could reduce the number of bushes of the same crop to a quantity you can cope with.

MINIMAL CARE

To keep the fruit garden going, remove any weeds and then mulch with well-rotted manure or garden compost. Pale green foliage and stunted growth is an indication of nutrient deficiency. This can be remedied by applying a rose fertilizer or a potash-rich fertilizer in early spring. Trained forms of fruit will need tying in and pruning (consult a pruning book – most fruits require both summer and winter pruning).

FROM FRUIT TO FLOWERS

If you want to use the site to grow other plants, most of the fruit will have to be removed. It is worth keeping an apple or pear tree, plus bush fruit, such as red currant or gooseberry, which are ornamental plants in their own right.

The area around the remaining fruit can be marked out as a bed – decide whether you want a formal effect or something more like a cottage

△ **EASY CURRANT**
An attractive plant, bearing delicious fruit, an established red currant is well worth keeping. Bushes are easily maintained, needing just winter pruning – cut off the tips of the main branches and cut back side shoots to one bud. Trained forms need pruning in summer and winter. Like blueberries, gooseberries and black currants, it is a long-lived fruit plant and should crop for at least 15 years.

garden. The soil where the fruit grew is probably fertile and moist and here clumps of daffodils will provide spring interest. Summer-flowering plants that like sun and rich soil include dahlias, roses and sweet peas. Where there were old paths, the soil is likely to be compacted, low in nutrients, and dry: here you can sow annuals for quick colour.

MOVING FRUIT PLANTS

A well-planned fruit garden will have been located in a sheltered, sunny site. If you want to free this up for another purpose, say a lawn, patio or flowerbed, you could move the fruit plants to other parts of the garden (preferably in the dormant season). Blackberries, currants and gooseberries will produce a reduced but respectable yield in partial shade. Black currants can be grown as part of a mixed hedge at the bottom of the garden. A trellis panel against a shed or garage wall could be used for a blackberry or a hybrid berry.

Trained fruit can often be moved to fences or walls elsewhere in the garden. A fan-trained fruit tree needs a wall or fence at least 1.8 m (6 ft) high and with room to spread for at least 2.4–3 m (8–10 ft). Cordons are fine for lower boundaries; space them 75 cm (30 in) apart. A fence or wall facing southwest or west is suitable for most trained fruit; colder north- or east-facing boundaries are suitable only for late varieties. A sunny fence or wall is ideal for pears or peaches, but not apples.

Raspberries need sun. They are difficult to train against a wall or fence, so are best grown as a screen, on horizontal wires attached to stout posts. In sheltered areas, an autumn-fruiting form can be grown as a free-standing shrub in a large border. Plant it 60–90 cm (2–3 ft) from other plants, and after fruiting, cut it back to the ground.

Strawberry plants are short-lived fruit, lasting only about three years, so they may not be worth moving. However, if you want to grow them elsewhere in the garden, you can take runners from a healthy plant and replant them. Strawberries can be grown in a container on a sunny patio or terrace, but the yields are small; plant six in a grow bag or three in a 30-cm (1-ft) diameter pot.

△ **CORDON PEAR**
A pear trained as a cordon against a warm wall is an attractive feature, as well as a space-saving method of growing fruit. This variety is 'Doyenne du Comice'.

◁ **FRUIT AND FLOWERS**
Espaliered apple trees, with ripening fruit, form a structured backdrop to this informal flower border. The tall, vigorous Nicotiana sylvestris bears clusters of fragrant, white flowers from late summer until the autumn frosts. It thrives in moist, fertile soil.

◁ **FRUIT SCREEN**
A row of raspberry canes trained against post-and-wire supports makes a productive divider or screen.

▷ **ORCHARD MEADOW**
*Converting a large fruit garden
to a grassy orchard is a low-
maintenance way of dealing
with it. The orchard remains
productive, is good for wildlife,
and provides plenty of space in
which to play and picnic.*

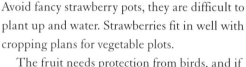

▽ **CORDON APPLES**
*Mixed varieties of apples grown
as cordons help to brighten up
a plain fence, providing both
blossoms and fruit.*

Avoid fancy strawberry pots, they are difficult to plant up and water. Strawberries fit in well with cropping plans for vegetable plots.

The fruit needs protection from birds, and if the plants are scattered around the garden, each one will need to be netted before the fruit ripens.

MAKING AN ORCHARD

Another option, if the layout allows, is to convert the fruit garden into an orchard. You could keep the existing fruit trees and remove the soft fruits, replacing them with traditional trees such as hazel *(Corylus avellana),* wild crab apple *(Malus sylvestris)* or pear *(Pyrus communis).*

The ground could be left to grow into a semishaded grass meadow, with wild daffodils, wood anemones *(Anemone nemorosa)* and bugle *(Ajuga reptans).* But most meadow plants prefer poor soil, so such a planting could be difficult if large quantities of organic matter have been put on the fruit beds. If you are planting new trees in a meadow, keep a radius of 60–75 cm (24–30 in) around them free from grass.

RENOVATING FRUIT TREES

Pruning can encourage a neglected apple or pear tree to crop again, but first you will need to assess whether or not this is worthwhile, given the age and health of the tree. Large trees over 4.5 m (15 ft) are best pruned by a tree surgeon, so consider whether the money required for this would be better spent on removing or replacing the tree. A modern dwarf rootstock could give you apples for much less space. Balance this against the fact that a new tree will take two or three years to bear fruit and seven years to crop fully.

If there are a number of apple trees, you might want to keep and renovate only the healthiest. Remember, though, that some varieties need to be cross-pollinated. A specialist fruit book or catalogue should list which trees are compatible, but you will need to know the variety name.

Renovation should be carried out when the tree is dormant, but not during severe frosts. If a fruit tree needs extensive pruning, stagger the work over two dormant seasons. Regardless of the tree's size, if you are at all unsure about carrying out this work, get a professional to do it for you.

To renovate an apple tree, first establish a good framework of main branches. Remove any dead or badly diseased branches, then take out any that are poorly placed, such as low branches that cross

REPLACING OLD PLANTS

⊘ Apples trees with bad scab or mildew could be replaced with new varieties such as 'Redsleeves', 'Saturn' or 'Winter Gem', which have improved resistance to disease.

⊘ An overvigorous cherry, or one whose crop suffers due to spring frosts damaging the blossoms, could be replaced by 'Sunburst', a variety that is self-fertile and crops late. Dwarf rootstocks can restrict the size of the tree, if necessary.

⊘ Gooseberries that regularly suffer from mildew can be replaced by varieties such as 'Rokula'. If spines are a problem, look for new varieties that are almost spineless such as 'Pax'.

⊘ There are several new blackberry varieties without thorns, including 'Adrienne', 'Loch Ness', 'No Thorn', 'Waldo' and the tayberry 'Buckingham Thornless', which is a cross between a raspberry and a blackberry.

⊘ New strawberry varieties come out each year, and many claim to be resistant to one or more diseases. Two good recent varieties are 'Florence' and 'Symphony'.

◁ **TRAINED QUINCE**
Most established fruit trees need little attention, although trained plants, such as this quince, require regular pruning and tying to maintain the shape.

over the tree and vigorous upward-growing ones. Cut back to a healthy main limb. Use a saw or pruning saw, undercutting first, then completing the cut from above to prevent the branch tearing (see also pages 212–213).

If a tree is stunted in growth with pale, starved-looking foliage, it needs thinning out so that more light can get to the fruit spurs. Feed, mulch and water the tree in spring. Cherries and plums are best pruned in early spring or immediately after cropping, to reduce the risk of silver leaf infection. Wound sealants are not now recommended, since they do not seem to help the healing process. It is better to cut cleanly with a sharp, clean blade.

If they are well cared for, fruit trees last many years: a good apple tree could crop for 50 years.

RENOVATING SOFT FRUIT

Bush fruit, such as currants and gooseberries, can be rejuvenated as you would a shrub by removing the old wood and letting light into the centre (see page 210). If a bush is unproductive or shows signs of virus, it is best to uproot and burn the stock.

Cane fruit, such as blackberries and raspberries, need annual maintenance. This involves removing the fruited canes, tying in new growth, and taking out the suckers. If you inherit plants that have not been maintained, it will be difficult to restore order. You will need to dig out suckers and any growth where the tips have rooted into the earth, and cut away the old canes. You can then either tie in the young canes to the existing supports, or uproot some healthy suckers and start again.

△ **CANE CROPS**
Cane fruits, such as raspberries, fruit on growth produced the previous season. Old canes must be cut off at the base – after cropping for summer-fruiting raspberries, and in late winter for autumn-fruiting ones. Raspberry plants more than 10 years old are best replaced, since they become susceptible to viruses.

VEGETABLE GARDENS

Growing your own vegetables is rewarding and ensures a ready supply of delicious produce, but a large plot takes up time and space. As with fruit, it is possible to scale down and simplify a vegetable garden to make it easier to cope with. Alternatively, you might want to use the site for something else.

▷▽ GROWING SPACES
While an allotment has its own ramshackle charm, you might prefer a more stylish approach to raising crops. The plot below uses an imaginative layout of raised beds, crisply edged in wood, and includes flowers, a water feature and seats.

Whether you intend to continue growing vegetables or find another use for the ground, begin by assessing the plot. Most vegetable gardens occupy a sunny and sheltered position, which is ideal for a terrace or for a variety of ornamental plants. The soil is likely to be fertile and enriched, although the paths between the beds will be compacted and possibly weedy.

Vegetable plots are usually divided into a series of beds as part of a rotation scheme. If a deep bed system is used, the beds are edged with boards or bricks. The paths might be simply grass or bare earth, or landscaped paths of brick or paving slabs.

Decide whether you need to make changes for practical or aesthetic reasons, or both. A series of attractively laid out brick paths is worth keeping; bare earth, on the other hand, becomes muddy in wet weather and you might want to lay a more practical path (see pages 200–201) or at least put down some gravel or bark with a retaining edge.

If you acquire the plot in summer, harvest anything that is there and clear spent crops as you go; rig up a simple compost bin nearby so all the green waste can be recycled. Clear the site of junk.

GROWING VEGETABLES

Inheriting a well-worked vegetable plot means that much of the back-breaking soil improvement and preparation has been carried out already. If you are keen on vegetables, such a garden provides an excellent opportunity for growing your own.

A good way to start is to work on one bed and cover the others with black polythene, secured to the ground, or old carpet – either will prevent weeds from taking over. Remove weeds from the plot you want to work on – seedling weeds can be quickly dealt with using a hoe, but perennials need to be dug out with as much of the root as possible (see pages 214–215). Applying weedkiller is another option (follow the instructions carefully).

To prepare the ground for planting, rake it with a soil rake until the surface is crumbly. You need to add organic matter, such as spent mushroom compost, each year in autumn, winter or spring. If you plan to dig the soil, the compost can be dug in at the same time. If you have a no-dig plot, then add a layer to the surface in spring.

It obviously makes sense to grow vegetables that you like eating, but also take into account how easy they are to grow. You are more likely to be successful with plants that require little care, such as garlic, which is just planted and harvested. Courgettes, squashes and runner beans need attention early on, but just a few plants will give plentiful crops (see page 139).

A POTAGER

If regimental rows of vegetables are not to your liking, allow them to rub shoulders with annual flowers to create a colourful, exuberant potager. A plot that is divided into four small square or rectangular beds often works well. Do not make the beds too wide, since you will need to reach into them from the paths.

Plants can either be mingled together or grown in small blocks, based on square or rectangular divisions of the beds. You could use perennials, but it is easier to experiment if you start with annuals. Limit the permanent plants to step-over apples around the edges or a standard gooseberry in the centre. Position a bamboo wigwam or a wicker tripod in the centre of each bed to support tall annuals such as sweet peas or runner beans. Then choose an edging for the beds, using brightly coloured, easy plants such as nasturtiums,

red or frilly lettuce, ruby chard, pot marigold or chives. Contrasting plants, such as parsley or carrots, can be grown in the remaining space.

With a potager, most of the colour will come in the summer months. In winter you will be relying on good structure, attractive paths or useful and good-looking objects, such as tripods, glass cloches or terracotta pots for forcing rhubarb. Winter-flowering pansies or violas or ornamental brassicas could be used to edge the beds; but if the plot is large, this planting for winter interest will require a considerable amount of extra work.

△ **SEATING AREA**
Vegetables grow best in a sunny, sheltered site, so, as in this attractive, informal plot, it is worth incorporating a seating area from which to admire the fruits of your labour.

△ **PERFECT POTAGER**
A well-designed potager is an asset in any garden. Here the brick paths have aged well and allow easy access to herbs and vegetables, whatever the weather. The box edging and lavender provide year-round structure and interest.

FORMAL FLOWERS

If you would rather convert the vegetable garden to another use, one option is a formal flower garden. The beds can be edged with box *(Buxus sempervirens)* to define them. Young box plants are cheaper and will establish more quickly than mature ones. Clear any weeds from the ground inside each bed and lay down a sheet of landscape fabric, covering it with gravel or bark chips until you are ready to plant. In time, you could plant the beds with summer or spring bedding in a formal pattern. Pave the paths, if necessary, and add an ornament or a large container in the centre of the plot as a focal point.

SECRET ROSE GARDEN

If the site is sunny and enclosed, another way of using the area is to fill it with scented roses and add a seat, or an arbour with a seat, from which to enjoy them. An arch with a climbing rose can be used to mark the entrance and several bush roses could be planted in each bed.

Alternatively, you may prefer to design a scheme with a standard rose in the centre and smaller patio roses around it. Stepping stones or a bark chip mulch over the beds will provide easy access to the roses for pruning. To extend the season of interest, underplant with low-growing evergreens, spring bulbs or spring bedding (see pages 114–115).

A HERB GARDEN

A vegetable plot with raised beds is ideal for conversion to a herb garden, especially if the rest of the garden is poorly drained. Mediterranean herbs like a sunny site with a well-drained soil of low fertility. However, there are other herbs, such as parsley, mint, and chives, that will thrive in the richer soil of a vegetable plot and can tolerate a bit more shade. The Mediterranean herbs might do well on the site of bare-earth paths.

In a large plot, it is best to concentrate on the shrubby herbs such as lavender, sage, rosemary and bay, as well as perennials such as bergamot and hyssop. These plants will remain in the ground for several years, whereas annual herbs must be sown each year. Herb gardens require structure to balance the loose habit of the plants, so make use of the beds and paths or incorporate a focal point such as an obelisk. If you prefer, add stronger colour to a herb garden by including a few herbs with bright flowers, such as pot marigold.

△ **DRAMATIC CROPS**
If you have enough space, globe artichokes are impressive architectural plants – each one takes 0.3–0.4 sq m (3–4 sq ft). Although perennial, they are not long-lived, usually lasting about three years.

▷ **EDIBLE FLOWERS**
A courgette in flower is a reminder to water the plant well – young courgettes will soon be cropping. Harvest them when they are small. The flowers can also be eaten, either stuffed with rice or made into fritters.

EASY VEGETABLES

Annual vegetables

The following vegetables need little attention during the growing season, so are suitable crops to grow if you are pressed for time.

Beetroot Very easy and can be left in the ground until you are able to harvest them. Young leaves are also edible. Choose bolt-resistant varieties.

Cabbage Can be grown almost all year, with spring greens, red cabbage in autumn and a Savoy type for winter. Choose bolt-resistant varieties.

Calabrese Tastes like broccoli, but is much easier to grow.

Carrots Need little space, but may not produce good roots in stony soil. Use a crop cover to deter carrot fly.

Courgettes Each plant needs 1 sq m (3 sq ft), but only a few plants are required to produce lots of courgettes. Harvest courgettes when small and firm.

Fava beans Hardiest bean and first to crop. In temperate climates, can be sown in autumn and grown under cloches for early crops. Very little watering needed.

Garlic Simply plant cloves in winter and harvest in summer.

Kale Hardiest winter vegetable and one of few brassicas to be almost free from pests and diseases. Curly kale can be grown as a cut-and-come-again crop.

Leeks Easier than onions, since they are not so fussy about soil conditions. Will stand in the ground until you have time to harvest them, but best eaten young.

Lettuce All types can be grown on most soils in sun, but they need watering. Cut leaves with scissors or tear off by hand; the plant will grow new leaves.

Radishes Summer types can be pulled three to six weeks after sowing.

Ruby/Swiss chard Leaves are similar to spinach, but stems can also be cooked separately and eaten; has a longer harvest period than spinach.

Runner beans Attractive, high yielding and take up little space.

Squash A good way to cover a large plot for little effort. Winter squashes store well if cut and ripened in the sun for a week before storing.

Perennial vegetables

Most vegetables are grown as annuals, but a few are perennials. Once planted, they will crop year after year, requiring no more care than perennial flowers.

Asparagus Can crop for 10 to 20 years, but need a lot of space and deep, rich soil. Keep the site weed-free and cut spears in late April. Feed growing fern with liquid feed. When ferns turn yellow in autumn, cut them down.

Jerusalem artichokes Tolerates rough ground, heavy soil, and shade. Reaches 1.5 m (5 ft), so is useful for summer screening. Cut back stalks in autumn and dig up tubers throughout the winter.

Rhubarb Healthy plants crop for 5 to 10 years. Mulch in spring with garden compost or well-rotted organic matter. Remove any flowering stems.

Sorrel Lemony, slightly bitter flavour. Useful for a partially shaded site. In mild areas and with cloche protection, it can be picked throughout winter. Pick outer leaves first, leaving inner leaves to grow. Remove seed heads. Lasts 3 to 4 years.

PATIOS

Most gardens have some form of patio or terrace. Often they are bleak and uninviting expanses of paving, providing nothing more than a mud-free entrance to the house. With a little thought and effort, though, they can be transformed into valuable outdoor living spaces.

△ **WELL-PLANNED PATIO**
This patio has plenty of space for tables and chairs, and groups of pots are cleverly placed to add colour and form where needed. The delicate arched pergola creates a subtle sense of enclosure, dividing the patio from the lawn without cutting off the lawn.

▷ **PROVENÇAL PATIO**
A cobbled floor in a Provençal-style courtyard looks charming, but it is not the most practical surface for a table and chairs.

Before undertaking any renovation work, decide what you want from your patio or terrace. Do you need a large, clear space for eating outside – perhaps with a barbecue – or do you require space for just one bench? If this is to be a living area, is either too little or too much sun a consideration? If there is too little, does the patio need to be resited, in which event, can you use the existing paving?

Consider also the condition of the paving. Is it uneven and a nuisance for chairs, or does it pose a danger to children and older people? Do the slabs or bricks become slippery with algae, needing frequent cleaning?

LINKING PATIO AND GARDEN

If the garden can be seen across the patio, it will function as a frame, and the way it links to the garden is very important.

Some patios are edged with rose beds, which can block access to the lawn, both visually and physically. Roses are also a depressing sight in winter, and will not provide you with a good view from indoors. In this case, work out where to make a route through to the garden. An unofficial path may have been worn by people taking a short cut through the roses. If this seems to be the best route, remove any plants here and lay paving slabs across to the lawn. It is important to use slabs that are wide enough for the purpose – a narrow exit will look mean, and plants on either side will tend to be trodden on. A few stepping stones laid in the lawn can be used to stop a bare patch developing.

ENLARGING A PATIO

It may be that there is simply not enough space to sit out on your patio, or that your seating area would be better located just a little further out into the lawn (either because it is sunny or there is a better view). Enlarging a too-small patio may be a big job, but it is worth the trouble and expense because it increases your living space. If the existing patio is made of loose-laid bricks or paving slabs, the job will be easier. Try to find new paving units that match the existing ones; otherwise choose a colour that is similar. If you want to plant among the paving, take out some of the original slabs to form planting pockets and reuse them in the extended patio, mixing the old pavings in with the new ones.

Paving must slope away from the house so that water can drain away. It also needs to be laid below the damp course; otherwise it can cause serious problems with rising damp or even with flooding if it is on a steep slope.

If you want to re-lay paving, see pages 200–201. If you feel you are unable to tackle such a job yourself, employ a landscaper or builder. Use a reputable builder who has had experience laying paving. Whoever you choose, ask him or her for advice on matching existing materials, and whether it will cost much more to lift the existing paving and re-lay it completely.

UNEVEN PATIOS

Some patios become uneven with age, which is irritating if you cannot find a flat place for your seat or table and have to wedge something underneath to stop it rocking. They may also be hazardous for the infirm and for young children.

△ MIXED MATERIALS
Using a mixture of materials such as slabs and cobbles lends a surface textural variety. Because they are difficult to walk on, cobbles also give a visual message to slow down and take care, which makes them useful for replacing some of the slabs on an uneven patio.

be strictly for visual effect, since it is difficult to walk on. Large stone pots or planters look effective in combination with cobbles, as do interestingly shaped rocks.

You may decide that no halfway measures will suffice, in which case the paving will have to be lifted and re-laid (see pages 200–201). This is a big and expensive project, so be sure that your existing patio is in the best place and is the right size and shape for your needs; otherwise this is the time to make changes.

CREATING AN ENCLOSURE

Patios that are completely open are dull and not particularly pleasant places to sit. Seats are always more inviting when there is a feeling of protection around them. Evidence of this is often seen in parks, when the benches out in the open are empty, while those placed in front of a wall or in a corner are occupied.

A simple solution is to place large containers over the most uneven areas of the patio. If you prefer, these can be embellished with smaller pots. Containers can otherwise be placed to steer people away from the dips and bumps – by delineating a path through the patio, for instance – or to surround the seating area so that the worst of the slabs are hidden.

If you do not want to re-lay the whole patio, replace the uneven slabs or bricks with gravel or cobbles set in sharp sand or dry sand and cement. This serves as a visual warning that the surface is not uniform. Large cobbles, which are more difficult to walk on, will also deter people from taking short cuts.

First, select the areas to be replaced and remove the paving, then stand back and consider the overall effect. If the slabs are clustered together in just one or two places, you will need to take out some others to give a more balanced effect. It may be possible to remove every other slab to create a chequerboard pattern, but such a surface would

Enclosure can be easily achieved by bringing the planting out from the wall or boundary, so that it starts to surround the patio. This will also create a frame for the garden, outlining the view from inside the house. Instead of, or as well as, using planting to give a sense of enclosure, you could erect a pergola (see below) or a simple trellis screen (see pages 60–61).

PERGOLAS

A pergola is a delightful addition to an area of paving, creating quite a different space. It gives instant enclosure and provides welcome shade and privacy, especially for eating areas.

When choosing or constructing a pergola for a seating area, check first that it will be both high and wide enough for the purpose by positioning your table and chairs where you want them and allowing enough space to walk around. A newly installed pergola may seem very large at first, but once climbers have grown over it you will be glad of the spaciousness.

If you do not have enough space for a free-standing pergola, a smaller, lean-to pergola can be made against a wall, to provide just enough shade and shelter for a seat. Try to position the pergola so that it casts shade at the hottest time of the day, while allowing the sun's rays to reach the seat in the morning or evening when it is cooler.

WATER FEATURES

A water feature will give a sense of peacefulness to a seating area, as well as providing a focal point. One option is a raised pool, which can either be formal – round, square or rectangular, in stone or brick – or a more natural-looking curved shape. This last, however, will need to be blended in very carefully, using stone or rock edging, since it can easily look out of place in such a setting.

Whatever form the pool takes, planting will help it to merge with its surroundings. Royal fern *(Osmunda regalis),* northern maidenhair fern *(Adiantum pedatum)* and ferny-leaved astilbes with feathery flowers work well. Large-leaved plants such as the rhubarb *Rheum palmatum rubrum* look stunning. All these plants need damp soil, and in an artificial environment such as a patio, you must provide this.

◁ **RAISED PATIO**
A clever solution to a change of level in a garden is to create a raised patio. Here, reclaimed bricks are laid in an attractive basket-weave pattern, and a low brick wall defines the patio's circular shape and retains the raised planting bed. Narrow brick and stone steps, closely planted on either side, link it to the lower area, which is paved with York stone.

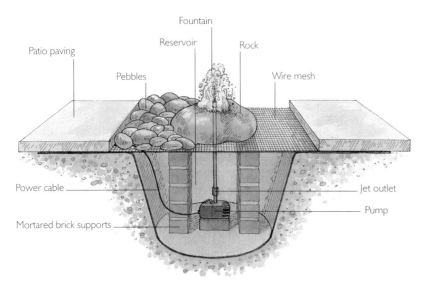

Fountain

Reservoir

Rock

Patio paving

Pebbles

Wire mesh

Power cable

Jet outlet

Mortared brick supports

Pump

△ **PATIO FOUNTAIN**

This simple water feature consists of a reservoir with a pump and fountain jet, over which is laid a firm wire grille covered with pebbles. The jet emerges from a hole drilled in the rock, and the water is recycled into the reservoir.

▽ **RAISED POND**

Instead of burying a fountain in the ground, as illustrated above, it can be built up. Here, a raised circular pond, built of brick, contains a selection of interesting rocks and pebbles, and a gentle bubble fountain, powered from below.

An alternative is to choose plants that have a lush look but can tolerate drier conditions such as *Hosta sieboldiana elegans,* the hart's-tongue fern *(Asplenium scolopendrium)* or cuckoo pint *(Arum italicum* 'Pictum').

Self-contained sculptural fountains, such as rocks, large pebbles or "millstones" of concrete or stone, can be effective on patios. A hole is drilled through the the stone or rock, and water is pumped up so that it bubbles over the surface, collecting in a reservoir below to be recycled (see illustration left). If your garden is hot and sunny, the sight and sound of cool water will be refreshing, and such features are attractive even when the fountain is turned off.

If the patio is bordered by a wall, you may be able to create a water feature that combines a pool and a wall-mounted fountain. Water is pumped up from the pool to the fountain, which is housed in a suitable outlet, such as a decorative wall mask, an old brass tap or a plain metal spout.

PLANTING

If your patio is just a dull area of paving and it is not intensively used, you could replace some of the paving material with plants. Check how the paving is laid. If the slabs, flagstones or bricks are laid in thick concrete with a deep hard core base, they can be difficult to remove. Again, consider the access routes needed or the framing effect that you want to create. Experiment with pots and tubs (see pages 44–51) to find out what works best.

When you are sure about the size and shape of the space you need, remove the paving slabs – either several together, which will allow for a group of plants, or one or two separate slabs for individual specimens. Dig out any concrete or stones underneath and remove at least 5 cm (2 in) of soil. Replace this with good topsoil, enriched with manure or compost. If you want to grow acid-loving plants, such as rhododendrons or azaleas, and your garden soil is unsuitable, you can use an acidic soil here. If the paving is mortared, it is advisable to line the planting holes to prevent any lime from leaching into the soil.

Sculptural plants are also effective, for example the cabbage tree *(Cordyline australis),* the tree fern

CLEANING PAVING

Paving can become green and slippery with algae, especially bricks and clay tiles. This may be caused by a lack of light and air, or by poor drainage. Clean any dirt and remove any overhanging branches. A proprietary cleaner or an algicide, from a garden centre, will remove the slime. If drainage is the problem, it may help to clean out the joints of the paving and refill them with sand; if this does not work, the patio may have to be re-laid completely.

◁ **SLABS AND GRAVEL**

Mixing widely spaced paving slabs with gravel creates a useful, attractive patio without going to the expense of laying slabs over the whole area.

▽ **PAVING PLANTS**

Creepers of different colours and textures have been planted in the gaps between the stone flags to enliven this plain grey patio. A striking foliage plant in a beautifully shaped pot and yellow-striped grasses complete the picture.

(Dicksonia antarctica), Euphorbia characias or the glossy-leaved Japanese aralia. Mediterranean plants such as *Phlomis fruticosa* and broom (*Cytisus* species) thrive in sunny paved spots.

Crazy paving can look wonderful planted with sun-loving creepers. Either plant between the cracks or lift a few smaller pieces of paving to make space. If the paving is uneven, you could remove the worst-affected pieces and put plants in their place. Remove any stones or loose concrete and add some good soil. Use small, rooted pieces of a plant, or make a hole big enough to take the entire rootball.

Many rockery plants are suitable for this type of planting. In sunny areas try *Thymus serpyllum* and *T. lanuginosus; Dianthus* 'Pike's Pink'; *Arenaria montana;* and *Arabis caucasica.* They will thrive in the reflected warmth from the stones, while their roots will be shaded and protected. Shady areas are more difficult: *Viola labradorica* should do well, and some of the saxifrages; *Campanula muralis* makes pretty green mounds with blue flowers over a long period. You could also try the northern maidenhair fern (*Adiantum pedatum*).

GARDEN STEPS

Leading enticingly into a secluded area or simply providing practical access from one level to another, attractive steps can enhance any garden. Whether you are improving existing steps, or creating new ones, make sure that they suit their surroundings and are both safe and well maintained.

△ **INFORMAL STYLE**
Railway sleepers form the risers of these simple but attractive steps, while gravel supplies the tread-surface. Large pots line one side of the steps, adding rhythm and structure (see page 149).

▷ **PAINTED STEPS**
Although quite steep and without a handrail, these steps are made safer by their bright blue colouring – an instant attention grabber. The rough timber is complemented by the plain gravel surface and the rocks and lavender at the base.

Function, location and safety are the three cornerstones of garden step design. While wrought-iron, stone or brick steps look appropriate leading from the average house into the garden, grand stone steps are a better choice descending from a formal terrace, and shallow, wide, rustic steps should lead up through a woodland area. If the design of existing steps seems inappropriate, consider replacing them – it is surprising just what a difference this makes.

Any rickety or damaged steps must be repaired or replaced urgently – perhaps providing an opportunity to change the design. Brick steps that have become loose and unstable will need re-laying, which is best done by a bricklayer.

PROPORTIONS OF STEPS

How easy and pleasant your steps are to use depends very much on their proportions. As a general rule, the steeper the steps, the more awkward they are to use. The height is obviously determined by the upright part of a step, called the riser. While a 17.5-cm (7-in) riser is acceptable in the house, it will feel uncomfortable outside, where the ideal height is 10 cm (4 in) – a lower riser slows the steps to a leisurely pace. The tread, or step depth, must be in proportion to the riser – the steeper the steps, the narrower the tread:

Tread	Riser
35 cm (14 in)	15 cm (6 in)
40 cm (16 in)	13 cm (5 in)
45 cm (18 in)	10 cm (4 in)

If an existing flight of steps is a little on the steep side and it feels unsafe, instal a handrail at one side. Alternatively, exaggerate the narrowness of the steps as a visual warning – perhaps by

◁ **FORMAL STEPS**
In this modern interpretation of a classical formal style, brick steps are given crisp definition by square-clipped box plants in square containers. Terracotta globes and standard roses reinforce the symmetry of the overall design.

planting shrubs close together on both sides and clipping them back to form narrow hedges.

A steep flight of steps may be eased by creating a resting place halfway up, such as a ledge or a bench to one side – provided you have enough space to place this in a safe spot. Arrange a few plants around the rest-point or a covering overhead; a covered seat is perfect in this situation.

Patio doors often open out on to one or two steps. If these are too narrow or steep, they give an unwelcome feeling of haste. Making the treads at least 40 cm (16 in) deep will improve matters considerably and will also provide additional seating for your next garden party.

The width of steps is also important. A width of 90 cm (3 ft) is adequate for one person; for two people, the steps should be at least 1.5 m (5 ft) wide. On a gentler slope, and where there is enough space, the very large mule steps seen in Mediterranean countries are a highly appealing option. These should be at least 1 m (39 in) deep,

with quite shallow risers of 10 cm (4 in) or less. Each riser is ramped gently upwards to the next one, so that two normal strides are needed to walk up them. These create a very easy approach to a slope and can be used with a pushchair or a lightly loaded wheelbarrow.

Wide steps may become tipped off angle or overgrown with weeds, but all is not lost. Keep the usable sections as steps – if they are steady and level – and convert unusable sections into planted terraces running down the sides of your steps. Remove the treads and any cement stuck to the tops of the risers. Dig out the insides of the steps, getting rid of any rubble, fill in with a mix of good soil and compost, and add suitable plants.

△ **NATURAL STYLE**
These appealingly natural rough stone steps are wide and generous enough for the self-seeded plants alchemilla, verbascum and Erigeron karvinskianus. The glossy ceramic pots are planted with Brachyscome iberidifolia.

PLANTING

Your terraces will form the ideal spot for rockery plants, which will be easy to reach and maintain from the steps. For an unusual feature, plant the non-flowering chamomile 'Treneague' to create a series of flat, green, scented cushions.

Most other kinds of steps also provide all sorts of opportunities for interesting planting. Many town houses, for example, have metal steps that provide the main access to the garden. These are usually either ornate wrought-iron structures or rather plain and utilitarian in style. Both types will benefit from hanging pots or small baskets, overflowing with brightly coloured flowers, fixed securely to the outside of the handrail. Ivy-leaved pelargoniums are good options for a sunny site, since they will trail down attractively. In a shadier location, ivy is effective, with busy lizzies supplying colour.

Keep your scheme simple and unfussy, with just one type of container and one or two plant varieties. Plant trailing climbers such as Chinese gooseberry *(Actinidia chinensis)* at the base of metal steps so that they curl through them; with vigorous growers such as this, you will need to pinch out any stray shoots a couple of times a year. For something a little more ambitious, you could build arches over the steps for your climber to scramble over, creating a mysterious, tunnel-like entrance to the garden. Make sure the arches are high enough, otherwise they may be difficult to negotiate.

Brick steps with concrete coping can be planted with self-clinging climbers such as Boston ivy. *Parthenocissus tricuspidata* is the most widely grown species, but the small-leaved 'Veitchii' variety is better for steps as it is neater in habit.

Grander stone steps with balustrading need a more formal treatment – a shrub on either side at the base, say. Choose evergreens, since they are substantial enough to balance the visual weight of the stone steps. Bay or box are classic choices, but make sure that they are kept symmetrical or they will lose their effect.

Looser-growing evergreens such as viburnums or rhododendrons can be left to develop their natural shape, but make sure you plant them far enough away from the steps, otherwise you will need to keep cutting them back.

With wooden steps, containers are an especially effective choice. Wooden plant boxes at either side provide a pleasing finish and make the steps safer by giving them a clear boundary. Use terracotta pots in the same way, but choose ones that are wide-based, as these are more stable and less likely to be knocked off. Likewise, avoid using tall pots with a narrow base in windy locations; low, wide ones are more secure.

▽ **CORNER STEPS**
Hard, geometric lines and symmetrically arranged pots produce the kind of design that works well where a change of direction is required – as with these steps in a corner.

▷ **POTS OF COLOUR**
Small pots of begonias are used to enliven these narrow metal steps, which are painted white to brighten up a dark basement area. Fixing the pots to the outside of the stair rods leaves more space on the steps.

◁ **PLANT COLLECTION**
Steps offer the perfect setting for smaller plants that either need special care or would not be fully appreciated in a dense border planting. Here, a mixture of tufted and mound-forming plants, including grasses and different sempervivums, flourish in a sunny location.

WOODEN STEPS

Although they can look very appealing, wooden steps are all too often unsafe, becoming especially slippery and dangerous if sited in damp areas. Make sure that they are not collecting moss, and brush them regularly with a wire brush to keep the surface rough. If this does not help, improve the grip by covering the treads with chicken wire, if you are not too fussy about appearance, or replace the treads with narrower sections so that air can pass in between. It is now possible to buy wood for steps with a ridged finish, which gives a much better grip.

Wooden steps overhung with branches from trees or shrubs may look romantic, but unless you have a hot, dry climate, they are almost certain to become slippery. Keep any branches cut back and fairly high above the steps.

MAKING WOODEN STEPS

For the outer areas of a garden, wooden steps are easy to construct. Straight logs or railway sleepers make ideal risers, since they are heavy and durable. The slope should be prepared properly and well graded. Establish the position of the bottom riser first and then work upwards. Dig out a level base and tamp it down firmly. Position the

log or sleeper, and secure it with a reinforcing rod, fixed about 30 cm (1 ft) from each end and driven into the ground. Alternatively, a wooden peg, treated with preservative, can be driven in front of the steps at each end. Fill the steps with 10 cm (4 in) of stones or hard core, to help drainage.

Make your tread surface from gravel or wood chips. Brick gives a more formal effect, but is suitable only for the square-edged sleepers and not rounded logs. Grass is a good surface for very shallow, wide steps, but this is a high-maintenance option and requires enough space for a mower.

If you cannot get hold of sleepers or heavy logs, a lighter set of steps can be made using wooden planks, but they will not last as long. Choose gravel for the tread surface because it will drain well.

▽ **RAILWAY SLEEPERS**
Steps made of railway sleepers and either gravel or wood chips work well in wilder or more informal areas. Make them wide enough to allow plants to grow over from both sides.

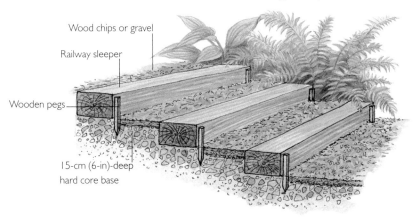

Wood chips or gravel

Railway sleeper

Wooden pegs

15-cm (6-in)-deep hard core base

PONDS

According to popular lore, a pond is one of the most appealing of garden features, a magnet for people and wildlife alike. In reality, too many ponds fall rapidly into a state of overgrown, murky, rank-smelling neglect. How do you restore a pond to prime condition – and keep it that way?

▽ **WILDLIFE HAVEN**
Frogs will visit the tiniest pond, even a birdbath, as long as there are plants nearby to hide in.

The success of any pond and the amount of maintenance it requires depend on three main factors: its location, design and construction. If the best practice has been followed in all these areas, then the pond will give a lot of pleasure and need little upkeep – unless you have opted to add a large number of high-maintenance plants or fish. If, however, the pond is badly positioned, too small or too shallow, or shoddily constructed with cheap materials, it will automatically leave a legacy of high maintenance and you may decide that it is better to build a new one.

Siting a pond near trees is a common cause of problems. For instance, falling leaves and plant debris may pollute the water. Covering the pond with netting before leaf fall prevents this, but the damage may already have been done if it has not been covered in the past. Perhaps tree roots have penetrated the pond liner, and you may have to choose between the pond and the tree.

KEY FEATURES OF DIFFERENT PONDS

POND TYPE	SIZE/SHAPE	SIDES/EDGING	SITE	TIPS
WILDLIFE POND	Any size. Shape is not critical when it comes to attracting wildlife, but a pond with curves will look more natural.	Sides should be shallow, with at least one side planted to give cover. Use natural edging materials such as rocks, pebbles or turf.	A secluded setting where the pond looks natural rather than man-made.	Make a steep-sided pond slope with materials such as old logs. Ornamental fish are best excluded. Planting can create a more natural look.
POND FOR FISH	Surface area is critical as it determines the stocking level. As a guide, each fish needs at least 0.2–0.3 sq m (2–3 sq ft). Any shape is suitable.	Use any type of material. Physical barriers are required to deter cats and herons, which are able to wade into sloping ponds.	Opt for a site that will create some shaded areas – under overhanging evergreens, for example.	Tripwires and netting can help deter predators. An outdoor power supply will be needed for a biological filter system.
POND FOR PLANTS	Any size or shape is fine, but always take the vigour of your plants and their required planting depth into account.	A shelf 45 cm (18 in) deep is needed for marginal plants. Bog plants may need a man-made bog.	Water lilies need sun and dislike water splashing on to their leaves – from fountains, for example.	Avoid fish as they uproot and eat plants. Most plants are best grown in containers. It may be possible to build a shelf or use floating planters.
FORMAL POND	Choose a geometric shape of any size that fits the garden design. If a fountain is included, the pond must be big enough to catch the water.	Opt for bricks, paving slabs, or wooden decking. Edging normally overhangs the water slightly to create a shadow line.	Most effective in a paved area such as a terrace. Fountains should be placed in a sheltered site.	Restrict the planting to a few bold architectural specimens and water lilies; the latter should be kept away from fountains.

ADAPTING A POND

Whether or not a pond's style or use can be changed depends on several factors (see table opposite). For example, the type and use of plants at the edge can help to make a pond look more or less formal, but its style is essentially dictated by the overall shape and the type of edging material, which are more difficult to alter.

A "pond for fish" in the table refers to easy-to-keep fish, such as goldfish. Adapting a pond to keep koi, for example, will be more difficult as they need water at least 1.5 m (5 ft) deep and an extensive filtration system to keep it clean and clear. This must be sited near the pond and is best built into the design at the outset. The pond should also have a bottom drain for easy cleaning.

If you want to restock a pond with both plants and fish, first establish the plants in late spring, then introduce the fish after three or four weeks.

CLEANING A SMALL POND

Green water is caused by algae and does not necessarily mean that the pond needs draining and cleaning. In fact, greening is likely to occur just after a pond has been cleaned and refilled, due to nutrients in the tap water. The following are reliable warning signs that a pond really does require cleaning:

⬦ Instead of a range of different plants, there will be just a few invasive plants.

⬦ The water is grey in colour most of the year, but particularly in summer. Black water in winter or early spring suggests leaves have accumulated.

⬦ Distressed fish may come to the surface frequently and gasp for air.

⬦ Pond dipping, using a glass jar, reveals very little insect life.

The best time to clean the average garden pond is either early spring or early autumn. A 9,000–14,000-litre (2,380–3,700-gallon) pond will usually take two people a weekend to clean. You will need protective clothing and gloves, as well as containers such as clean plastic buckets – filled with pond water and with an aerator inserted – as holding bays for fish or wildlife. Use a pump to empty the pond. As the water level drops, net any fish and put them in the containers.

Remove pond plants, which will be growing in aquatic baskets or will have rooted in the mud. Divide them like other perennials (see pages 206–207) and replant the youngest and healthiest sections. You may need new baskets, filled with aquatic compost, since the old ones often become distorted. Pond plants can become invasive, so it is always worth planting them in baskets.

The thick sludge at the bottom of a pond needs to be removed in buckets. It can then be tipped over vacant ground or dug-over beds, but rescue any frogs or newts that you find. A pressure sprayer may be hired or bought to clean algae from the pond liner. Most types are electrical, so you will need access to a power point and mains water; use a residual current device (RCD) to protect yourself. Pump the pond out again and repair any leaks (see below).

Finally, refill your pond with tap water, but leave it for at least three days before returning any fish, to allow the chlorine to evaporate. Ponds go green after cleaning, but adding extra plants will help to clear the water.

LEAKING PONDS

If the water level of your pond is dropping, this might be caused by a problematic water feature or a leaky lining. If you have a pumped feature, such as a fountain, turn the pump off and observe whether water is still lost. A fountain that is too powerful for a small pond will spill water outside it, particularly in a windy site. Water can also be lost from poorly built waterfalls, cascades and rills.

If you are sure that a feature is not to blame, check for leaks. Flexible liners are easily pierced by stones or a sharp-edged plastic planting basket – lift these in and out carefully, or use fabric planters. A rigid liner, such as one made of fibreglass, can crack when stressed, for example if it is trodden on and has not been properly bedded in.

▽ **DECKING PLATFORM**
The pond's surround should be designed as thoughtfully as the pond itself. A decking platform provides an attractive area from which to view this pond.

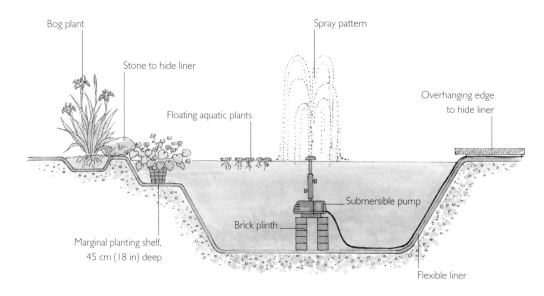

▷ POND PROFILE

Here, a shelf for baskets of marginal aquatics and a separate boggy area have been incorporated into a pond with a flexible liner. Overhanging paving slabs hide the liner while protecting it from the ageing effects of ultraviolet light. The pump is placed on a plinth, so silt accumulates at the bottom of the pond, not around the pump.

Bog plant

Stone to hide liner

Spray pattern

Overhanging edge to hide liner

Floating aquatic plants

Submersible pump

Brick plinth

Flexible liner

Marginal planting shelf, 45 cm (18 in) deep

▽ PLUMED FOUNTAIN

A tall-spouting, multiplumed fountain makes a dramatic feature – choose a sheltered site with a dark background for the best effect.

Leaks are usually found around the water line, so it may not be necessary to drain the whole pond, unless it needs cleaning as well.

Polythene or PVC liners are fairly cheap and are not worth repairing if the material has gone brittle due to old age or exposure to ultraviolet light. Liners that are not brittle but have been accidentally punctured can be repaired with patching kits.

Butyl rubber liners are expensive and should last around 40 years, but they do sometimes become punctured. Clean and dry the damaged area thoroughly first, and then repair the liner with butyl tape or by heat welding.

Leaks in pre-formed fibreglass ponds are easy to repair with a kit, available from boat makers or garages. Follow the instructions and safety guidelines on the repair kits carefully. If you are not sure what the pond is made of, you might need to test the product on the lip of the liner.

Isolated cracks in concrete ponds can be fixed with a pond mortar. If there is widespread cracking, the pond must be completely drained and painted with a special paint or sealant (you could get a professional in to do this). An easier option is to make a drainage hole in the concrete and line the pond with a butyl liner, but first work out how to deal with the edge of the lining.

Leaks in natural or clay-lined ponds can be caused by tree roots, but are difficult to locate. They can be repaired by smearing clay over the damaged area, but this really is a job for an expert.

◁ **FORMAL PLANTING**
Use imaginative planting choices to play up the overall style of your pond. The formal design of this water lily pond is underlined by box edging and symmetrically arranged containers filled with summer flowers.

SAFETY MATTERS

Ponds do bring potential dangers that must be considered and dealt with; but do not let safety issues detract from the fact that they also bring great enjoyment and are valuable to local wildlife.

The main hazard is drowning. Children under the age of three are most at risk, although older people can also trip and fall in, so check for trip hazards. If the garden is used at night, the pond edging should be lit. Keep paved edges free from slippery moss and algae. Covering the pond with builder's mesh or another material capable of supporting an adult will make the pond safer (see photograph).

Battery-operated child alarms are available, which are placed in the water and activated if a person falls in. These are of limited use, since you must be within earshot to hear the alarm and must also remember to renew the batteries. Physical barriers such as fencing can help, but children may still drown after climbing under the fence or going through open gates.

LARGE PONDS

Clearing a large pond can be difficult; you may need to bring in professionals with power equipment. If this is beyond your budget, ask a local conservation group that has done similar work elsewhere for advice. If there is no one locally, a national conservation body may be able to point you in the right direction.

Most companies will want to visit before giving you a quote. However, when you make initial inquiries, it is worth knowing the volume of your pond and an estimate of the depth of silt, since many firms will only tackle jobs of a certain size. To work out the volume, multiply the surface area in square metres by the water depth in metres and multiply the answer by 1000, which will give the volume in litres. If the depth varies, work out an average figure for depth first. The surface area of a rectangle is the length multiplied by the width. For a circle, the surface area is r x r x 3.0, where r is the radius in metres. If the pond is an informal shape, make a rough calculation by breaking it down into simpler shapes on graph paper.

The firm may also ask about access to the site for machinery, so consider this as well. As the work will be disruptive to the surrounding garden, do not replant or hard-landscape that area until later on.

PUMPS

Modern pumps usually require less maintenance than older models; if you inherit an old pump, consider replacing it. Pumps need to be cleaned and serviced annually, which can be done at the end of the season if the pump will not be used in winter. If a pump powers a filter for fish, it is worth having a spare one in case of failure. Submersible pumps are fairly easy to clean, but consult the manual first. Surface pumps are more complicated and are best given a yearly service by a pump expert.

DISUSED STRUCTURES

Do you have a large garden with a swimming pool or tennis court that has fallen into disrepair or is unwanted; or a smaller garden with a stray lump of concrete left over from some foundations? Space-consuming and costly to remove, these structures can easily form the basis of creative garden features.

If you are the not-so-proud owner of a disused structure, it may actually be that your only option is to remove it – say you have a large, unwanted pool and your heart is set on levelling the garden. But remember that this kind of operation is expensive. A pool, for example, is a very big hole, needing tonnes of rubble, subsoil and topsoil to fill it, plus equipment and manpower. In most cases, however, more creative solutions are at hand.

SWIMMING POOL

If you want to get rid of a swimming pool altogether, you don't necessarily have to level the ground completely. Filling the hole up partially creates interesting changes of level and is a slightly less expensive option. Building terraces on different levels is another idea for those not afraid to spend a little money. Some levels might have larger paved areas for seating, and each one

▷ **PERGOLA ROOF**
An overhead structure such as this wooden pergola transforms the atmosphere of an enclosed pool area. It will also alter the microclimate, especially when covered in climbers, giving welcome shade and some protection against frost.

could provide a different specialized planting zone, enabling you to grow a wide range of plants requiring different soil types (see pages 92–97).

Sunken garden A very different solution is to create an unusual sunken garden – possibly using the pool's water-holding capacity to include a pond and an area for bog plants. If you want a pond, this is best located at the deep end, with a jetty leading out to it. Once these have been built, a bog garden can be added (see pages 92–93). You could also construct islands or a walkway around the edge, perhaps leading from the bottom of a set of steps going down to the pool area. Try creating a sculpture garden with dramatic lighting that highlights the pieces and sculptural steps leading into the pool.

Making changes Alterations of some kind will be needed for most alternative uses of pools. Your

pool may have a blue lining, for instance, which will immediately betray its former use. If this lining is plastic, it will have to be removed, but a concrete surface can be painted in neutral colours such as soft brown, cream or grey – or whatever will help it to blend with the rest of the garden.

A flight of steps will often need to be built for access into the pool, with about seven risers for entry at the shallow end. The steps should ideally be made of concrete or stone as wood and brick will become slippery too easily.

A deep hole such as this does present dangers. If the pool conversion is in a terraced garden, it might be possible to plan it so that the drop is minimized to a safe level on all sides. Otherwise, the area must be fenced off.

Planting The microclimate of such a large cavity will be sheltered. Take advantage of this both for your own comfort and to grow tender plants.

Pools are usually sited in sunny places, so it is worth incorporating a seating area. If it receives too much heat and sun, you could partially cover the space with an awning or a pergola draped with a vine. Alternatively, grow a fig in a large pot so you can enjoy the aromatic leaves. Other scented plants to try include rock rose, lavender, rosemary and some of the evening-scented flowers such as nicotiana and night-scented stocks.

Plants that are slightly tender in your area will grow happily here. To provide additional warmth and protection, you could instal an acrylic plastic or reinforced glass roof over half of the pool.

TENNIS COURT
Typically measuring 35 x 18 m (38 x 20 yd), a tennis court occupies a large area. Consider whether you can use some or all of the surface exactly as it is – perhaps as a play area for other games, or as a dog run or a compound for small animals. Alternatively, the space could become home to a specialist plant collection, such as citrus fruits growing in containers, with a greenhouse for winter protection.

△ **MODERN STYLE**
This contemporary solution to the problem of a disused pool makes good use of architectural elements – stepping stone rocks, a decking path and a rectangular planter filled with sedums.

The possible uses of the space will depend on what the surface is made of. Older courts are grass or compacted clinker and cinders. Later courts are made of asphalt or other materials such as concrete.

Lawn or meadow An old grass court can be made into a lawn, surrounded with a hedge or trellis screens, and possibly including planting beds. It could also be made into a wildflower meadow (see pages 108–109).

Whichever option you choose, consider the view from outside – blend the straight lines of the court with shrub beds of substantial evergreens. You could plant a grove of trees in your meadow, or a small orchard (see pages 132–135).

Gravel garden An old cinder court makes an unusual growing medium. Left to itself, it will support plants that like light, sandy soil, and in time an interesting plant colony will take root.

A cinder or asphalt court can be converted to a gravel garden. With asphalt, you will have to make raised beds and fill them with suitable soil, covering areas in between with the gravel. With a cinder court, there is no need for raised beds. Break up the areas to be planted, add some topsoil, plant suitable species (see pages 94–95) and mulch the whole area with gravel. You could also add found objects such as driftwood, rocks or metal structures (see pages 168–169).

Garden room Exploit the distinct, separate nature of a tennis court by making it into a garden room with a specific purpose or mood. You could create a formal parterre or knot garden, with a geometric layout and box hedging, and herbs, flowers or a mixture of both in the beds (see pages 172–173). Alternatively, consider making a kitchen garden – this has a similar formal layout, and the tennis court fence will support espalier or fan-trained fruit trees.

Following the tradition of great gardens such as Sissinghurst or Hidcote, you might want to use the "room" for a stunning display of choice plants or for a colour-themed planting. It might also provide the perfect location for a secret garden, hidden behind a hedge or trellis. This could be either a restful green area with a still, reflective pool for quiet contemplation or a romantic retreat featuring a summerhouse, a seat at each end, overflowing flowerbeds and paths that converge on a central rose arbour.

Fedge The fencing around a tennis court – usually chain link, 3–4 m (10–13 ft) high – can become a useful screen. It should readily support climbing plants and in doing so forms a "fedge", a cross between a fence and a hedge. Twining climbers such as clematis or potato vine *(Solanum jasminoides)* will form a brilliant wall of colour in summer. For an evergreen screen, use ivy – either a range of dark green varieties, perhaps with different leaf shapes, or several variegated types to supply a rich mix of creams, yellows and greens.

CONCRETE BASE
Disused bits of concrete foundation can be quite an eyesore. People often make vain attempts to hide them by laying turf or a thin layer of topsoil over the top and adding plants – only to have their secret revealed during a dry spell when the turf turns brown or the plants die.

If you have such a structure, the options are either to remove it completely or to reuse it as the base for a garden building or feature.

If the base is deep or is reinforced concrete, you will need machinery to get it out. A large hammer drill can be hired, but using it is heavy work, requiring steel-capped boots, a mask and protective glasses and gloves. If you cannot reuse the broken-up concrete in any way – as a base for paving, for instance – you will need to dispose of it. The simplest option is to rent a skip, but it may be easier to hire a builder to do the work.

There are a lot of options to consider before starting work, and you need to plan for them in advance, as necessary. You might decide to lay decking or a patio on your concrete base (see pages 200–201), or build up the sides to make a raised pond or a raised bed, providing a habitat for plants that need special soils. Think about how such features will blend in with the existing garden. Is the area large enough and sunny enough for a patio? Will a raised bed look out of place? You can merge the new feature into its surroundings with plants; alternatively, a screen of some sort may be necessary (see pages 60–61). You might decide that a builder is needed to help with many of these options, or even with simpler tasks such as restoring the ground after digging out the concrete and laying turf, or laying the broken concrete as a paving foundation.

Arbour or pergola Erecting an arbor or pergola on the base is an attractive option. This will involve drilling holes in the corners to take the uprights, and you might need to lay paving to provide an appealing finish. Check first that the area is large enough for the planned structure. If necessary, the structure itself can be slightly smaller than the base, leaving a plinth on the outside or a step along the front. This will provide space for containers or simply for sitting out.

Raised pond If you have the remains of an old shed base in your garden, this may form the ideal starting point for a substantial raised pond. A sheltered site close to the house could even become a hot tub or Jacuzzi with decking surround.

Taking the shed's rectangular outline for its shape, your pond will readily harmonize with a formal garden or with the clean, simple lines of an architectural garden. A range of materials can be used for the retaining walls, from simple brick with classic coping, or railway sleepers lined with butyl for a modern, natural look, to rendered and waterproofed concrete blocks for an abstract or minimalist feel. If in doubt, you can always try to match the materials used in the rest of the garden or the architectural style of your house.

Raised bed If the soil type in your garden restricts your planting choices, a raised bed will enable you to use a different growing medium and introduce all kinds of new plants.

Ideally, a raised bed needs light shade and little wind. Build it with low walls of bricks, railway sleepers or logs, and fill it with soil suited to the plants you want to grow (see pages 92–97). One possibility is an alpine garden, which needs sun and good drainage. If they will suit the style of your garden, drystone retaining walls provide the perfect foil for alpines. Some rocks can be half-buried on top of the bed as well, providing further niches for tiny plants. Tilt them backwards slightly into the soil, so that any water runs off quickly. The soil should be sandy and not too rich.

▽ **FORMAL POND**
A concrete base is an ideal foundation for a formal raised pool. This pool's square shape is reinforced by a surround of clipped box and echoed by the outer hedges.

GARAGES

The average garage tends to be something of a blot on the landscape – a large, unwieldy structure built for practical use rather than beauty. Strange, then, that it is so often ignored when undertaking a major garden redesign, as it can easily be integrated into the whole, or adapted in interesting ways.

If your garage is in a poor state of repair or is too narrow for your car and you do not need the building for another use, take the opportunity to decide whether you actually need a garage at all. Is there a better way of using the space? A level, hard landscaped area near the house is a real asset in a small or sloping garden – it could provide the base for a patio or the foundations for a conservatory or greenhouse (see also pages 156–157). A location that is warmer, sunnier and more sheltered than the rest of the garden should be exploited to the full. This might be the spot, for example, to try growing Mediterranean plants or exotic wall shrubs that are of borderline hardiness in your area.

INTEGRATING A GARAGE

Integrating a garage into its surroundings is not as hard as it sounds. Garage walls that face on to the garden can provide a large surface for climbers. Plant one of the more vigorous species and let it romp away: *Clematis montana* and its varieties provide flowers from late spring to early summer; honeysuckles, like the evergreen *Lonicera japonica* 'Hall's Prolific', offer deliciously scented summer flowers; and vines, such as *Parthenocissus* species, supply spectacular autumn colour.

For a more formal look, buy or make several identical trellis panels, paint them in a colour that contrasts with the garage wall, and mount them at equal intervals along its length. Wall shrubs such as pyracantha or flowering quince (*Chaenomeles* species) can be trained as espaliers between the trellis panels. If you have a double garage, a wisteria can be trained up the gap between the two doors and across the top.

There may be no soil at the base of your garage wall. In this case, use planting containers or build a raised bed, but check first that you are not blocking off any damp course.

If you have a detached garage and there is no path linking it with the house, the garden surface will suffer considerable wear and tear. It is worth laying a path, or perhaps even building a covered walkway. Use plants to make the link attractive, choosing species that will tolerate being brushed past, such as hebes.

▽ **CONCRETE CANVAS**
The rear of a garage can be quite an eyesore – but not if you use it as a backdrop for vigorous climbers and wall shrubs. Pyracantha is a tough evergreen that can cope with cold, shady walls and provides visual interest for much of the year. Here, two different varieties have been grown together: the yellow-berried 'Soleil d'Or' and the orange-red 'Mohave'.

ADAPTING A GARAGE

If you do not need the garage for a car, try adapting it for another use. Some garages are constructed in such a way that the sides can be removed, leaving the uprights and the roof. This will, in effect, create a covered arbour, which can be planted with scented roses, honeysuckle or jasmine. An architect will advise on whether the structure can be changed in this way; the work itself is best carried out by a reputable builder.

If level ground space is at a premium, taking down the front half of a garage will free up some space, but still give you the back of the garage to use for storage or as a potting shed. Again, it is best to consult an architect to see if this is possible with your garage, and to employ a builder, since the work is potentially dangerous. Once the garage door has been removed, the roof and walls can be taken down to the desired length. Remove the lintel carefully, before it becomes unsupported.

The ends of the exposed brickwork or blocks will need to be rendered and a wooden frame attached to them. A door, small window and overlapping weatherboards can then be fitted to the frame.

CONVERTING TO A CARPORT

Part of a driveway or the base of a dismantled garage can often be used to house a carport, providing shelter for a car and for people getting in and out of it. But a carport is more than just a roof with legs – from a gardener's point of view it is also a sheltered pergola that can be used to support a wide range of climbers and cascading plants. A typical carport has metal poles or timber posts for uprights. These supports are ideal for climbers such as wisteria, clematis, honeysuckle, jasmine, trumpet vine *(Campsis × tagliabuana)* and climbing hydrangea *(Hydrangea anomala* subsp. *petiolaris)*. In frost-free regions, you could also consider growing vines such as star jasmine *(Trachelospermum jasminoides)*, *Mandevilla,* potato vine *(Solanum jasminoides)* or Chilean glory flower *(Eccremocarpus scaber)*. Fit wires or netting to the uprights so that the climbers can take hold.

If you want to build a carport from scratch, check whether you need to obtain planning permission.

▽ **CLIMBING COVER**
The vigorous deciduous climber Clematis montana *will quickly clothe an ugly carport. Leaves, flowers and other falling plant debris could, however, become a nuisance, and you may find that evergreens provide a better solution*

◁ **GARAGE CONVERSION**
If you can safely dismantle part of a garage, you will free up ground space yet retain a useful covered area – perfect for a workshop or, as seen here, a potting shed.

SHEDS

Behind every successful garden is a fully equipped and well-organized shed. Given their important role, it is surprising that sheds are often hidden away or disguised with trellis. With a little imagination, even the most basic shop-bought types can be turned into attractive garden assets.

△ **INTEGRATED SHED**
A large shed can be used to support vigorous climbing plants that also help it to blend in with its surroundings – roses and sweet peas happily fulfil the task here.

Storage space for garden equipment; a valuable covered work area for numerous tasks from mending a mower to propagating plants; a quiet retreat from the family (especially if it has lighting) – the humble garden shed has earned a vital place in many people's lives. So, how can you also make it an integral part of your garden design?

SHED LOCATION

If you have inherited a shed that seems oddly sited, try to work out why it was put there – it might be hiding an eyesore such as an ugly wall, or providing privacy – and decide whether it would be better elsewhere. In a long garden, having a shed some way down the space saves a lot of time, particularly if fruit and vegetables are grown at the bottom of the plot. A shed used for storing tools or for working needs to be near paths, and if you want to instal electricity, it should be fairly near the house.

SHED CONDITION

The other main factor to consider is the shed's condition. Sheds vary in their durability and this depends on the quality of the materials and the care taken in the construction. Open and close the door several times to see if it sticks (common in winter and less so in summer) and check the locks and hinges, replacing or oiling them if necessary. Once you have cleared any junk, jump up and down in the middle of the floor, then push against the sides and the roof – the floor, sides and roof should be solid and firm. If the wood flexes, the construction of the shed is flimsy. Large knotholes or gaps between the planks weaken a shed, and such wood is best replaced to avoid potential problems or hazards.

If you want to use your shed as a workshop or potting shed, you will need space for a bench or worktable and enough headroom – or you might have to consider buying a bigger one. A shed with windows is a good choice, since it will give natural light to work by. If there is no artificial lighting, you may want to lay a power line (or preferably have one laid by an electrician) and instal lights inside and out.

If you have a very small garden and the shed is occupying space that you need for another purpose, consider selling or dismantling it and using the wood around the garden. You will probably be left with a concrete base, for which there are many uses (see pages 156–157). Tools and equipment could be kept in a garage or cellar. If you want to keep them in the garden, buy a tool cupboard or a wooden chest that will double as a seat. Further storage could be built into a patio, perhaps attached to a raised bed or barbecue.

INTEGRATING A SHED

Your shed may be in the best
position from a practical point of
view, but it may not be very well
integrated into the garden. The
best way to blend a shed in is with
planting. Climbers such as a clematis
or a rose are an obvious option, but
rather than letting them spread over
the shed, train them on a trellis
panel fitted to the shed on wooden
battens. If it would suit your garden
better, use a screen made of rustic
poles. Evergreens such as ivy, laurel
or holly will clothe the shed with
foliage all year round, but they need
to be clipped into shape.

A shed in a kitchen garden could
be planted with beans or peas, or an
espaliered fruit tree or two trained against the
trellis. Instead of, or as well as, climbers, you
could plant small shrubs or place containers
around the shed (see pages 44–51).

DECORATING A SHED

A lick of paint or wood stain gives a new lease on
life to a shed, but you can take this idea one step
further and turn it into a fantasy feature. The
decorative possibilities are endless and include
striped bathing huts, gothic follies with finials and
arched windows, and Dutch-inspired sheds.

If an inherited shed is too small for a workshop
and you have children, you could transform it into
a playhouse, letting them help you to decorate it
as a gingerbread house, a clubhouse, a railroad
signal box, or whatever they like.

REPAIRING THE ROOF

One of the first things that will deteriorate on a
shed is the roof. Roofing felt can rot or come away
from the nails that hold it and may start to let in
water. There are various grades of roofing felt.
For a shed, you need one that is 20–38 kg
(44–84 lb) per 10-m (11-yd) roll. It should be
fixed in place with large-headed clout nails,
spaced 10 cm (4 in) apart. Fitting gutters to the
shed will help to protect the wood from rot.

◁ **STENCILLED SHED**
*Bring a touch of artistic expression to the plainest
wooden shed with colourful stencilled effects,
such as this simple brickwork pattern.*

▽ **SIMPLE STYLE**
*Painted white with a blue trim and bedecked
with pink impatiens, this shed makes a striking
summer feature. For winter colour, the impatiens
could be replaced with winter-flowering pansies.*

GREENHOUSES

A run-down greenhouse is ugly, inefficient, and often dangerous; a safe, clean, well-maintained one is perfectly simple to achieve and brings huge bonuses – letting you raise plants cheaply from seed, start plants off before placing them outside, and grow vegetables that may not ripen outside, such as tomatoes.

The first rule of running a greenhouse is to remember that, while work can be kept to a minimum (see opposite), greenhouse plants need regular watering and pest and disease checks. So, if you are away for long periods or have very little time, a greenhouse might not be a practical option.

SITING A GREENHOUSE

Location is a major consideration. Greenhouses need light, but not too much direct sunlight – ideally, the longest side should run from west to east. It should be accessible in wet weather, with space at the side for getting plants used to outdoor conditions. A nearby tap is useful, as plants in a greenhouse need frequent watering; avoid using stored water for seedlings.

It is also useful to have a source of electricity for lighting and heating, so bear this in mind when choosing a site.

Avoid areas where children play. If you have a wooden greenhouse, replace the lower glass with solid wood to make it safer for toddlers. Don't site a greenhouse under overhanging trees – they will block out light and falling leaves can be a nuisance.

MOVING A GREENHOUSE

If a greenhouse is in the wrong place, it can be dismantled and moved. Dismantling may also be needed if there is a problem with the foundations or if a damp course is required. Remove the glass carefully and store it in a safe place, then dismantle the framework. Label the parts to make them easier to reassemble and keep small fittings together in a container.

The new site must be level and compact. Use slabs or bricks on a hard-core foundation for the base, or buy a metal base for an aluminium greenhouse. If you want to plant in earth inside the greenhouse, mount the "bed" on a strip of bricks, laid on a simple strip foundation of hard core and concrete set in a narrow trench. Rising damp can be a problem in wooden greenhouses, so lay a strip of PVC or bitumen felt between the frame and the base.

MAINTAINING THE FRAME

Aluminium frames need no maintenance, but check wooden ones for rot or woodworm. Rot is most likely where the wood is in contact with the ground, where there is rising damp or if there are leaking gutters. Treat the cause of the rot first, then cut out any soft, spongy wood and replace it with treated softwood or a naturally durable wood such as cedar or redwood. If the wood has crumbled away or there are small holes with sawdust nearby, this is a sign of woodworm. Cut out affected sections and treat the area with a woodworm killer. Clean the gutters. If there are none, it is worth installing them, with a downpipe and a butt. If there is an earth floor, kill any weed growth with a substance such as glyphosate, and lay a polypropylene membrane, followed by gravel or paving. If you want to keep a soil border, soak it with garden disinfectant and fumigate the greenhouse with smoke cones once it is repaired and draughtproof.

△ **GARDEN ANTIQUE**
Old greenhouses such as this Victorian one can be restored to full working order, but you may need to seek advice from a restoration specialist or a garden history society.

◁ **FUNCTIONAL STYLE**
*Aluminium greenhouses are
not the easiest structures to
integrate into a garden, but
this one looks perfectly at home
in the centre of a functional,
screened-off vegetable plot.*

FITTINGS AND ACCESSORIES

Contact the manufacturer of the
greenhouse if you want spare parts,
such as bases, replacement glazing
bars and glazing clips, or if you want
to improve the ventilation by buying
automatic or louvred vents.

Shelves or staging will maximize
growing space. Aluminium staging
can be bought that bolts to the frame.
For a wooden greenhouse, make
slatted staging with roofing battens.

To stop the greenhouse becoming
too hot in summer, use brush-on
shading wash. In winter, insulate it
from cold with bubble insulation – a
minimum temperature of 5–7°C
(41–45°F) is needed to overwinter
plants. The best way to provide heat
is with a greenhouse fan heater.
Rather than relying on the heater's
thermostat, use a max–min
thermometer to check temperature.

◁ **FOCAL POINT**
*A clematis-covered metal
arch plus symmetrically
placed box spheres
have transformed this
ordinary-looking greenhouse.*

MAINTAINING THE GLASS

Dirty glass can be cleaned with hot water, using a
few drops of dishwashing liquid and a soft brush,
or with special cleaning fluids. Rinse the glass with
clean water afterwards. Dirt accumulates between
overlapping panes of glass; use a plastic plant label
to dislodge it. Replace broken glass and glass that
has a frosted appearance with horticultural glass.

To remove a pane of glass, unhook the glazing
clip and lift it out (wear gloves). In older wooden
greenhouses, the glass may be held in place with
putty, which can be chipped out with a knife.

MINIMAL GREENHOUSE GARDENING

If you have inherited a working greenhouse, you can raise your own half-hardy
annuals from seed, which will provide you with plenty of summer bedding plants
for borders and containers – a quick way of brightening up a garden. Tender
perennials can be bought as young cuttings or small plants and grown on in the
greenhouse, which is much cheaper than buying pot-grown tender perennials in
early summer. Tomatoes are a popular crop and are easy to grow if you water and
feed them regularly; home-grown ones have a much better flavour, and you can
also try unusual varieties. Many flowering indoor plants, such as gloxinia, are easy
to grow in a greenhouse and can be taken indoors when in flower. In the autumn,
tender perennial patio plants can be brought under cover and kept frost-free.

CONSERVATORIES

A conservatory is a unique space – a transitional zone midway between house and garden. Unlike a patio, this enclosed area provides a delightful living or eating space all year round, or you can exploit its warmth and light by growing a range of beautiful, exotic plants.

A conservatory can be designed either for plants or for people. It is difficult to create one that is suitable for both without making compromises, so be clear about your priorities before taking any further steps.

ASPECT

If you inherit a conservatory, you may not be able to change the orientation, but it helps to know how different aspects will affect what you can grow.

Ideally, a conservatory should face west or east, since these aspects are less extreme in winter and summer. In the northern hemisphere, south-facing structures can become unbearably hot in summer – for both plants and people. A north-facing conservatory is more pleasant in summer, but can be gloomy and cold in winter. Also, the lower light levels mean that many exotic plants might not bloom, although foliage plants often do well. In the southern hemisphere, north-facing conservatories can be too hot in summer and chilly in winter.

LINKING WITH THE GARDEN

Many conservatories automatically end up looking like they belong more to the home than to the garden, but linking the two is a simple matter. Try using the same tiles and similar plant containers for the conservatory and for the area just outside. You probably have a clear view of the garden from your conservatory, so make sure the view is pleasant, perhaps hiding or framing certain objects by placing large plants on the patio.

LIVING SPACES

If your conservatory is to be used mainly as a living space, you will no doubt want to include some soft furnishings. To stop these from staining or going mouldy, choose plants that tolerate lower humidity. Group plants together to make watering easier, or create displays in the garden or on a patio that can be seen from the conservatory.

A SPACE FOR PLANTING

If you want to concentrate on the planting opportunities that a conservatory brings, remember that many of the more interesting plants need high humidity. Avoid soft furnishings and choose a floor surface that will cope with spills. Any blinds should be made from metal, plastic or treated wood – not fabric.

Decide how much you can afford to heat the space in winter, and use this as the basis for your plant choice. Create different levels of planting, so that sun-tolerant taller species and climbers will shade smaller plants that dislike direct sun.

BORDER SOIL

Most conservatories have a complete floor, so plants need to be grown in containers. However, sometimes a border of soil is left along a wall. This

▽ **LIVING SPACE**
Linked to the living room by the use of similar floor tiles, this conservatory is very definitely a place for people. Plants can still be enjoyed, however, in the form of container displays seen through the large glass doors.

ensure that other plants get enough light. You must also work out how you need to control heat and light at various times of the year.

Summer The conservatory may get too hot for plants or for people, especially at midday, and you will find that dry air wilts plants and allows red spider mite to take hold, so you might want to move plants outside. Blinds or shading will be needed. Shading, which is painted on the outside, is efficient at lowering the temperature and worth considering for plant conservatories. External blinds keep more heat out of the conservatory, but are expensive. Internal blinds provide shade, but will not reduce the heat. Automatic ventilation improves conditions for both people and plants. Grouping plants together, misting and using trays filled with wetted pebbles helps to keep the humidity levels high. Regular watering is essential.

Winter Heating will be needed if you want to grow tender plants, or for a warm living space. Most plants have a minimum temperature below which they cannot survive. A "warm" conservatory should be heated to a minimum of 15–18°C (60–65°F); a "temperate" one to a minimum of 10–15°C (50–60°F); and a "cool" one to a minimum of 5–10°C (40–50°F). Heating a whole conservatory to the warm level will prove expensive, but you may be able to screen off a small section and just heat that.

Cold, damp conditions can encourage the spread of grey mould (*Botrytis*) – it is vital to remove any infected growth promptly.

Remember that light levels are low in winter, so keep the glass clean. Watering should be reduced to a minimum when plants are not actively growing.

△ **VINE CEILING**
A grapevine (Vitis vinifera) can be planted in a soil border or trained through from outside. Grown up wires fixed to the frame, it provides shade in summer while the under-glass warmth helps ripen the grapes.

◁ **TENDER EXOTICS**
Warm temperatures are needed for exotics such as a fan-trained Mandevilla x amabilis, blue-flowered Plumbago auriculata and Datura arborea with sweet-scented white trumpets

EASY PLANTS FOR A CONSERVATORY

Gloriosa superba (glory lily) Climber with yellow or red flowers. Grows from tubers each spring.

Passiflora (passion flower) Hardy or tender climbers, with a range of impressive flowers.

Pelargonium Drought-tolerant plants, especially good for a sunny window sill. Several varieties have scented leaves.

Philodendron scandens Fast-growing foliage climber for shade.

Plumbago Easy, climbing plant with blue, red or pink flowers. Can be kept small or grown as a specimen plant.

Small flowering pot plants that can tolerate light shade include streptocarpus, fuchsia, begonia.

can be enriched, mulched and planted just as you would a border outside and needs less frequent watering than pots. In a neglected conservatory, either replace the border with soil-based compost or water with a special disinfectant, since pests and diseases may have built up in the soil. Plants grow more vigorously in border soil, so make use of a wall and the roof – try growing a fan-trained peach or fig on the wall, for example, and a grapevine or other climber up to and across the roof.

AFTERCARE

The key maintenance tasks are to water and feed plants regularly during the growing season and to tie in new growth on climbers. Inspect plants regularly for pests and diseases, which can take hold very quickly under glass. Most climbers will need pruning to restrict their growth and to

WALLS AND FENCES

Sound walls and fences are essential for providing security and privacy, as well as defining legal boundaries clearly. One of the most prominent surfaces in the garden, they must be carefully integrated into the whole design through a careful choice of materials and clever use of plants.

Your first consideration should be whether you want to tackle any alterations or repairs to your walls or fences. Think about this as soon as you have clear access to them, and before you start any new planting.

Walls and fences often delineate boundaries, so do your research beforehand. Are you sure that you own the structure? Are there local height restrictions? If you live in a conservation area, there may be local covenants, or even rules about the materials you can use. It is better to find answers to these questions sooner rather than later.

REPAIRING FENCES

A fence is only as strong as its supporting posts. If they rock when you try to shake them, they will have rotted below ground. Check each one: it is possible that some may still be sound even if others are rotten (see pages 200–201).

The bottom of a fence is liable to rot where it is in contact with the ground. Your fence may have a horizontal gravel board that protects the rest of the fence from rot. Gravel boards are designed to be easily replaced and should come away without damaging other parts of the fence.

Wooden fence panels that have been damaged or that do not offer enough privacy are easily replaced since most are a standard size. Close-board fencing is held together by horizontal arris rails. If an arris rail has only a slight split, a metal repair bracket can be fitted over it. However, any warped rails will need to be replaced.

REPAIRING WALLS

Common wall problems that can be dealt with by a competent amateur handyman include repointing the mortar (see page 200) and laying coping – adding a new top by using coping stones or brick will help to protect the wall and improve its overall appearance.

If you have any of the following problems, it is best to employ a professional, such as a builder or a landscaper:

⌀ A retaining wall that is crumbling or stained at the front (indicating a drainage problem).

⌀ A load-bearing wall, such as one supporting an outhouse roof, that you think might be unsafe or one that is bowed.

△ **ORNATE FENCE**
If the fence is an attractive feature in its own right, choose plants that complement rather than swamp it. Here, yellow pokers of Kniphofia echo the shape of the fence posts.

▷ **CLOTHING A WALL**
Climbing roses have long been seen as the classic wall shrub. The glossy-leaved, yellow evergreen Choisya ternata 'Sundance' likes sun or light shade and reaches a height and spread of 1.5–1.8 m (5–6 ft).

∅ A free-standing wall in need of repair that is either more than 1.8 m (6 ft) high or is located in an exposed and windy location.

PLANTING

Satisfied that your boundaries are sound, you can now turn your attention to planting, which does wonders for walls and fences that are either unattractive or not solid enough. Shrubs are a low-maintenance solution, or use climbers and wall shrubs where space is limited. If the wall or fence is solid, attach a support such as wires or trellis. This should protrude from the boundary by 5 cm (2 in), which makes training easier and improves air circulation, reducing the risk of fungal diseases.

Galvanized wire, with a thickness of 10–14 gauge, can be fitted horizontally across walls or fences using vine eyes. Different types of vine eyes are available, for hammering into a wall or screwing into wood. They should be attached along the wall or fence every 1.5–2 m (5–6½ ft). For most climbers, they can be spaced vertically at 30 cm (1 ft) intervals; for more vigorous types on a large wall, space them at 45 cm (18 in). The wires must be taut – for long lengths or for heavy climbers, use straining bolts to give extra tension.

Thin wood, wicker or plastic trellis is fine for annual or non-woody climbers, but for woody climbers and wall shrubs use heavy-duty wooden trellis. It is worth fixing the trellis to battens – allow three battens per 2 m (6½ ft) height of trellis – to improve air circulation behind the panel. If a wall needs regular painting, fix up a trellis that can be unhooked and moved away from the wall – by securing a trellis panel to the bottom batten with a hinge and using a hook and eye to attach the trellis to the top batten.

Trellis panels on top of a low fence or wall provide more space for climbers and create extra privacy. Metal plates can be bought for joining fence posts and trellis posts together.

Trellis panels can be fixed to a wall by first attaching 10 x 5-cm (4 x 2-in) timber uprights to the wall. Use a masonry bit to drill holes through the timber and into the brickwork. Insert wall plugs, then screw 10-cm (4-in) screws through the wood and into the wall.

Always take aspect into account when planting. In the northern hemisphere, south- or west-facing walls or fences offer more shelter and warmth than an open area, although the soil can be too dry for some plants unless it is mulched and improved with organic matter. North- or east-facing aspects can be cold, exposed, and often shady – but the ground may retain moisture well (the opposite applies in the southern hemisphere). Remember, bricks or stones retain heat better than wood does.

▽ **WALL SHRUB**
Ceanothus will thrive rooted in the drier soil found near the base of a warm wall. These summer-flowering wall shrubs are fast growing, so site them where they have plenty of room to spread.

JUNK

Neglected gardens often contain all kinds of interesting objects. With just a small degree of lateral thinking, these can be given a new lease on life as decorative or useful items, adding individuality, wit and even beauty to a garden – and appealing to the gardener's instinct for recycling.

There is no special skill to using junk – just the ability and willingness to see potential in the most unlikely objects. Gardens are extremely forgiving places, and much of what might be considered "junk" can be transformed into something more attractive and interesting by the natural processes of ageing, weathering and self-seeding. For example, an old piece of corrugated iron will rust to a lovely colour and texture and might even become covered with self-seeded houseleeks (*Sempervivum* species), which turn a dazzling yellow in early summer. You might want to make this the basis of a natural alpine garden.

SOURCES OF JUNK

The search for junk can, of course, be broadened beyond your own garden, to include friends' gardens, dustbins and dumps. Houses that are undergoing renovation are great places to find old bathtubs and even ornate (but cracked) commodes, which can make unusual containers. Always ask before you remove anything.

The beach is a traditional hunting ground for found objects, such as driftwood, shells, buoys and other artefacts washed up by the sea. The use of such objects was beautifully demonstrated by the artist and film maker Derek Jarman in his

△ **WEATHERED ROOT**
This old tree root looks quite at home at the foot of a wall, where it acts as a foil to the shapes of the plant leaves.

△ **MANGLE SCULPTURE**
Linked to its setting by a coat of blue paint, this old mangle introduces an industrial note that contrasts dramatically with the frothy planting of petunias and artemisias.

▷ **SCRAP METAL**
Junk can be pulled apart and reassembled creatively – witness this metal archway over a seat. In time, the climbers will weave effectively through its sparse structure.

seaside garden at Dungeness in Kent, England. With its simple driftwood and stone sculptures, and tough plants that will survive the harsh environment, it is an object lesson in sense of place.

USING JUNK

Junk can be used to create all manner of unusual and original garden features – a refreshing change from the fake classical statues or wishing wells that are available at so many garden centres.

The simplest option is to use the object as is, placed on its own in an appropriate setting. Try it out in several locations to see if it complements the atmosphere of the space (see pages 68–69). You might want to paint it a different colour to tie in or contrast with a flower colour scheme – for

example, using gold paint on an old tin used as a container, to go with the reds and oranges of the planting, or blue as a contrast to cool mauves.

Another approach is to pull the object apart and rebuild it as something else, possibly combined with other pieces. Old forklift truck pallets, for instance, can be broken up to make an inexpensive picket fence or compost bin.

As well as the colour and texture, think about the materials and the lines of the object. Rounded shapes, such as a metal dustbin converted to a planter, can be echoed by plants with fat round leaves or contrasted with spiky foliage.

The really wonderful thing about junk is that it doesn't matter at all what you do with it, because it cost you nothing in the first place. So forget the rules, splash some paint about and have fun. You might amaze yourself.

△ **FIRE SURROUND**
Painted in vivid naive blue and red, with gold flourishes, this old fire surround now has the look of an altar to a garden god. The surrounding green foliage provides a suitably plain foil.

◁ **BEACH ART**
This flotsam and jetsam was found and arranged with an unerring eye by the artist Derek Jarman at his influential seaside garden in Kent, England.

RE-CREATING A GARDEN STYLE

Most gardens work best when their style echoes the landscape and location in which they lie, and borrows various elements from it. These elements include the key trees and other plants – and the overriding colours – that define a style; the hard landscaping features and other materials that contribute to it; and the finishing touches, including containers and planters, that complete the picture.

To give you the inspiration to take your garden design a step forward, this chapter looks at the major features of a dozen different garden styles, some of which may fit your own garden.

△ **RIPE PLUMS**
Easy and undemanding, plums can be grown as free-standing trees or fan-trained against a kitchen garden wall. They are rarely troubled by disease and need little pruning.

◁ **JUNGLE STYLE**
This scene, with an isolated steamer chair surrounded by water in a jungle garden, evokes a strong image of plantation life in the Far East early in the 20th century. It demonstrates how, with flair and imagination, you can create such a style in a suburban garden.

MEDIEVAL STYLE

The romantic picture of a knight in a flowery mead presenting a bunch of gillyflowers to his lady is belied by the reality of this type of garden, where the serfs were busy planting vegetables in plain, square beds, while the physick garden of the monastery was filled with plants with healing virtues.

MEDIEVAL STYLE

Suitable for
Small courtyards

Separate garden rooms

Flat areas

Hard landscaping and features
Latticework arbour

Wattle or lattice fence

Plain round stone pool with single fountain

Turfed seat

Different coloured gravels within box hedging

Planting
Dwarf edging: box, germander, santolina

Fruit trees: mulberry, apple, cherry, medlar, fig, pomegranate

Madonna lily (*Lilium candidum*)

Rosa gallica

Early European gardens were practical affairs, enclosed with walls against the outside wilderness, growing food for the table and herbs for medicinal and culinary purposes. The layout was orderly, unnatural – a blessed relief when nature was still so untamed – and the garden was a refuge, a controlled place, where plants were grown in straight lines and little raised beds.

The style has continued in some form for many centuries and is today echoed in gardens with a formal layout. We find this type of garden in medieval tapestries and old manuscripts, in stories of courtly love and illustrated prayer books. In later gardens, little hedges were planted around the beds, which were sometimes planted with flowers for the house. Occasionally, there

were no plants except for the surrounding hedges, the space between being filled with different coloured pebbles. The elaborate knot gardens of Tudor times, with tight little hedges in curlicue shapes, the grand parterres of 18th-century Versailles, and the elaborate Victorian bedding schemes so beloved of municipal park gardeners are all connected to the same tradition.

During the centuries of turmoil of the early Middle Ages, monastery gardens carried on the Persian tradition of the walled paradise garden. Their quiet, enclosed, cloistered quadrangles were usually divided into four sections, with a central fountain and perhaps a few fruit trees in tubs.

Monasteries had separate vegetable and herb gardens, where the plants were grown in simple

△ **RUSTIC SIMPLICITY**
In this garden, laid out in a style often used in medieval gardens, the beds are slightly raised for free drainage and edged with wooden boards. Vegetables were grown apart from herbs, and these in turn were divided into those for the kitchen and for medicinal use.

▷ **FORMAL SIMPLICITY**
The layout of this garden shows the transition from the simple vegetable plot (above) towards the more formal knot garden style. The box edging defines the quartered pattern of the design, while the fruit tree in a circular bed in the centre creates a focal point.

rectangular beds, usually raised to
assist drainage, and edged with
wooden boards. There would also
have been an orchard and a fishpond
stocked with fish.

Castle gardens, at first grim,
defensive affairs, evolved in time
into the later medieval pleasure
garden, divided into different areas.
There might have been a flowery
meadow, a grassy area for games and
dancing, with daisies, violets, crocus
and heartsease growing through the
turf, and even, surprisingly, taller
plants such as bellflowers and
columbine. Raised turfed seats were made; later
they were planted with aromatic chamomile.
These gardens were also adorned with fountains,
bathing pools and arbours.

There would have been an area enclosed with
a fence, perhaps of latticework and sometimes
decorated with carved animals on the gateposts,
where the chatelaine grew herbs and simples. The
squared-off beds might have been edged with wood
or stones, or plants such as box, cotton lavender or
thrift. In addition they might well have contained
some of the new plants brought back from the
Crusades: Crown imperials *(Fritillaria imperialis),*
damask roses, carnations and hollyhocks.

Gradually the shape of the beds became more
complex, and during the late 15th century
patterns, or knots, were created, using the clipped
edging plants. These patterns were simple and
decorative or, later, highly stylized, sometimes
representing a heraldic device, and the areas they
enclosed were filled with different coloured
materials, from brick dust to pebbles, or even coal.

This style has been carried on in some form in
most centuries because it is simple and practical.
If you have some of the elements of a formal
garden already, or wish to develop a separate small
garden area, you can re-create the effect. There
are certain key elements. It must be contained and
separate, either enclosed with a wall or with a
high fence. Flowerbeds must be straight edged or
elaborately curved into patterns and edged with
dwarf hedging. Paths can be of turf or gravel.

◁**MODERN POTAGER**
*Flowers and vegetables are
planted for visual effect in this
fanciful pastiche of medieval
garden style. The grey-green of
the cabbages contrasts with
the deep green box edging,
and standard roses and topiary
bushes complete the picture.*

▽ **KNOT GARDEN**
*The full-blown, elaborate knot
garden at Barnsley House, in
Gloucestershire, England, relies
for its effect on the flowing lines
of intertwined knots in favourite
designs – such as lovers' knot
and fleur-de-lis – punctuated
by taller clipped bushes.*

AMERICAN COLONIAL STYLE

The term colonial garden conjures up images of a lovely old clapboard house, surrounded by white picket fencing, with neat, trim beds full of flowers in bright, naive colours to go with the gingham curtains hanging at the windows – and an apple pie baking in the oven.

AMERICAN COLONIAL STYLE

Suitable for
Clapboard or shingle houses, Georgian or Colonial style houses

Hard landscaping and features
White picket fencing

White-painted wooden archway

Wooden arbour with seat

Brick or gravel path

Planting
Black-eyed Susan

Box edging

Canada and martagon lilies

Herbs

Hollyhock

Lilac

Michaelmas daisy and New England aster

Peony

Tulip

Stonecrop

◁ **BLOSSOM AND BULBS**
Although the garden is open and full of spring sunshine, it is nevertheless firmly enclosed with wooden fencing. In early colonial gardens, only a few flowers would have found space – pride of place went to useful herbs and vegetables.

The origins of this style in America lie with the "dooryard gardens" of the early settlers, in which the woman of the house would grow the herbs necessary for the kitchen and for medicinal use, in the days when the doctor might be a day's journey away. The plot would be enclosed by a simple wooden fence of whitewashed pickets, or palings, and would be divided into beds by paths.

Potherbs would be grown on one side and medicinal herbs on the other. A few favourite flowers, such as irises, peonies and lilies, would be included, and the path to the front door might be lined with stonecrop (*Sedum spectabile*) and pinks. The porch would be planted with a shrub on either side, often a rose or lilac, but otherwise the early gardens would have had little in the way of decoration; there just wasn't time for it.

These gardens were based on traditional gardens back home in Europe. The English manor-house style became influential, particularly around Boston, in the Massachusetts Bay Colony. The emphasis here was on symmetry, with a central path, perhaps a knot garden, and trained evergreens. From Holland came a similar formal style, with topiary and clipped hedges; the Dutch brought to their settlements in Pennsylvania and New York a strong gardening tradition and great knowledge of plants.

The settlers brought seeds and cuttings, carefully nurtured during the long Atlantic crossing. Early writings speak mainly of edible and medicinal plants, but some of these were also ornamental, such as marigolds, pinks and feverfew. Gradually the colonial garden acquired native species: both crops, such as maize, which the Native Americans cultivated, and ornamentals, such as dogwood, Martagon and Canada lilies, sunflowers, black-eyed Susans and Michaelmas daisies (*Aster novi-belgii*), and New England asters (*A. novae-angliae*) from the local grasslands.

This is a charming style for the garden of a classic clapboard house or a small brick Georgian-style house, also known as Colonial. The keynote is symmetry. Straight lines or simple curves were used for the paths; beds were rectangular or square, or a circle divided into quarters by paths – the link to the earlier knot garden style is evident. In this style the centre was filled with flowerbeds.

If you wish to have a lawn, it should also be simple and symmetrical, but generally you would not expect to see a lawn, bearing in mind the garden's practical origins. However, many larger gardens, such as that at George Washington's Mount Vernon, have fine, sweeping lawns.

The fence is either white picket or of open latticework, with a wooden front gate. A hedge looks good behind the fence, but 1 m (3 ft) is high enough, and a wooden archway is charming over a gate, painted white to match the fence. Paths can be of brick, gravel edged with brick, or crushed oyster and clam shells. Flowerbeds and lawn can also have a brick edging, or a low box hedge if the winter climate is not too cold.

Planting should be in bright, unsophisticated colours – if you don't wish to be strictly in period, bedding plants look good, since the splash of colour combines well with the clear outlines. Tulips and fruit trees recall the Dutch input.

▷ **COLONIAL TRADITION**
Adapted for a more modern effect, this attractive front garden still retains the white picket fence and front door trelliswork. A formal, box-edged flowerbed is filled with santolina for year-round effect and annuals for summer colour.

▽ **CLASSIC COLONIAL**
The Blair garden in colonial Williamsburg has brick paths and a rough, hand-split post-and-rail fence above a clipped hedge. A grander touch is added by the steeply roofed garden house. Planting is simple and traditional.

ENGLISH COTTAGE GARDEN

A thatched cottage in the country, with roses around the door and a garden bursting with flowers and produce, forms part of many people's daydreams. There's an old apple tree; bees buzzing among foxgloves, Canterbury bells and columbines; and the air is heavy with the scent of honeysuckle.

Such images of peace and quiet and fresh air can be found on birthday cards, in advertisements and in countless paintings. Poets such as William Wordsworth (1770–1850) wrote about the simple life of country people, and the artists Helen Allingham (1848–1926) and Kate Greenaway (1846–1901) produced charming, sentimental pictures of cottagers and their gardens in paintings and children's books.

The idealized cottage garden became popular as a concept in the early years of the 20th century, a reaction against the elaborate formality of the 19th century, but, in fact, the real cottage garden is a practical place and shows links back to the medieval garden. It collected bits and pieces from many traditions, in the same way that cottagers collected slips and seeds from the great houses, and so preserved plants when the gentry moved

ENGLISH COTTAGE GARDEN

Suitable for
Front gardens of smaller houses. Not appropriate for modern houses

Hard landscaping and features
Path of brick or cobbles

Wooden or rustic archway

Box or lavender edging

Sundial and birdbath

Planting
Apple tree

Columbine

Foxglove

Holly

Honeysuckle

Lilac

Lupin

Pink

Climbing rose

Snapdragon

on to another fashion. In this way, you might find an arbour copied from a castle garden, topiary hedges from the Dutch tradition, or a herb bed laid out as a knot garden.

All this, however, would have been alongside the main business of the garden – food provision. Flowers had to be tucked in wherever space allowed, although some would have survived in the herb garden long after their use as simples was forgotten. In the main beds would be vegetables, such as cabbages, potatoes and other root crops to last through lean winter days.

The modern cottage garden was made popular by such great gardeners as Margery Fish (1893–1969), who rescued many plants from oblivion by collecting them from her country neighbours, growing them on and writing about them. Hellebores, masterwort (*Astrantia* spp.), many varieties of windflower and geranium were used in mixed, apparently artless, plantings that were a far cry from the staked-up prima donnas of the country-house herbaceous border.

To follow this style you do not need to grow vegetables in with your flowers. It is, however, important to have a strong framework to contain the overflowing flowers and foliage. The main element is the front path, straight up to the cottage door, with a rich jumble of flowers spilling in from either side. Brick laid in a herringbone pattern is attractive, although the original surface would have been made from whatever lay at hand – that delightful cobbled pathway was made from stones or flints thrown out while digging the beds – nobody had money to spare to buy materials. Edge the path with bricks and box or lavender hedging, or simply flowers mixed with herbs and salad vegetables.

In the rest of the garden you can select from the rich historical palette of centuries – a herb bed laid out in a pattern; a sundial in a circle of paving; a trellised arbour, or covered wooden seat; or a rustic archway. Again, these would have been made with whatever was at hand – the wood might have been prunings from the fruit trees, the bricks or slabs from a tumbledown house – nothing quite matched, creating the "lived-in" effect that is now so fashionable.

△ **TIME STANDING STILL**
Little has changed in this garden. Many elements of the old cottage garden remain – tall foxgloves, sweetpeas growing up a brushwood frame, and a pale pink climbing rose. And the ivy-covered shed, built in stone, with a slate roof and faded blue door, was probably the original privy.

◁ **MODERN PASTICHE**
This garden achieves cottage style through the emphasis on its straight, gravelled front path, with flowerbeds on either side. The plants are an exuberant mixture in a riot of colours, from huge, creamy white dahlias to pink and purple phlox, rust-coloured heleniums, red and white nicotiana, and mauve asters. Jasmine and climbing roses clothe the house front.

◁ **WORKADAY GARDEN**
In this more ordinary traditional cottage garden, the path is patched together from irregular stone slabs and gravel. It leads past an old fruit tree, through flowerbeds filled with poppies, daisies, lychnis and lady's mantle to a whitewashed shed adorned with a red climbing rose, the compost bin and a rainwater butt.

WALLED KITCHEN GARDEN

The huge, walled vegetable gardens of a large estate – providing a continuous supply of fresh vegetables, soft fruit, prize peaches, grapes from the greenhouse and cut flowers – are fast becoming a rarity; but on a smaller scale such gardens are still feasible and highly desirable.

WALLED KITCHEN GARDEN

Suitable for
Larger houses and gardens; best in cooler climates

Hard landscaping and features
Gravel path; brick, board or tile edging

Arches for walkways

Cloches, forcing-pots

Planting
Box or lavender hedge

Flowers for cutting: carnations, dahlias, chrysanthemums

Fruit: apple, apricot, cherry, currants, fig, grape, nectarine, peach, pear, plum, raspberry, strawberry

Salad crops: beetroot, cucumber, lettuce, tomato

Vegetables: artichoke, asparagus, beans, brassicas, carrot, peas, potatoes, turnip

A walled garden is a wonderful invention in a cool climate. Although the enclosure of gardens is a timeless tradition, Victorian Britain is often considered to have taken the art of kitchen gardening to its limit. The great gardens in Britain face south, if possible, sloping gently towards the sun. They are mostly rectangular, enclosed on all four sides by brick walls 3.7 m (12 ft) high on average, and protected from the north and east winds especially, with a line of trees planted outside the garden. The gardens were ruled with a rod of iron by the head gardener, whose house was often actually built into the wall on one side of the garden.

The walls were used to the full, both for protection and for the warm, heat-reflecting surface they provided. The sunny, south-facing wall was the most valuable. Apricots, nectarines and peaches, early cherries and choice plums would be grown here, with figs on the west wall, together with apples and pears. These would also fruit well on the east-facing wall, although they would be later varieties, less likely to suffer frost damage to their blossoms in spring. The cool, north-facing wall would support Morello cherries, red, black and white currants, and some hardier apples and pears.

The space in front of the fruit was also well employed. The south-facing bed was often much wider than the others and was used for early crops of turnips, peas, potatoes, and beans and later for lengthening the cropping season. Salad crops

◁ **SUMMER BOUNTY**
The potting shed was often attached to the end of the greenhouse, and the errant branch of a grapevine can be seen here. The late summer garden, visible through the window, has yielded a full harvest, including potatoes, cabbage, beetroot, cucumber, beans, sweetcorn and carrots.

were also grown here early in the year, protected by glass cloches. The cooler borders, too, had their uses, since crops and fruit grown there would ripen later than those in sunny positions, so prolonging their availability for the dining table.

The layout of the garden was prepared with scientific precision. Outside the walls would be the potting shed, mushroom forcing house, toolshed and other necessary workshops. Inside, greenhouses were generally positioned at the top, sunniest part, with the cold frames lower down. Larger gardens would have several different houses for the different crops, such as figs, grapes and peaches. There might also be a show house in the middle, growing flowers and flowering plants for the house. In smaller establishments, the single gardener would have to make do with one long greenhouse, divided into compartments.

A central walkway would run up the middle of the garden, often ornamented with fruit trees trained as cordons or espaliers on each side. This was the main pathway for viewing the garden. It was generally gravelled and sometimes there would be hooped iron archways for climbers over it. At either side would be flowers for both cutting and ornament – perhaps a small, clipped hedge of box or lavender. There would also be side paths in front of the garden-wall beds; the larger, central beds were used for growing main crop vegetables, such as potatoes, peas, beans and brassicas.

If you are fortunate enough to have a walled garden to work in, you will probably not aspire to such heights as these; but they are pleasant gardens to live in, since their microclimate is generally warmer than that outside the walls. The keynote of a formal layout of paths is worth retaining; if you don't have much time for maintenance, a plain, rectangular lawn, divided by paths, will give a simple, tranquil effect. If you can manage it, espaliered fruit trees are an incomparable asset, both for their beauty and their high productivity.

◁▽ **POTAGER STYLE**
High hedges, rather than walls, are used in this modern kitchen garden. It is laid out in a formal style, with paths of slabs and pavers, and beds edged with box or sage. The terracotta pots are used for forcing early crops of rhubarb, and the young fruit trees are wired up, ready for training.

▽ **TRADITIONAL LAYOUT**
This beautifully kept walled kitchen garden slopes south, with a shed built into the wall on the north side. Gravel paths, edged with box, have fruit trees trained on hoops at either end. Each row of vegetables is labelled with the name and date of sowing, and soft fruit is given a separate bed.

ENGLISH COUNTRY HOUSE

The quintessential English country-house garden evokes the era of

lawn-tennis parties on summer weekends; tea on the lawn under a huge

cedar; and a stroll down the winding walk through the little wood, or along the

herbaceous border to admire the new colour schemes approved of by Miss Jekyll.

ENGLISH COUNTRY HOUSE

Suitable for
Most gardens, except those of small modern houses; larger plots on acid soil may incorporate a woodland element, smaller sites will concentrate on the herbaceous borders

Hard landscaping and features
York stone path

Curved brick steps

Summerhouse

Large wooden seat

Circular lily pond

Sundial and birdbath

Planting
For woodland: azalea, ferns, magnolia, rhododendron

For herbaceous borders: delphinium, globe thistle, gypsophila, hosta, tree mallow, phlox

The small, country-house gardens of Surrey, England, grown in acid, woodland soil, have set an example still followed every year in many of the famous show gardens at the Chelsea Flower Show in London. They contain banks of brilliant rhododendrons, artfully natural rockeries, with brooks tumbling through them, and choice alpines nestling in the hollows of the rocks. This,

together with the fine lawn edged with its herbaceous border, is perhaps the most typical "English garden" style, having elements of the 18th-century English Landscape style in its apparently natural woodland, and of the cottage garden in its medley of perennial flowers. It became the style of the new garden suburbs that were developed in the early 20th century.

This style developed as a reaction to the over-elaborate 19th-century gardens. Garden designer William Robinson (1838–1935), in his magazine *The Garden,* thundered against the use of garish carpet bedding, demanding a return to what he called "wildflower gardening", using a far wider range of perennial plants in softer colours, and taking account of leaf texture and plant form.

The influential Gertrude Jekyll (1843–1932) employed her intimate knowledge of the cottage gardens in her native Surrey, then a quiet country locality, and her training as an artist, to develop herbaceous borders using subtle colour schemes. In partnership with the architect Sir Edwin Lutyens (1869–1944), she made many extremely beautiful gardens, with strong, formal layouts including steps, walls, rose gardens and lily ponds.

In the outer reaches of these gardens, however, she used her familiarity with the native woodland of Surrey to great effect in flower gardens planted in "forest clearings". She, too, complained about the "commonplace treatment" accorded to many gardens, with their "ruthless destruction" of the natural woodland, in order to make place for "common nursery stuff, such as laurels and a heterogeneous collection of exotic conifers".

Jekyll advocated the retention of existing woodland combinations such as juniper, holly, birch and mountain ash, and the judicious addition of plants that respected the natural character of the soil. In many instances this was acid, and so the classic plants of her woodland walks were calcifuges, such as rhododendron and pieris underplanted with heathers or lithospermum. These were chosen very carefully for colour and planted near the house lawns – as the paths wove more deeply into the woods, the planting became more subtle, with groups of wild ferns and, perhaps, an occasional "flowery

incident" of trillium or Solomon's seal. The intention was to lead imperceptibly from cultivated to wild scenery.

The flower borders of these gardens were generally long and wide (at Munstead Wood, the house designed for Jekyll by Lutyens, the main border was 5.5 m (18 ft) wide and 55 m (180 ft) long). The borders were often backed by a high wall, with a path in front; or perhaps a pair of borders would form a flowery walk.

There were also small, enclosed gardens, with symmetrical beds, often edged with box, echoing the knot garden tradition of earlier centuries. Planting in these beds was composed almost entirely of perennial plants; although the work was less than the enormous labour required for Victorian bedding schemes, it still required a large number of gardeners for staking, tying-in and placing of potted lilies and the like to fill in any gaps. Planting usually followed a colour theme: pink, purple and white, for example.

△ **TRADITION UPDATED**
This long herbaceous border uses a modern colour scheme of red and white lupins and red roses, with pink and deep purple geraniums and yellow potentilla. The wide York stone path allows the plants to spread, and the seat at the end, under a yew hedge, both forms a focus and looks out across a flowering meadow.

△ **WOODLAND GEMS**
In the Savill Gardens at Windsor, England, the acid soil allows a traditional woodland planting of rhododendrons and orange Azalea mollis. In the distance can be seen the still waters of the lake, reflecting the trees.

◁ **COLOUR THEME**
Wisteria flowers prolifically on the walls of this English country house, clambering past the upper windows. Its pale lavender flowers are echoed by a large plant of Abutilon 'Suntense' and a border of herbaceous perennials spills out on to the paving.

NORTHEAST WOODLAND

The American garden equivalent to the English woodland garden developed around the big houses in the woods of New England. But this style of garden, which is fundamentally created as a clearing in the woods, is echoed in many other parts of the country as well.

AMERICAN NORTHEAST WOODLAND

Suitable for
Any style of house in woodland

Hard landscaping and features
Flagstone paving

Bark paths

Rustic furniture; benches

Gazebo

Pond

Planting
Azalea

Dogwood

Ferns

Hosta

Hydrangea

Maple

Mountain laurel

Pieris

Spruce

This type of garden is extremely simple, hewn as it is out of the all-enveloping forests. These gardens have an acceptance of the grandeur and the landscape of the northeastern United States that gives them a timeless appeal. In the best examples, the form of the garden is an extension of the existing topography, and plants are brought right up to the house from the adjoining woodland. The essence of the style is its simplicity and its compatibility with the surrounding countryside; the key to it lies in the treatment of the natural scenery.

At the front, a substantial drive may lead up to the house. Often there is an elegant front entrance, furnished perhaps with columns, and plants in tubs at either side. The beds are filled with simple, sturdy evergreens, such as spreading junipers and spruce, with azaleas – often of only one variety – to give colour, and silver birches, dogwoods and maples for height and autumn effect. The ground beneath them is covered with a dense mat of ivy or pachysandra, which gives the beds an abstract rounded shape.

Practical paving, sheltered from the weather, leads around the house to the side door, past the service area and the woodpile. At the back, for the hot summer, is a shady porch and a generous flagstone terrace or, on a sloping site, a wooden deck, with rustic or natural wood benches, tables and chairs.

This might be surrounded by formal beds, filled with roses and bedding plants, or it may simply

△ **WOODLAND VIEW**
A path of red clay pavers leads to this shingle house and bench overlooking the woods. Simple, easy-care planting includes leadwort and fountain grass.

◁ **FIERY RED AND GOLD**
Maples are one of the key ingredients of the spectacle of the New England autumn. They grow best in well-drained but moist soil, in sun or light

lead on to the spreading lawn, which is shaded in places with venerable shrubs, such as the peegee hydrangea *(Hydrangea paniculata)*, grown with age to the size of a small tree, or the redbud *(Cercis canadensis)*. There is not much sculpture, but large stones are often placed to draw attention to groups of small, delicate plants. There may be a large tree, with a wooden seat beneath it, or, with a touch of formality, a stone bench and even an urn with a bright spot of colour from such bedding plants as busy lizzies.

Behind these, the lawn stretches to the surrounding woodland; it is planted at first with a few more ornamental shrubs, perhaps mountain laurel *(Kalmia latifolia)*, or rhododendron, fothergilla, pieris and leucothöe. In the woodland proper, the tall trees – most of them deciduous – are pruned up to let in light and make room for understorey trees and shrubs, including azalea, dogwood, aucuba, Carolina allspice and daphne. Shade-loving woodland plants (many of them

native species), such as grasses or ferns, hosta, wood anemone, bunch berry, lily-of-the-valley, trillium, violet, trout lily *(Erythronium americanum)*, shooting stars *(Dodecatheon meadia)*, foam flower, wild geranium, wild ginger and wild sweet William, are massed in drifts under the trees.

Dirt or bark paths meander through the trees, and if water is available, there will be a stream and pool, or a natural-looking man-made pond. There might even be a gazebo in a clearing; this is often screened if biting insects are a problem.

These are spring-flowering gardens, and after the first flush of colour, they settle into a cool greenness during the hot summer, when the only colour may come from pots of annuals, until the glorious autumn hues start to show on the leaves of the trees. In winter, a carpet of snow covers the spreading evergreens so that their mounded shapes stand out against the dark trunks of the deciduous trees.

△ **CITY WOODLAND**
This garden was designed by landscape architects Oehme and Van Sweden for a classic suburban property in a typical 1,000-sq-m (quarter-acre) plot. It consists of quite simple hard landscaping in bluestone pavers and dense planting around the existing mature shrubs and trees.

ITALIAN GARDEN STYLE

Water staircases, fountains, water parterres, grand flights of stairs and classical statues denote the Italianate garden, inspired by the Renaissance gardens of Rome and Tuscany. This style – elegant, urban, sophisticated, even when set in the heart of the country – is determinedly and proudly man-made.

ITALIAN GARDEN STYLE

Suitable for
Large gardens;
unlimited money and
labour; hillside sites

**Hard landscaping
and features**
Stone steps and
balustrades

Stone paving

Classical urns

Statues

Terracotta pots

Marble or stone
pools and fountains

Planting
Bay

Box

Cypress

Ferns

Fig

Geranium

Lemon

Myrtle

Olive

The style we think of as Italian has its roots in ancient Rome, in the villas sited on the hillsides above the city, with their shaded courtyards and colonnades, and carefully planned views of distant hills. Gardens such as that of the Emperor Hadrian at Tivoli became the inspiration for Renaissance men such as Cosimo de' Medici (1389–1464). At his villa at Careggi, near Florence, he gathered a group of intellectuals, known as the Platonic Academy, who discussed philosophy and literature in the setting of the classical garden.

An early example of the Italian style, Cosimo's garden was laid out symmetrically, with clipped bay trees, box hedges and cypress trees. There was at least one fountain, for which water was specially brought in. It was later decorated with a sculpture by Verrocchio (1435–88) of a putto with a fish: this custom of employing great architects and sculptors to build and ornament gardens is one of the attributes of Italian landscape.

Gardens like those of the Villa Gamberaia at Settignano, the Villa Lante at Bagnaia, Lazio, and

△ **MODERN FORMALITY**
A formal layout and clipped bushes and trees give this contemporary Italian garden refreshing shade and greenness in summer. Flower colour is not as important as form and style.

▷ **LA FORCE, TUSCANY**
This is a classic Italian garden, with clipped topiary hedges leading to a stone fountain and pool. The large stone urns on substantial pillars give emphasis and stature to the layout.

the famous fountains at the Villa d'Este near Rome demonstrate the elements of this style. They are powerfully architectural, generally laid out from one main central axis, delineated with paths, terraces and grand sets of steps. Often, especially on hillside sites, water gives the star performance, cascading from its source in a grotto (inhabited by statues of Mercury and nymphs) and foaming down water staircases to emerge in elaborate fountains, formal pools and vast parterres of water, not flowers. The many buildings are often set to face each other on either side of the garden, or are carefully sited to catch a distant view.

These gardens are mainly deep green in colour, although occasionally they are ornamented with regular rows of terracotta pots with geraniums and flashes of colour from the fruits of orange and lemon trees. Tall spires of cypress, lines of clipped box, glossy-leafed myrtle and dripping fountains clothed with ferns combine to give a welcome coolness – both real and illusory – under the heat of the Mediterranean sun.

Italian gardens were especially popular in the 19th and early 20th centuries, when there was money to spare for expensive stonework, statues and balustrading. In the 1930s, Randolph Hearst attempted a Roman garden for his swimming pool at San Simeon, near St Luis Obispo in California, but the style is more usually inspired by the Renaissance and, outside Italy, is often combined with beautiful formal lawns.

In Victorian times, the Italian style became blurred with fussy detail and a mass of colour from bedding schemes and exotic plants, but glimpses of Italy may be seen in the pergolas of country-house gardens, with their columns of stone or brick, often ending in a fountain or (as at Edwin Lutyens' Hestercombe in Somerset) in a framed view of the countryside. Interestingly, another great gift from Italy, that of al fresco dining, is not part of this style. The long lunch under a vine-covered pergola is too rustic for the worldly Italianate garden.

▽ **ORNATE STONEWORK**
This elaborately carved stone fountain, backed with natural rock and almost overgrown with plants, is in the garden of La Mortola (the Giardini Hanbury) in northern Italy. Such features are an essential element of Italian garden style.

◁ **CLASSIC FORMALITY**
The gardens of the Villa Gamberaia in Tuscany are among the most famous in Italy. This view shows a typical path, lined with clipped bushes of various types and sizes interspersed with heavily laden orange trees in huge terracotta pots.

FORMAL SMALL GARDEN

Following the Italian style closely, this modern garden has an elegance that stems from its precise and geometric layout and the nature of the materials used, which are weighty, rather grand – and tend to be expensive. The garden forms the perfect backdrop for stylish, sophisticated entertaining.

FORMAL SMALL GARDEN

Suitable for
Any small plot, but especially a town garden

Hard landscaping and features
Stone paving

Urns or pots and statues

Painted or stone seats

Fancy treillage

Brick walls with York stone coping

Versailles tubs

Planting
Bay

Bergenia

Camellia

Eucryphia

Evergreen magnolia

Galtonia

Hydrangea

Skimmia

In its most refined form, this garden is a stage set, designed and built professionally, generally for busy (and wealthy) clients, who have no time to fuss about and want a garden that looks good at all times, no matter what the season or the weather. Although ideally suited to grand receptions, this style is, of course, also perfectly suitable for a family lunch or a quiet gossip with a friend. It is not, however, really a garden for those who like to potter about tending their plants, although a compulsive collector could have fun introducing new *objets d'art* into it.

The essence of the style lies in its formal, classical architectural character. The shape is defined by strong lines and a clear axis, emphasized with focal points such as seats or urns. As with the original Italian style, this is a built garden, and frequently there may be no lawn and only very few plants.

The ground surface is usually paved with York stone or similar slabs, and there may be some raised beds capped with matching stone. If there is a change of level, the steps should be made of brick or stone with stone treads. If finance does not allow this, it is acceptable to use a gravel surface, as long as it is strictly contained within a well-delineated framework of brick or stone.

Enclosure is provided by high walls, if possible of brick or stucco finish, but painted trelliswork is often used either instead of, or in combination with, this. Elaborate walls of treillage (trelliswork) can be

▽ **GRACIOUS LIVING**
In this London garden, designed by Jonathan Baillie, formality is established by the paired lions and row of clipped box domes in white-painted pots that stand out against the dark ivy on the walls. The brick terrace is paved in herringbone pattern.

▽▽ **SIMPLE SYMMETRY**
A formal layout of paving surrounds the small lawns in a New York City garden designed by Jeff Mendoza. Plantings of agapanthus and hydrangeas maintain the balance, while the focal point – the seat – is flanked by terracotta pots.

made, adorned with archways, railings and, occasionally, urns and mirrors, to give a theatrical impression of depth or the illusion of several different spaces. Columns and balustrades, pavilions and gazebos all have their place in such a garden, provided they are carefully orchestrated within the grand plan. Stone statues, urns and cast-iron vases are all appropriate.

Again, water is an important, although not essential, element, either in the form of a stone structure, perhaps a raised pond, with a single fountain jet, or more elaborate arrangements with sculptures of lion's heads or figures of water gods or nymphs gushing water into a pool. In smaller spaces, a wall fountain can be set to trickle into a carved basin, or an old lead cistern could make a simple water feature.

The garden is well furnished with seats and tables, either of painted wood or wrought iron, or perhaps carved stone benches. Nothing as easy and relaxed as a deck chair, hammock or swing seat should be allowed.

Containers may be planted with brilliantly coloured geraniums or clipped topiary bushes. If there is a conservatory, orange or lemon trees, or an olive or oleander in a tub can be placed outside during the summer and wheeled back under cover for the winter.

Planting relies heavily on permanent evergreen features, generally deep glossy green – evergreen magnolias, eucryphia, common laurel *(Prunus laurocerasus),* and bay. Flower colour may be vibrant, with the deep reds and pinks of camellia or peony, or cool white, with heavy white mophead hydrangeas and waxy-flowered gardenias – but the garden is not reliant on flowers for impact and effectiveness.

If a lawn is required – usually only if the garden is fairly large – it must be symmetrical, generally a long, narrow rectangle, perhaps with rounded ends, and the shape should be outlined, either within the overall pattern of the paving or by a paved edge to the lawn.

◁ **STARK ELEGANCE**
In this restrained design, white paving, close-clipped hedges and plain green ground cover contrast with annuals in pots and a luscious white hydrangea.

▽ **COURTYARD GARDEN**
A white arched wall acts as a perfect foil to formal hedges and paving. White daisies and pelargoniums in classical urns are the only flowers allowed.

JAPANESE GARDEN STYLE

The Japanese garden is epitomized by the tale of the young Buddhist monk who, having carefully swept the leaves from a path, is told by the abbot his work is not done; so he starts again. After his third attempt, the abbot shakes the branch of the tree; five leaves fall on the path. The work is complete.

JAPANESE GARDEN STYLE

Suitable for
A separate garden "room" or space in a large garden

Hard landscaping and features
Groups of stones; stepping stones; path made from stone

Raked gravel and sand

Bamboo structures

Stone lanterns

Pond and bridge

Planting
Azalea

Bellflower

Camellia

Cherry

Cleyera

Ferns

Hollies

Japanese iris

Maple

Gardening has always been revered as an art form in Japan and has been used as a way to express spiritual values and philosophy. Indeed, the Japanese word for garden, *niwa,* was first used in literature to mean a place purified for the worship of the gods.

This has resulted in gardens that are intangibly powerful and often inexplicably moving to experience. It can be seen in both the earliest surviving sacred gardens, such as the Ise Inner Shrine, which is simple and austere with straight lines of stone blocks and a surface of shining white stones, and the grand landscape gardens, such as the Shugaku-in villa garden, with its vast pond and panoramic view of distant hills, subtly blending natural scenery with artificial landscape.

Shugaku-in demonstrates the use of "borrowed scenery", incorporating a view from outside into the garden proper. Gardens are always based on the natural scenery of the area – either by copying a natural setting, or with a miniature version of it, or an abstract representation of a natural scene.

Many famous gardens are quite small and are made to be viewed or contemplated from a single viewpoint. They are often simply furnished with arrangements of two or three rocks in either a gravel or mossy surround.

The influence of Zen Buddhism led to the creation of the dry landscape garden – perhaps an arrangement of rocks in gravel, representing water falling over a waterfall, with the gravel raked into wave patterns as the "river" flows towards the plain, as in the garden of the Daisen-in.

Alternatively, there may be a completely abstract composition, as in the famous placement of 15 stones in fine white gravel in front of the abbot's quarters at Ryoan-ji. Stones play a large part in Japanese gardens, from the sacred rocks of

◁ **SIMPLE PERFECTION**
In the famous dry landscape garden of Ryoan-ji – a garden from which all superfluities have been removed – white sand is raked into a flowing pattern and 15 rocks are grouped together. There are no plants, just a borrowed landscape of distant trees.

▷ **MEDITATIVE GARDEN**
Stepping stones have been laid on the gravel in this Japanese stroll garden in New York. The contemplative mood is enhanced by the planting – green leaves with a single flash of red – and by the dappled shade cast on the gravel.

the Shinto shrines, worshipping the divine in nature, to the artful arrangements of the Zen monks, which used the form and layout of the stones to express human emotion. Beautifully shaped rocks were valued so highly that they were considered suitable gifts for an emperor.

Paths are generally made of stone, sometimes rectangular cut slabs edged with small irregular pieces, more often of randomly shaped rocks beautifully arranged. Stepping stones are often used, set in gravel or in a mossy surround.

The tea garden was another development influenced by the Zen tradition. Basically, it was made around the path linking the garden gate to the teahouse. In order to induce a mood of calm repose in the guest, the garden must be carefully designed to remove all worldly distractions. The famous stone lanterns and stepping stone paths associated with Japanese garden style are elements of the tea garden, as is the ritual stone water basin, which invites the visitor to wash his hands and rinse his mouth in purification. The basin is placed low, requiring the guest to humble himself in preparation for the ritual.

Plants play a very different role in Japanese gardens from that of European tradition. There is not the same collector's passion that led cottagers to save slips of plants, and grand house owners to plant whole arboreta with newly discovered conifers. The appreciation of flowers is linked to their place in the calendar – the cherry blossom in spring, the bush clover in autumn.

The shape of a plant is vitally important, and trees such as pines may occupy a critical position in a garden composition and be pruned skilfully to the required shape. Evergreens are often clipped into stylized mounds, echoing the form of distant mountains, and azaleas may even be cut back before they bloom, since in some places the shape is considered more important than the flowers. A much narrower range of plants may be used, with ferns, one or two shrubs and perhaps one flowering plant, such as the bellflower, used in profusion.

The true Japanese garden style, in fact, cannot be copied – in reality to call this a garden "style" is to misunderstand its significance. But the principle of respect for the natural scenery of the place, the practice of "less" rather than "more", and the reverence for a garden as a haven of quiet contemplation is certainly worth following.

◁ **GARDEN LIGHTS**
Pedestal lanterns, used to light the way in Japanese tea gardens, are popular in re-creations of the style. This example is in Portland, Oregon.

△ **SERENE SECLUSION**
Still water, wooden bridges and mass planting of one species are often features of Japanese gardens. The effect of the irises is enhanced by their reflection.

INFORMAL SMALL GARDEN

This type of modern garden is ideal for busy people who have a practical approach to life and little time or inclination to do more than maintain and enjoy an uncluttered outdoor living space. Design is paramount, and plants are chosen mainly for their foliage and shape, or are in containers.

INFORMAL SMALL GARDEN

Suitable for
All but period houses

Hard landscaping and features
Brick or concrete paving; gravel

Raised beds

Natural wood trellis or fencing

Pergola

Planting
Artemisia 'Powis Castle'

Cordyline

Cotinus coggygria 'Royal Purple'

Grasses

Hosta

Japanese aralia

Phormium

Stag's-horn sumach

Tulip

Verbascum

An altogether more relaxed style than the formal Italianate courtyard, the informal garden is influenced by the asymmetry and simplicity of Japanese gardens. Many of the elements found in them, such as natural-looking water features and arrangements of rocks, may also appear here.

This is not an overflowing cottage garden, although it has many variants. Plants are chosen for their form and leaf shape, as much as for their flowers, and single specimens may be placed in isolation so that their beauty can be appreciated.

Because it draws on the modernist tradition of functionalism, it is generally a practical place, made for use as well as ornament. The modern informal garden is easy to maintain and perfectly adapted to contemporary living.

The layout is usually quite carefully planned, in keeping with the idea of efficient use of space – utility areas are practical and well screened with squared trellis or vertical wooden slatted fencing. There will be a generous eating area, sensibly positioned to catch the sun in cooler climates, with provision for shade from a pergola or a parasol over the table. Often a smaller seating place in a different part of the garden will provide a retreat for reading or a quiet doze. Seating is of natural wood, with simple, clean lines, or perhaps is ultramodern, in stainless steel and canvas.

Paving is used extensively; it either is of natural materials, such as granite pavers or brick, or employs the sharper lines of concrete slabs or block pavers. If the budget is low, this can be combined with gravel, which is also often used as a planting medium in gravel gardens that recall the dry gardens of Japan. They are not, however, as starkly simple, but are generally planted up with species that enjoy the sharp drainage this medium provides. Steps will tone with the paving, and may be brick, with brick or concrete treads, or sometimes railway sleepers with gravel treads.

Raised beds, often made with railway sleepers, or in brickwork, suit this style very well. The beds may be used to support the uprights of a pergola or a wooden screen dividing the more "built-up" part of the garden from the lawn area. Containers are also widely used, either in combination with

◁ **RELAXED LIVING**
The long lines of the easy-care decking make this tiny garden seem larger. Plants are grouped to enclose the seating area and to display their leaves and the shapes of the containers to greatest effect.

△ **STRONG SHAPES**
Many elements of the informal style are present in this garden, with its bold foliage plants. Agave, Japanese aralia, senecio and artemisia give shape and texture; flower colour is provided by an hydrangea.

◁ **CACTUS GARDEN**
The striking forms of the plants in this garden in Sydney, Australia, create a sculptural composition. They need little care, and combined with the tiled paving, give maximum effect for minimum upkeep.

△ **VIBRANT COLOUR**
The bright pink walls that surround the practical, slab-paved eating area provide the strongest colour in this small garden in Vancouver, Canada. Grasses and other foliage plants form the main planting.

raised beds or on their own. They tend to be in simple shapes and range from plain terracotta pots or concrete planters to wooden tubs. A piece of modern sculpture can be used to draw the eye to a focal point, or be hidden in a corner or among the plants so that it is come upon unexpectedly.

In smaller gardens there may be no lawn, but on larger sites the lawn will flow out from the paving, and there might be a wilder part of the garden, with the grass left longer and surrounded by native shrubs and flowers.

Although not a "plantsman's" garden, it can vary enormously, and large flowerbeds can form a satisfying element of the composition. In general, the planting will be chosen for all-round effect, and foliage will be important. Colour schemes are often novel: for instance, a planting of black *Ophiopogon planiscarpus nigrescens* and black tulips with white daisies, or the subtle tones of furry, grey lamb's ears (*Stachys byzantina*) against the russet leaves of *Heuchera* 'Palace Purple'.

CALIFORNIA STYLE

Designed for a warm climate, the California-style garden is intended as an extension to the house, an open-air living space. Certain key features such as a patio – or a deck – and a pool are common, but essentially the garden is purpose-built, alongside the house, to take advantage of each individual site.

This is a highly social type of garden, for play and entertaining. Land is expensive, so it tends to be small; it is usually designed and built at the same time as the house and requires little upkeep.

The style developed in the 1930s and '40s, as a reaction against the then-popular classical gardens, with their symmetrical layouts, lawns and flower gardens, which derived from European traditions. The "California School", influenced by landscape architects Thomas Church and Garrett Eckbo, rebelled against these conventions; they were affected by various factors.

At the time, new social developments, such as the increasing use of cars, led many families to move out into the suburbs. A new confidence, and an enthusiasm for the modern, showed itself in the design of fashionable houses, which were planned ergonomically to use the site in the best possible way.

The garden was now seen as an extension of the house – the smaller plots, as an outdoor room. On bigger sites in the Californian hills, house and garden were created to form a living sculpture, blending into the dramatic landscape in the manner pioneered by the architect Frank Lloyd Wright (1869–1959) in the early years of the 20th century. Other influences came from the conceptual gardens of Japan and from the flowing shapes of modern abstract art, which showed in the free-form lines of pools and decks. A strong Spanish influence is evident in tiled courtyard gardens, with fountains and ornamental pools that form a useful cooling element and celebrate the importance of water in this dry climate.

This, then, is a built outdoor living space designed for beauty and utility. Different functions are assigned to different areas, starting with the public entrance, front garden and driveway, and maybe a carport. This leads to the backyard for keeping rubbish and for outdoor hobbies.

Then come the main living areas, for eating, swimming, playing with the kids and general relaxation – planned for shade and privacy, where necessary; shelter from wind; and maximizing any natural assets, such as a view or mature tree. Paved patios are a common feature in California

gardens, surfaced with exposed aggregate concrete
precast concrete slabs or tiles. Lawns are still
popular and are often heavily irrigated, although
as environmental awareness grows, the use of
water in this way is increasingly unpopular, and
ground-cover plants may be used instead.

Screening, used extensively both for visual and
wind protection, is generally made of wood, either
louvred split-wood for open fences or trellis
frames. Sometimes there are glass insets, when
the function of the screening is to break the wind
rather than hide an unattractive outlook. Masonry
walls, often painted in bright colours, may also be
found, made from concrete blocks or poured
concrete. Overhead screening from the sun is
provided by wooden structures, ranging from a
simple post-and-beam pergola to more elaborate
trelliswork and the heavy shade provided by a lath
house, made from slats of wood nailed together.

Decking is a common element of this style;
often it is redwood decking, in asymmetrical

shapes, sometimes on different levels, or
cantilevered out over the valley, with a spectacular
view. There are plenty of seats and tables on the
decking, and raised planters, which may form
additional seating. Garden furniture includes
wooden or ultramodern tables and chairs, full-
length loungers, or cushions on benches.

Sometimes a built-in barbecue is
sited where it receives shade and
protection from the wind. Most
gardens are well lit at night, for
parties around the barbecue and by
the pool and for the dramatic views
seen from inside the house.

Plants are regarded as only one of
the decorative elements, along with
sculpture, rocks and driftwood.
Shrubs and trees with architectural
forms are important, and the garden
may be designed around a mature
tree. Shrubs are used for screening,
less often for their flowers, which are
provided by containers filled with
annuals such as busy lizzies and
begonias (in frost-free areas they are
treated as perennials). Gardens
often have a tropical air, with palms,
bougainvillea, camellias, gardenias
and tree ferns growing outdoors.
Drought-tolerant California natives
are often grown, and single-species
ground-cover planting is popular
and almost maintenance-free.

△ **ABSTRACT ELEGANCE**
*This smooth, white, concrete
pool, with its spare, minimalist
lines, single-jet fountain and
modern sculptures, is an essay
in the California style by garden
designer Thomas Church.*

◁◁ **QUIET RETREAT**
*Sunbleached wooden steps and
decking lead in a bold zigzag
pattern to a relaxed seating
area, complete with blue-and-
white loungers. Wooden fencing
and trellis covered in creepers
provide privacy in this Los
Angeles garden.*

◁ **MODERN LIVING**
*Another view of the Los Angeles
garden shows the Spanish-style
house and its raised sun deck.
Palm trees growing on the roof,
a clipped tree in a large
terracotta pot, and drought-
resistant plants, some with
architectural forms, emphasize
the air of modernity.*

NEOCOLONIAL STYLE

Overtones of long-past life in the British colonies are everywhere evident in this type of garden, where tropical-looking climbers drape a wide veranda, the air is heavy with the scent of exotic flowers, and the encroaching plants loom large, with leaves in all shades of green.

NEO-COLONIAL STYLE

Suitable for
City and suburban gardens; modern or wooden houses

Hard landscaping and features
Decking or veranda with cane chairs

Bamboo screens

Stone or concrete paving

Bark mulch

Natural-looking pools

Planting
Bamboos

Bougainvillea

Canna lilies

Evergreen magnolia

Ferns

Gunnera

Japanese aralia

Jasmine

Kiwi fruit

Loquat

A garden such as this may seem entirely inappropriate for the average suburban or city home, but in fact it makes a very usable style. It is quite possible to create a tropical-type jungle or a shady veranda drooping with vines in a different environment. Gardens in the Deep South of America, northern New Zealand and parts of Australia and Africa will already have many of its components, such as a covered porch and a humid, frost-free climate, but it also works well in inner city environments, where winds are low and temperatures higher than in surrounding areas.

The main requirement for this garden is that you enjoy looking at and growing plants, the stranger and more unusual ones especially, and that you are not too worried about things getting out of hand – if you are successful, they will, but an exotic jungle should not be well behaved.

The underlying structure is important – strong lines contain the exuberance of the planting. The paved terrace (and, indeed, the house itself) gives the impression that at any minute it is liable to be overrun by clinging vines – stout woodwork is necessary to give support, and any permanent fence structures must also be strong, although light, movable bamboo screens are very effective.

Paths lead out through the "bush", every now and again opening out into small clearings, where you might find an ancient canvas chair or small bush hut with a canvas or thatched roof. The garden's boundaries are completely hidden and almost impossible to find.

Ground surfaces can be hard; either stone or concrete slabs are fine, but of a dark rather than a pale colour and with a dull surface. Decking looks great, but it must be raised above the ground to allow air to circulate below or the surface will grow moss and become too slippery. Bark and wood chips both work well for the paths in the main part of the garden.

Lawns are not suitable for this style, since with all the damp and shade they will tend to moss. In fact, this is a much better surface in this situation, as are tiny ground covers such as mind-your-own-business *(Soleirolia soleirolii)*, although this cannot be walked on.

Water is an essential and can wind through the garden in rills and streamlets, emerging as bubbling fountains at black water holes or in lazy, quiet pool areas. These should have pebble banks and boggy surrounds, overhung with ferns and moss and hanging creepers. Wooden planks, covered with wire to counteract their slipperiness, cross the stream at various places, and in large gardens the water can open out into a lake, with a decking platform at one side to fish from – or even a boat tied up to a tree.

With plants for such gardens you can really experiment. Even in temperate climates, surprisingly tropical-looking plants will grow: stalwarts such as Japanese aralia *(Fatsia japonica)* and fatshedra; gunnera, with its amazing huge leaves; a tall, shiny, elegant evergreen magnolia; all types of bamboo with narrow black stems or wide, bright green ones. In temperate regions, you could also try the Tasmanian tree fern or the hardy banana *(Musa basjoo)*.

A veranda, with a corrugated iron roof, pale blue or faded green wooden railings and wooden decking, and hung with bougainvillea, wisteria or jasmine will provide a platform from which to survey the territory and complete the scene.

△ **TELLING CONTRAST**
On the terrace of this South
African house all is order, with
flowering plants in pots and a
clipped tree, but beyond, the
dense, encroaching greenery of
the garden is visible.

◁ **LUXURIANT GROWTH**
Clinging tendrils of wisteria
invade this veranda from the
lush planting below, where
cordylines and bamboos
overhang the path of stones
set in bark mulch.

△ **MYSTERY STAIRWAY**
Concrete stepping stones lead
up into the dark heart of the
bush in this jungle garden.
Magnificent tree ferns, ivy
and grasses enhance the
tropical effect.

GARDENING BASICS

N ow that you have thought about and planned the garden you want, it is time to put your ideas into action. Here you will find practical advice on clearing the site and successful replanting. The tasks in every garden may be similar, but how you tackle them will vary.

For this reason it is vital to take stock first and get to know your garden and what will be involved in changing it. No matter how daunting your garden may seem at the outset, be assured that there are tools, techniques and expertise out there to help you. This chapter will give you the basic know-how you need to get started, whatever your garden problems.

△ **NEW PLANTINGS**
When adding new trees to your garden, make sure they are top quality and are planted correctly. They need a good start to help them become established and compete with the existing plantings.

◁ **OVERGROWN BORDER**
Autumn is the ideal time to tackle a congested border. Many perennial plants that have been left to grow into large clumps can be lifted, divided into smaller sections and replanted in the cooler months.

CLEARING THE SITE

There is no magic wand you can wave to make a messy site ready for planting. If the builders have left you with piles of rubbish, or brambles are rapidly creeping over the plot, there is simply no point putting in new plants until you have cleared the site and prepared the soil.

△ MINI DIGGER
Using a mini digger is a quick and economical way of moving soil or debris, and it will take out old hedges or unwanted paths. To preserve the quality of your soil, use a mini track excavator only when the soil is dry. You can hire the machine with or without a driver.

▷ ROTAVATOR
Use the rototiller to turn over weed-free soil that is moist, not wet or dry. Press down as you go so that the soil is turned over to a depth of about 23 cm (9 in).

First, sort through the non-living debris. As a precaution against spills, cuts and scratches, always cover your arms and legs and make sure your tetanus shot is up to date. Wear protective gloves and stout footwear if there are rough or heavy items to be moved. Once the surface debris has been cleared, use a garden fork to probe any raised areas of earth. Often these contain partly buried waste, such as plastic bags, old bricks and nails, all of which are best removed now, rather than left until you want to plant.

Collect items you might use later and arrange for the rest to go to a waste disposal site. For large quantities, it is worth hiring a skip. The cost is based on the volume; typical skip sizes are 1.5, 3, and more than 4.6 cubic metres. Companies charge a nominal daily hire fee as well as a charge per load dumped. Gather all the debris in one place so that you can estimate just what size skip you need and save money by not needing to fill two loads.

Don't be tempted to use unofficial waste collectors – they may give cheap quotes but often dump waste in the countryside. It is safer not to burn waste made from material such as plastic, chemicals and treated wood.

UNWANTED PLANTS
Large trees should be taken down by a tree surgeon; other unwanted plants can be removed by unskilled labour. Always get tree stumps removed promptly. Woody growth can be reduced in bulk by using a shredder. Don't take plant waste to landfill sites; instead try to recycle it either by adding it to the compost bin or by using chipped bark as a mulch.

Weeds need to be tackled as a priority. If you are not planning to plant for, say, a year or two,

roughly cut down the weeds with a scythe, garden shears or brushcutter, then smother them by depriving them of light. Cover the weeds with old carpet, black plastic, or polypropylene sheets, or even several layers of newspaper held in place with bricks. Where the ground is on show, cover unattractive sheets with a layer of bark chips.

If you cannot wait for the weeds to be smothered, either dig them out or use a systemic weedkiller, such as one based on glyphosate. Don't compost perennial weeds with roots attached, any weed in flower or setting seed, or diseased plants. Small quantities of weeds can be put in the dustbin, but if you have a lot, burn them if you are permitted to do so in your area.

USEFUL TOOLS

You will need to buy a garden fork, a wheelbarrow, and some planks for access. Where there is a lot of heavy debris and hard core, get a builder's barrow, since it will withstand abuse better than a garden wheelbarrow. A scythe to cut down tall weeds is worth buying if you plan to have a wildflower meadow; otherwise try to borrow one and get an experienced person to show you how to use and sharpen it safely. Heavy-duty power equipment will speed up clearing tasks. You need to be fairly strong to use it safely, but it can be hired (along with safety gear and a trained contractor).

Brushcutter A noisy, petrol-powered alternative to the scythe, the brushcutter will cut down tall weeds quickly. Some machines have a nylon line that can tackle only coarse grass and young nettles; others have a metal blade that cuts through vegetation such as brambles, old nettles and saplings up to 2.5 cm (1 in) in diameter, but these machines are potentially more dangerous.

Rotavator This machine will till the soil prior to planting, thereby saving the need to dig a plot. It is best used on weed-free soil, since it tends to chop up perennial weed roots, which then resprout. The alternative is to rotavate three or four times, leaving at least three weeks between rotavating, until the weeds are exhausted.

Stump remover Tree surgeons often supply this tool as part of tree removal. There are two types: one winches the stump out, the other grinds it out. Tree stumps can also be killed using chemicals.

Pressure washer Attached to a hose, this blasts water under pressure and will clean areas of paving after site clearance without having to use strong chemicals. It can also be used to clean wooden decks and furniture.

Pressure sprayer Use a pressure sprayer for weedkilling over a large area. You pump by hand to compress the container, and the diluted weedkiller is released from a hand-held lance with a nozzle on the end. Some sprayers have a handle, others are knapsack sprayers, carried on your back. You will need goggles, protective gloves and waterproof footwear.

▽ **HEDGE TRIMMER**
A powered hedge trimmer will trim a hedge much more quickly than garden shears. Electric models are cheap, lightweight and not too noisy. Petrol ones are heavier and noisier, but if you can handle them, they are efficient, long-lasting machines.

▷ **WOOD SHREDDER**
A shredder is an electric or petrol-driven machine that reduces branches and prunings to shreddings. In this way, instead of wood being burned it can be used on the compost heap, to mulch around plants, or as a weed suppressor in flowerbeds.

FIXING GARDEN STRUCTURES

Before replanting it makes sense to tackle repairs to any existing garden structures that you are planning to keep. Priorities would include repairing ramshackle fences or walls and any other landscape features that are unsafe or could become hazardous.

Repairs to garden structures can be undertaken at any time of year, but avoid freezing or very wet weather. Late autumn is a good time to repair unstable structures before winter winds cause damage; in addition, access to walls, fences and plant supports is easier while plants are dormant.

GARDEN WALLS

Bricks need to be frost resistant, or they will soon crumble. Assuming the correct bricks have been used and the wall is basically sound, it is worth protecting a wall from weather damage by dealing with crumbling mortar and protecting the top. Repointing the wall will keep joints watertight. For an attractive finish, match any repairs with the existing mortar and use the same joint type. You can best protect the top of a wall by fitting coping stones. These are shaped so that water runs off them, and they often overhang slightly, so water is shed away from the wall.

PATHS

On a flat site, a gravel path is suitable for both formal and informal garden styles and is easy and cheap to make. The merit of this type of path is that it is fairly long lasting but can be dismantled and the material reused if you change your mind later. A variation on the method of laying shown below is to lay plastic sheet or polypropylene membrane on a firm soil surface and then to add 2.5–5 cm (1–2 in) of medium-sized gravel.

REPOINTING BRICKWORK

YOU WILL NEED
Hammer, cold chisel
Goggles
Large and pointing trowels
Mortar
Wood with a straight edge

To make the mortar, mix two parts sand to one part cement. Add water in small amounts and mix well until the mortar stays on a trowel when it is turned upside down. The easiest way to finish a joint is to have the mortar flush with the brickwork (see below).

1 Use a chisel and hammer to chip out any weak or loose mortar between the bricks. The more of the old mortar you can get out, the better chance you will have of getting the new mortar inside the joints and of its staying in place.

2 Using a pointing trowel, work some mortar into a circular shape. Tilt the small trowel so it is at right angles to the large trowel. Cut a strip of mortar with the pointing trowel and push it forward using the underside of the trowel.

3 Push the mortar between the bricks, then slide the trowel along to release the mortar. Repeat the process, sliding the next lot of mortar into the first. Run the tip of the trowel over a straight piece of wood to remove excess mortar.

▽ **A GRAVEL PATH**
Gravel comes in different sizes: small 1.2 cm (½ in) gravel is difficult to walk on if it is more than 2.5 cm (1 in) deep, so use it over a layer of larger, 2.5 cm (1 in) gravel or hoggin (clay and stone mixture).

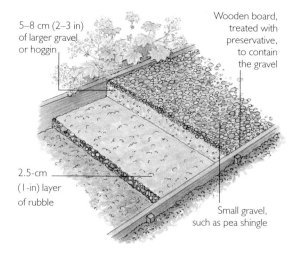

5–8 cm (2–3 in) of larger gravel or hoggin

Wooden board, treated with preservative, to contain the gravel

2.5-cm (1-in) layer of rubble

Small gravel, such as pea shingle

PATIOS

To level an uneven paved area made of slabs, first find out what is underneath the paving. Use a pick, crowbar or old spade to lever up a few of the uneven slabs. You may be lucky and find the paving lies on a bed of sand, perhaps held in place with blobs of mortar, or you might be faced with solid concrete. If the concrete is less than 10 cm (4 in) deep, you will probably be able to chip it out yourself. Thicker layers, and those with steel reinforcement, are best tackled by a contractor.

WOODEN POSTS

Posts that wobble when leaned on or pushed have rotted underground. If you catch the rot in time, you can bolt on a concrete spur to the sound post, otherwise you will have to replace it. The length of post needed depends on how it will be sunk into the ground, where you live, and how much weight the post is going to have to bear. Those held in place with hard core, then concrete, need a quarter of their length underground. If you use metal spikes instead of concrete, much shorter posts can be used

Using a spirit level, check frequently to make sure the posts are straight. To save having to dig lots of holes, it is worth hiring a post-hole auger.

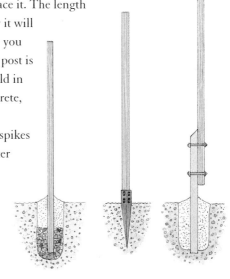

Hard core and concrete   Metal spike   Concrete spur

LEVELLING AN UNEVEN PAVING SLAB

YOU WILL NEED
Bolster chisel
Hammer
Hand trowel or spade
Bedding material, eg sand
Garden rake or tamper
Stiff brush
Protective clothing

Wear gloves and heavy-duty footwear when handling slabs, and goggles when chipping mortar. The slab may be uneven due to blobs of mortar on the underside or to underlying layers of hard core, sand, or aggregate. You may be able to even up the slab by removing the mortar and adding extra sand. You may need to add or subtract bedding material depending on whether the slab formerly sat too high or too low. Typically, you will find a layer of sand or sand and gravel mixed, and a thicker layer of hard core or finer rubble.

1 Use a bolster chisel and hammer to remove any blobs of mortar from the underside of the uneven slab.

2 Remove each underlying layer in turn and keep it in a separate pile. Discard any materials contaminated with soil.

3 Replace the layers in order. Firm down each layer with a tamper or the back of a garden rake. Check each layer is level.

4 Replace the slab, check it is even and level with its neighbours. If it is not, lift it up and add or take away sand until the slab is even.

5 Brush sand over the top of the paving using a stiff brush; it should settle into the joints. If the rest of the joints are mortared, brush in dry mortar and water gently.

▷ **PATIO CROSS-SECTION**
If you want to grow plants between paving slabs, leave the joints unmortared.

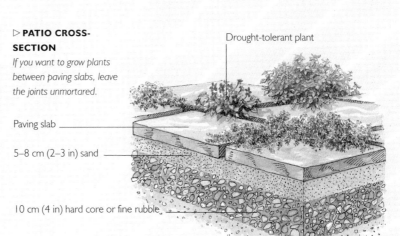

Drought-tolerant plant

Paving slab

5–8 cm (2–3 in) sand

10 cm (4 in) hard core or fine rubble

PREPARING THE GROUND

Once you have cleared the weeds and debris from your site, the ground can be marked out and prepared. Although you may be anxious to get on with the actual planting or building, taking time to do the basic work thoroughly will pay dividends in the long term.

You can tackle ground preparation a feature at a time, starting perhaps with a lawn or border, but if you are having a lot of hard landscaping done by a contractor, it is just as well to get all of this done first, before introducing any plants.

MARKING OUT

A laminated scale plan of the new-look garden is invaluable for marking out. Divide up the plot into paved areas and planting areas, taking measurements from a fixed point to avoid introducing errors. Now is the time you might want to make some practical adjustments: for instance, if the paving you have chosen will need a lot of cutting to fit your design, you can make life easier by tweaking the dimensions of nearby beds so that none of the slabs will need cutting.

You can judge informal shapes by eye, and there are various ways of marking them out. You can use a hose or leave a trail on the ground using a can of spray paint or a narrow-necked bottle filled with dry, free-flowing sand. A formal design of straight paths, squares or rectangular beds needs more precision, so arm yourself with a builder's square, pegs and string (see page 216 for advice on marking out circles).

PAVED AREAS

First strip the topsoil from areas that are going to be paved and add it to beds that are to be planted, then tamp the subsoil with a plate compactor. Depending on the depth of topsoil removed, you may need to add some hard core to raise the level to the required height. A paved area needs proper

◁ **PRECISE MEASURES**
Formal shapes need to be precisely measured. Use a wooden builder's square, pegs and string to make sure that any right-angled corners really are 90 degrees.

▷ **CURVED BEDS**
Before marking out an informal curved bed, experiment with different shapes by laying a garden hose on the ground and adjusting it until you have the shape you want.

drainage: a slight gradient, such as 1:80, falling to a bed or lawn is usually adequate.

PLANTING AREAS

Where you are starting to plant from scratch on soil that has been compacted by heavy machinery or was previously vacant ground, it is worth digging over the area first (see right). Usually this is a one-time task for ornamental beds, such as shrub borders, or laying a lawn. It gives you the opportunity to see what the soil is like and to remove any buried debris such as dead weed roots. Adding organic matter, such as well-rooted manure, will also help to open up the soil. Once the ground has been dug, it can be left over winter and planting can take place in the spring.

A heavy clay soil benefits most from digging, but timing is important. Aim to dig in autumn when the soil is moist, but not baked hard or very sticky. Sandy soil can be dug at any time. Digging is strenuous; if you are not used to manual work, spread the task over several months and take a break every 20 minutes or so.

SINGLE DIGGING

YOU WILL NEED
Stout footwear
Spade
String and pegs

Mark out the plot with pegs and string. Remove any turf or vegetation and divide the area into strips about 30 cm (1 ft) wide. Keep your back straight when digging, insert the spade vertically into the earth, and throw soil forward into the next trench, not to your side.

1 Start in a corner. Dig down to one spade's depth (a "spit"). Put the soil from the first trench to one side outside the plot to be dug (it will go into the last trench). Finish digging the first trench before moving on to the second.

2 Put a layer of organic matter in the bottom of the first trench and add the same amount to each trench as you go. Stand on the third strip to dig out the second trench; turn the soil into the first trench. Cut through and remove any roots .

3 Finish digging out the second trench, add organic matter, and turn the soil from trench three into it. Continue thus until the last trench; add organic matter, and fill it with the soil from the first trench. Don't walk on the soil you have dug.

LEVELLING GROUND

YOU WILL NEED
Spirit level
String and pegs
Length of straight wood
Garden rake

For most planted areas, the only levelling you need to do is to rake over the ground after it has been dug over. Rake in one direction all over the area, then again at right angles, picking up any large stones as you go along.

For a formal bed, or where you want to make a lawn, it is worth getting the ground really level. Any bumps or hollows in the ground will make mowing difficult – in some parts the grass will be scalped and in others it will grow too long. Mark out the area so that you have a grid of pegs at equal intervals, say 1.5–2 m (5–7 ft) apart.

1 Lay a piece of wood across the top of two neighbouring stakes. Use a carpenter's level to check if the pegs are level. If they are not level, adjust them by hammering one in farther until the carpenter's level indicates they are level.

2 Tie brightly coloured string tightly between the pegs. The ideal pegs to use are flat-topped but are shaped so string can be tied under the head without slipping. The string must be secure and tied at the same level on all the pegs. The string now marks a level line.

3 Use a garden rake to rake the soil level with the string line. Use the back of the rake to move large amounts of earth into hollows and the front to pull earth away from bumps.

PLANTING

Start by planting long-term plants, such as trees, shrubs, and climbers. Use these as a backbone for your planting scheme; later on you can add smaller or more temporary plants to provide seasonal highlights. Combine plants with similar care requirements so that they will thrive with minimum attention.

Allow long-term plants space to mature; check the mature height and spread in a reference book. You can plant shrubs and climbers closer than recommended if you are prepared to control their growth by pruning, but this may spoil the natural shape of the plant and is rarely practical for a tree.

WHEN TO PLANT

Hardy container-grown plants can, in theory, be planted at any time of year, but it is much easier and more pleasant to plant in either spring or autumn. Summer planting means almost daily watering and

the plants will struggle to get established. In general, deciduous plants are best planted after leaf fall, during the dormant season. Evergreens are best planted in early autumn or in spring. Delay planting tender plants, such as summer bedding, until they have been acclimatized to the outside and the last frosts have passed.

PLANTING BASICS

Whatever the plant, even if it is drought tolerant when established, make sure it is well watered before and after planting. Dig a generous planting

PLANTING A TREE

YOU WILL NEED
Spade
Organic matter
Bamboo cane
Stake, hammer and tree tie
for trees more than 1.2 m
(4 ft) tall

The step-by-step photographs show you how to plant a container-grown tree more than 1.2 m (4 ft) tall. For smaller trees you can skip the staking steps.

A stake needs to be in place for only a couple of years, so untreated softwood is fine. The stake should be no more than one-third the height of the tree when it has been hammered into the ground.

1 *Clear an area of about 1 sq m (10 sq ft). Water the tree thoroughly. Dig a large hole, twice the size of the rootball. Mix the dug-out topsoil with a soil improver such as garden compost if it is available.*

2 *Hammer in a wooden stake, just off centre for a container-grown tree to allow space for the rootball, but in the centre of the hole for a bare-root tree.*

3 *Remove the tree from its container. Position the tree in the hole so that the surface of the soil is at the same level as it was in the container. Lay a straight piece of wood or cane across the hole to check the level.*

4 *Backfill the mixed topsoil and soil improver into the hole. You may need to tie the tree stem to the stake with raffia while filling the hole or ask someone to hold it to keep it vertical. Firm the soil as you fill the hole.*

hole, twice the size of the rootball, and clear a space around the plant so that it does not have to compete with grass, weeds, or other plants.

TREES

The way to plant a typical container-grown tree sold in a garden centre is detailed below. Trees less than 1.2 m (4 ft) high do not need staking unless the site is very exposed. A bare-root tree is planted in a similar way, but more care is needed to prevent the roots from drying out. (Soak the roots in a bucket of water while the hole is being dug.) In addition, when refilling the hole, make sure there is soil all around the roots.

SHRUBS

When planting a shrub border, set the shrubs out in their pots before planting to make sure they are in the right positions. Dig a large hole for each one, as you would when planting a tree; there is no need to stake shrubs. Fill large spaces between young shrubs with annuals or mulch with bark chips, which are more attractive than bare earth.

PLANTING CLIMBERS AGAINST A FENCE

YOU WILL NEED
Vine eyes
Wire and pliers
Bamboo canes, raffia

Put up all the horizontal wires about 30 cm (1 ft) apart before planting, rather than adding the higher ones later. Tie in the plant growth with raffia or soft string, using a figure-of-eight loop and simple knot.

1 Screw vine eyes into the fence posts; the wires should be held at least 5 cm (2 in) away from the fence. Thread the wire through the eyes, tighten it, and use pliers to twist the ends around the taut wire.

2 Clear the ground around the planting area, especially any weeds coming from under the fence. Plant the climber 15–25 cm (6–10 in) away from the fence, but tilt it towards the fence.

3 Insert canes to create a fan shape and attach them to the wires. Cut away the ties holding the plant to the original cane. Spread out the stems and tie them to the canes and the lower wires.

5 Once the hole has been filled, firm the earth in place with your foot; this will make sure the roots are in contact with the soil. Do not mound up soil around the tree stem, but put any excess on other planting beds.

6 You will need an adjustable tree tie so that as the girth of the stem increases, the tie can be loosened. A buckle tree tie is easy to adjust; nail the tie to the stake, not the tree.

7 Water the ground around the tree after planting and thereafter during dry spells for the first couple of years. A 5-cm (2-in) layer of bark chips covering the bare ground around the tree will help to retain moisture.

△ **WALLS**
To attach wires to a brick wall, use these special nails, which are hammered into the mortar.

DIVIDING PERENNIALS

YOU WILL NEED
Garden fork
Hand trowel
Damp hessian or compost
Knife or border spade

Autumn or spring is the best time to lift and divide perennials. Most need to be divided every four years or so – a plant that has ceased to flower, or flowers only at the edges of the clump, is a prime candidate. Choose a day when the soil is warm and moist, but the weather is not too hot or windy.

1 *Ease a garden fork under the clump. You may need to loosen the soil all around the clump first before lifting it. Move the plant to an area of empty ground nearby.*

2 *Discard any old or diseased portions of the clump, retaining only the young healthy sections. Cover the roots of plants not being divided with moist compost or damp hessian.*

3 *Pull the clump apart with your hands, or use a knife or sharp spade if the crown is too tough. Each section needs a healthy shoot and a fistful of fibrous roots to be viable.*

4 *If there is a lot of foliage, remove some of the older leaves. Replant young, healthy sections in a drift (see box below), spacing them all the same distance apart and water them in well.*

PLANTING IN DRIFTS

YOU WILL NEED
Watering can
Hand trowel
Sharp knife

Bare earth, such as at the front of beds or between long-term plantings, can be filled quickly by adding low-growing perennials or bedding plants. Correctly spaced, these plants will soon grow together to form a drift of colour.

1 *Give plants a good soaking before planting. Compost in small pots is prone to drying out, but peat-moss-based compost is easier to rewet if you add two drops of washing-up liquid to a full watering can and stir well before watering.*

2 *Space out the plants to fill gaps in the border. To make a drift, arrange the plants informally, not in rows as you would for a formal bedding scheme.*

3 *Remove plants from their pots or packs. Bedding strips, in which the plant roots grow together, must be cut into sections with a sharp knife. Use a hand trowel to dig a hole, and firm the plant in gently with your fingers.*

CLIMBERS

To get climbers to grow up trees or tall supports, or over bushes, dig a hole some distance from the support and lead the climber towards it, using a bamboo cane or a piece of rope. Where you want a climber to cover a fence, wall or eyesore, put in horizontal wires to which you can tie the climber. When planting a climber or wall shrub against a wall, tree or hedge, dig a hole some 15–25 cm (6–10 in) away, where the soil will be more fertile and moist. Add a bucket of organic matter to the excavated topsoil, water the plant well after planting, and add mulch around it to compensate for the poor, dry soil.

PERENNIALS

These plants are fairly tolerant and can be planted in spring, summer or autumn – those of borderline hardiness in your area are best put in in spring or summer. Any variety of perennial can be planted in a group of three to five plants, which will then grow and merge to create a drift. You can also line them up to edge a bed, or a large plant can form a single specimen. Buy perennials in small pots in spring or later on as larger plants, which can be divided before you plant them out.

BULBS

Dry bulbs are dormant, so if you cannot plant them straightaway, store them in a cool, dry place for a week or two but do not forget about them. A hand trowel is adequate for planting a few bulbs, but a bulb planter or spade can be quicker when planting large quantities. Most bulbs prefer a free-draining soil; if the soil is heavy and wet, a shallow layer of grit or sharp sand at the bottom of the planting hole will help to prevent the bulbs from rotting. Bulbs are usually covered with twice their height of soil, but check the packaging for precise planting details for different types of bulb.

BEDDING PLANTS

You should delay planting out tender plants until after the last frost date. Prior to this the plants must be acclimatized to outdoor conditions gradually over a seven to ten day period. This can be done either using a cold frame (a small glass or plastic chest with a lid) or by moving plants out on to a sheltered patio during the day then bringing them in at night. Bedding plants that are used informally are planted in drifts, in the same way as small perennials, but for formal patterns, set the plants out first, spacing them accurately. If unseasonal frost is forecast after planting, cover the plants with a double layer of garden fleece overnight and remove it when the danger of frost is passed. It is important that bedding plants are not left in their small pots too long or they will be at risk of drying out or running short of nutrients. If planting is delayed, either pot them into larger pots or give them a dilute liquid feed.

MOVING PLANTS

You can move trees and shrubs (including fruit-bearing ones) and replant them in new positions, provided it is done at the right time of year. Most perennials can be given a new lease of life by lifting mature clumps, dividing them and replanting the young sections. Often the best way to tackle a border full of perennial weeds is to lift out the plants you want to keep, heel them in in a holding site, then proceed as you would with vacant ground (see pages 202–203).

TRANSPLANTING SHRUBS

YOU WILL NEED
Garden fork
Strong bag or hessian
Spade
Watering can

Transplant evergreen shrubs in mid- to late spring; move deciduous shrubs any time in the dormant season – from autumn to spring. To encourage a large shrub to develop new feeder roots, slice through the roots all around the plant several months before transplanting it.

1 Cut a trench around the shrub, 30–45 cm (12–18 in) away from the stems. Sever any roots around and under the shrub with a sharp spade or pruning saw. Insert a fork under the shrub and lift.

2 Ease the shrub into a carrying bag or on to hessian. Work quickly to cover the roots to stop them from drying out. The tips of evergreens may wilt rapidly.

3 It helps to have the new planting hole already prepared before you move the shrub to its new position. If the shrub is too heavy for one person, get help or use a wheelbarrow.

4 Plant the shrub in the usual way, firming the soil down with your foot. Water the plant in well. A wilting evergreen shrub should recover after a day or two.

AFTERCARE

Aftercare of new plants need not be time-consuming. An easy way to reduce maintenance is to apply a mulch to the soil surface, which will cut down evaporation from the soil and block out light so that weed seeds cannot germinate and compete with the new plants.

Mid-spring is the best time to apply a mulch; the soil is starting to warm up and is full of moisture from the winter rains. The ground must be free of perennial weeds before the mulch is put on.

WHICH MULCH?

There are two types of mulch, loose and sheet. Loose mulch can be applied around plants, or a sheet can be put down before planting; often the two types are combined.

A loose mulch on its own must be at least 5 cm (2 in) deep to be effective; a 8-cm (3-in) thick layer is even better, but is often not cost effective. Loose mulch will need topping up every year, although as the plants grow there will be less bare ground that needs to be mulched, and, in time, organic mulches rot down and improve the soil.

Sheet mulches are low maintenance and long-term, but they can restrict your planting schemes. A thin layer of loose mulch on top will improve their appearance. Two of the cheapest sheet mulches are newspaper and black polythene. Several layers of newspaper make a surprisingly effective mulch, but it lasts only one season. Black

LAYING DOWN A SHEET MULCH

YOU WILL NEED
Sheet mulch
Scissors/sharp knife
Hand trowel
Spade
Loose mulch

Sheet mulches are only practical on bare ground that has not yet been planted. They work well for ground-cover schemes using shrubs or evergreen perennials that will be left in place for several years. The ground must be cleared of weeds, and any soil preparation, such as digging in organic matter and raking, should be completed before laying sheet mulch.

1 Lay the sheet mulch on the ground and flatten it with your hands. You need an overhang of 10–15 cm (4–6 in) at each edge.

2 Using the coloured grid on the sheet mulch to space the plants, position them where you want them to go. Remember to take their final spread into account,

3 Cut a cross in the sheet large enough to accommodate the plant, and peel back the corners. Dig out a hole twice the size of the plant's rootball.

4 Take the plant out of its pot and plant it in the usual way. Replace the peeled back sheet, cutting off enough to make it lie flat around the plant stem.

polythene is effective, but it is tricky to get it to lie flat and it does not let water drain away, so puddles can form – if this happens, make some drainage holes with a garden fork. Purpose-made sheet mulch, such as woven polypropylene or bonded-fibre fleece is easier to lay, effective and durable, but expensive to lay over a large area.

An attractive option around small plants is cocoa shells, a waste product from the chocolate industry. They are pleasant to handle, but must be watered in to prevent them from blowing away. Bark chips are the most widely used loose mulch and are ideal for woodland shrub borders. Large chips of actual bark last longer and look better than wood chips. Farmyard manure and spent mushroom compost are cheap and worth using in larger gardens. Spent mushroom compost contains lime; this makes it ideal for vegetables, but not as good for fruit or acid-loving plants.

Gravel in various grades and colours is attractive for rock gardens, paths or gravel gardens. It does not contribute to soil fertility, but can improve drainage and cool the soil surface in summer.

FREE MULCH

Set up a compost bin so you can recycle plant waste from the garden (and the kitchen) to use as a mulch and soil improver. Don't put diseased plants, perennial weed roots or seeding or flowering weeds into the bin, or mix green, sappy waste with shredded, woody waste. It should rot down in six months or so.

OTHER AFTERCARE

Loose organic mulch will help to feed your soil as earthworms pull it down into the soil, where bacteria break it down. In most ornamental borders, no further feeds will be needed. Plants that do need feeding include those in containers; fruit, vegetables and lawns; and plants that have been bred to produce large flowers, such as roses and dahlias.

△ **SEEP HOSE**
On a newly seeded or planted bed, a seep, or leaky, hose that allows water to ooze out gently along its length is an efficient way to water. The hose can be attached to a timer on an outside tap.

▽ **LOOSE MULCHES**
Many different materials can be used as a loose mulch. Take into account not only their appearance but also their durability and cost. It is much cheaper to buy a load of loose mulch than a lot of small bags.

5 *Secure the edges of the sheet to hold it in place by making a V-shaped trench with a spade and pushing the edges of the sheet down into the ground.*

6 *Cover the sheet with a 2.5-cm (1-in) layer of loose mulch of cocoa shells (shown here), bark chips or gravel to disguise its appearance*

Cocoa shells

Bark chips

Gravel

Garden compost

PRUNING

While tackling overgrown trees is best left to a tree surgeon, pruning other established plants such as shrubs is straightforward and can be very beneficial. Apart from pruning to curtail a plant's growth, you can prune to stimulate flowering, encourage young growth and maintain a neat appearance.

▷ SHORTEN NEW GROWTH

Prune while shrubs are young to keep them compact and neat. Take off half to two-thirds of the new growth, but do not cut into the older wood. Remove any dead shoots.

▷ CUT DOWN ALL STEMS

Prune all stems either down to 5 cm (2 in) from the ground or to a low stump. Start pruning a year after planting, then repeat the process every one or two years thereafter.

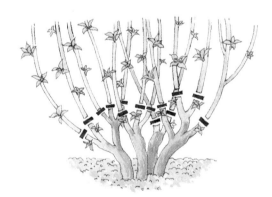

▷ CUT OUT ONE STEM IN THREE

Start when the shrub is about three years old. First, cut back the oldest and weakest stems to just above ground level. If the shrub is still overcrowded, take out a few healthy stems from the centre of the bush.

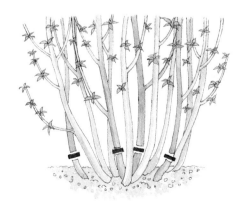

Most shrubs that need pruning can be dealt with by one of the methods shown left. If you know the scientific name of the shrub, you can check the pruning method or the time to prune in a plant reference book; if you do not know its name, you should use the "one-in-three" method (see below).

PRUNING METHODS

The most common method is the one-in-three. It is used on many spring-flowering shrubs after flowering. By having a third of the oldest stems removed each year, the shrub keeps an open shape, with no tangle of congested stems. Stand back and look at the shrub between cuts to make sure you are left with a balanced shape.

Some shrubs can cope with hard pruning; that is, all their stems can be pruned either down to 5 cm (2 in) from the ground or to a low stump each year. Hard pruning of vigorous shrubs stimulates a lot of young growth so it is often used for shrubs with colourful winter stems, such as the dogwood *(Cornus alba),* or where the young foliage is particularly attractive. You need to mulch and feed a shrub after annual hard pruning, since it can weaken a plant; if growing conditions are poor, hard prune only every other year.

Be wary of cutting into the old wood of shrubs such as brooms and sun roses, since they rarely sprout from old wood and you will be left with a gap or could even kill the shrub. However, they do benefit from pruning, which keeps them neat and flowering well. The secret is to prune them while they are young and to take off just half to two-thirds of the new growth. Do not cut into the older wood unless there are dead shoots; if there are, just remove them.

CLIMBERS

Since climbers are nothing more than floppy shrubs, in many cases the pruning is similar. Old woody stems, for example, are cut out to leave room for new stems. An important difference is that new growth needs to be tied in to supports.

The pruning time for clematis depends on its flowering time. Most clematis fall into one of three groups.

Group 1 Spring-flowering clematis flower on the previous season's growth and need pruning only if they are overgrown. Prune right after flowering if necessary.

Group 2 This group includes the large-flowered hybrid clematis that often flower early on the old wood and again later on the new wood. Wait until late winter or early spring to prune.

Group 3 Plants in this group flower late in summer on the current season's wood. They make new growth from the base of the plant each year, so cut back hard in late winter or early spring.

Before pruning a climbing rose, find out if it is a true climber or a rambler – pruning methods differ (see below). More drastic pruning, such as cutting all the stems to the ground in late summer, can help neglected ramblers.

△ **LAVENDER BUSHES**
These are worth pruning annually, but only start a year or so after planting. In spring, look for new growth at the base of the plant and cut back to the new growth. This usually means to within 5–10 cm (2–4 in) of the ground.

▷ **RAMBLER ROSES**
Prune after flowering. For every new stem emerging from the base, cut one old or weak stem right down to the base. Tie in the new shoots, keeping them as horizontal as possible to promote flowering. Prune all side shoots to two or three sets of leaves from the stem.

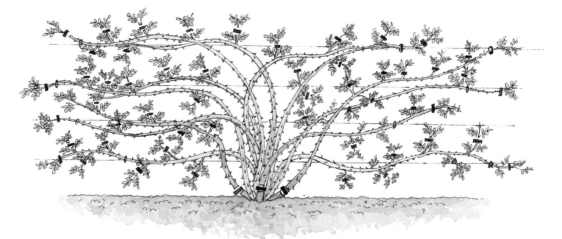

▷ **CLIMBING ROSES**
During the dormant season, cut out any dead stems and remove weak or thin growth. Don't worry if there are no new stems coming up from the base of the plant. Shorten those side shoots that flowered during the summer.

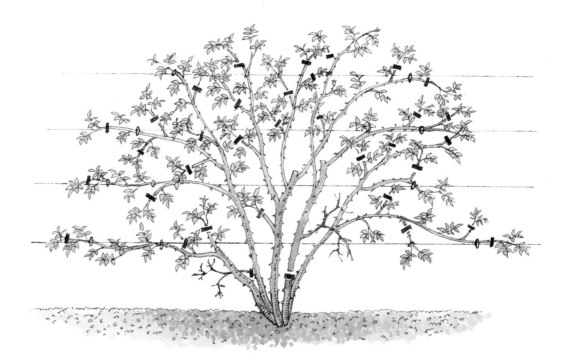

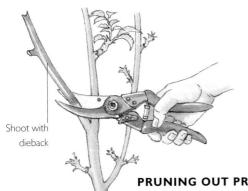

Shoot with dieback

Shoot to be removed

▷ **REVERTED SHOOTS**
Sometimes a shoot that is unlike the others will appear – the most common example is a variegated plant that produces an all-green shoot. Cut such shoots out as soon as you notice them or they could take over the whole shrub.

PRUNING OUT PROBLEMS

Apart from pruning certain shrubs routinely to promote flowering or to encourage young growth, you can prune to remove problem branches, which, if left, could cause harm to the shrub. This pruning out of problems as they occur applies to all shrubs, even the ones that are not pruned routinely. Illustrated above are some instances in which pruning can help.

In addition, a severe winter can take its toll on shrubs: winds can snap branches; cold winds can scorch foliage; and late frosts can catch the young growth of shrubs such as pieris. When this occurs, wait until the worst of the winter weather is over and then cut back to healthy wood.

WHEN TO PRUNE

Late winter or early spring is a good time for routine pruning, but when you are growing a shrub for its flowers, check that you will not lose the display. Early-flowering shrubs produce their best blooms on the previous year's growth, so prune soon after flowering to allow the shrub time to produce new flower shoots for the following year.

△ **DIEBACK**
Cut out a dead or diseased shoot as soon as it is seen to stop infection spreading to the rest of the shrub. Cut back to healthy wood just above a bud. Put prunings in the dustbin or burn them, and dip blades in a chlorine solution between cuts to stop the spread of infection.

▷ **CROSSING BRANCHES**
Crossing branches, or branches growing very close together, may rub against each other, and their protective outer bark may become damaged, making them prone to infection. Cut out the weakest or most damaged branch.

Shrubs that bloom after midsummer flower best on the current season's growth. Prune these in early spring to stimulate new growth. If you prune late-flowering shrubs after flowering, new growth will not have time to mature before winter, so evergreen shrubs are usually pruned in spring, after the last hard frost.

Summer pruning is sometimes needed in addition to pruning in the dormant season – for example, to control long whippy growth on wisteria and to maintain the shape of trained forms of fruit such as cordons.

Prune *Prunus* family in early summer, rather than in the dormant season, to reduce the risk of silverleaf entering the plant through pruning cuts. A few plants, such as vines (*Vitis* species), bleed when cut, and this can seriously weaken the plant. To limit the damage, don't prune when the plants are actively growing; midwinter is the best time.

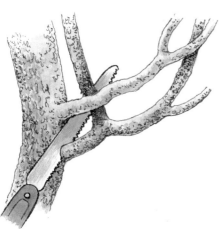

▷ **REMOVING SUCKERS**
Some shrubs are grafted on to a more vigorous rootstock. If this throws up its own shoots, known as suckers, they must be removed. Dig back the earth to find where the sucker emerges from the main stem, and pull or cut it near to the stem.

▷ **SHAPING THE TOP OF
A HEDGE**

*If you inherit a hedge that has
been cut square across the
top, it is possible to taper the
top, as shown, to minimize
snow damage. However,
tapering the sides of a conifer
hedge should be started while
it is young, since most conifers
will not resprout from old wood.*

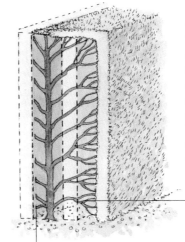

◁ **REDUCING THE
WIDTH OF A HEDGE**

*You can reduce the width of
hedging plants that respond
well to drastic cutting back.
In year one, cut back one side
hard, almost to the main stem,
prune the other side normally.
The next year, cut back the
second side hard and prune
the other side normally.*

Normal pruning

Cutting back hard

HEDGES

You can renovate hedges such as box, beech, hawthorn and holly by cutting back hard, but only a few conifers, such as yew, will sprout from old wood. Renovate deciduous hedges in the dormant season and evergreens in spring, and then clear weeds and debris from under and beside the hedge. Follow with a balanced feed, and mulch well to encourage fresh new growth.

FRUIT TREES

Renovate apple trees in the dormant season. A tree more than 3.5 m (12 ft) tall is best dealt with by a tree surgeon or professional fruit grower, but it is worthwhile to attempt to prune a smaller tree yourself (see below). Mark the branches you intend to cut with chalk or spray paint, then stand back and check the effect before making the cuts.

PRUNING TOOLS

Hand pruners will cope with stems that are 1.2 cm (½ in) thick or less, which is all most people will need. If you have to tackle thicker stems, such as those on old shrubs, you will need heavy-duty tools, such as long-handled loppers, a telescopic pole pruner for high branches, and a pruning saw for really thick branches. For hedges you need garden shears or an electric or petrol-driven hedge trimmer. One-handed shears are useful for clipping heathers or box edging, since they allow you to hold the trimmings in the other hand.

Before putting tools away, clean plant sap off the blades and close them. Wear protective clothing when tackling prickly shrubs: long sleeves and tough gloves that protect your wrists, as well as your hands, are a good idea. Goggles will protect your eyes from twigs.

▽ **RENOVATING AN
APPLE TREE**

*A neglected apple tree will be
tall and congested, with a lot
of thin twiggy growth. It can be
rejuvenated by removing dead
wood, crossing branches,
vertical branches and excessive
thin growth. The end result
should be a more open
framework of branches.*

Apple tree before pruning

Apple tree after pruning

WEEDS AND WEEDING

Even if you cleared the garden before planting, weeds will still keep appearing, not only in beds and borders but between paving, on drives, and in lawns. A combination of hand weeding and chemical weedkillers will help you to get the upper hand.

▷ **HAND FORK**

Tug at a perennial weed by hand, and you will get the top growth but leave behind extensive roots that can resprout. Instead, when the soil is moist, use a hand fork to ease out the whole plant.

▽ **DUTCH HOE**

A crop of annual weed seedlings can be quickly dealt with by pushing and pulling a Dutch hoe just below the surface of the soil. Hoe on a warm, windy day and the severed seedlings can be left to shrivel up.

It is difficult to eradicate weeds completely, particularly if they have had the upper hand for several years, but there are several tools and techniques that can help to control them. To decide how to tackle weeds, you first need to know whether they are annuals or perennials. Annual weeds produce copious amounts of seed, which can survive for years in the soil. Every time the soil is dug, a fresh crop of seedlings will appear. The real problem weeds, however, are the perennial ones: once their roots are in the soil they can keep regrowing from them.

ANNUAL WEEDS

For a few years, expect flushes of annual weeds every time you disturb the earth. A combination of hoeing and hand-weeding will get rid of them at the seedling stage. Mulching will prevent annual weed seeds from germinating since it deprives them of light, but seed may be blown on top of the mulch; if this happens, pull out any seedlings by hand. Annual flowerbeds, vegetable plots and other areas of bare ground can be hoed regularly. Use a Dutch hoe and keep the blade really sharp so that it cuts through the weed seedlings as it is pushed and pulled near the surface of the soil.

PERENNIAL WEEDS

Digging out perennial weeds is worthwhile as long as you get as much of the root out as possible, then throw away the weed rather than composting it. Where it is not practical to dig weeds out, it is worth using a systemic weedkiller. These chemicals are sprayed on the plant's leaves, and are then carried down inside the plant to the roots. Do not expect to see instant results – it will take a week or so to see signs of decline. A product based on glyphosate is particularly effective, although some weeds have such deep or extensive roots that a second application may be needed.

Glyphosate breaks down rapidly on contact with soil, so the ground can be replanted within a week of treating the weeds.

To deal with perennial weeds among garden plants, apply weedkiller to the weed only. There are various applicators, varying from sticks that you wipe over the leaves to hand-held sprays or aerosols. When using a spray, remember that wind can carry fine droplets on to nearby plants. Take care when using chemicals near ponds and waterways.

LAWNS

You can dig out lawn weeds by hand, but you must take care to remove the minimum amount of soil. A special tool with a long, thin blade, known as a daisy grubber, exists, but it is time-consuming to use. A spot weeder, in either spray or stick form, will deal with most broad-leaved weeds, but if coarse grass is a problem, try repeated slashing with a knife to weaken it. For a very weedy lawn, it is best to use a "weed and feed" dressing, which can be applied to the whole lawn from mid- to late spring through to autumn.

HARD SURFACES

Weeds such as grasses that come up between cracks in paving can be cut out with a weeding knife or an old kitchen knife. Where a whole driveway or path has weeds, you will need a path weedkiller. This will not only kill the

▽ **DRIBBLE BAR**

Dribble bars can be bought as an attachment to fit on to a watering can of the same make. They offer an economical way to apply weedkiller evenly over a large area such as a lawn.

◁ **WEEDING KNIFE**

Use the blade on the outside of the knife to cut weeds growing between paving, then turn the knife over and hook out the weeds with as much of the root as possible.

existing weeds but should also prevent more weeds from growing for up to a year. These weedkillers are fairly strong chemicals, which must be kept away from garden plants; take care that the wet chemical does not run off the path or get carried on your shoes to the lawn.

SAFETY

Although the packaging and applicators supplied with weedkillers have improved so they need only minimal handling, always follow the instructions on the box when using chemicals. Buy only as much as you need in a season and store any surplus in a safe place, away from children.

◁ **SPRAYER**

A quick and economical way of dealing with a large area of perennial weeds is to buy concentrated weedkiller and use it diluted in a sprayer. The diluted weedkiller comes out under pressure through a nozzle on the end of a lance. Never use a sprayer that has had weedkiller in it to disperse liquid fertilizer: residue weedkiller can damage your plants.

LAWN CARE

If you have renovated or changed an existing lawn, keep it healthy and in good condition with a suitable mowing regime and an annual feed. Where a new lawn is needed, you can use seed or lay turf; do the work preferably in spring or early autumn.

▷ **KEEP A CLEAR EDGE**
A lawn edge near a flowerbed will gradually break down. Restore a crisp edge using a straight-edge and half-moon cutter or sharp spade.

Caring for your lawn does not mean just dosing it with chemicals to keep it weed-free, or meticulously trimming the lawn edges every week. Modern lawncare aims to keep the grass healthy enough to fight off most problems.

While the grass is growing, it will need mowing regularly, with any feed or weedkillers applied in late spring to early summer. A lawn that suffers from drought over the summer is best left to recover by itself – there is little point in watering it. Autumn is the ideal time to rake out any dead grass and repair lawn edges.

MOWING AND EDGING

Grass that is cut little and often will be less stressed than grass left to grow long then scalped, so you need to mow regularly during the growing season. If you cut off just 1.2–2 cm (½–¾ in) each time you mow, you can take the grassbox off the mower and leave the clippings on the lawn.

Lay a mowing edge, such as a line of bricks or paving, slightly lower than the lawn. You can then mow straight over them and dispense with regular trimming of the edges.

FEEDING AND WEEDING

It is well worth feeding a lawn so that it grows vigorously and can compete against weeds. Products exist that contain both feed and weedkiller; some are available with mosskiller, too. The best time to apply these is when the grass and weeds are actively growing. Even application is important or the effect will be patchy. Buy or hire a wheeled spreader to help apply dry products; use a watering can and dribble bar for liquids. In shady, damp sites, moss competes with grass, and here you will need to reduce the shade, improve the drainage, or apply mosskiller annually.

▷ **MAKING A CIRCLE**
Take a length of string or rope the diameter of the final circle, and tie the ends together. Insert a stout broom handle firmly into the ground. Loop one end of the string over it, and the other over a small, sharp stick. Holding the string taut all the time, mark out the circle.

RAKING

Fallen leaves are best removed from the lawn with a leaf rake, wheeled leaf sweeper or garden vacuum. Dead grass and dead moss – known as thatch – build up on the soil surface and must be scratched out with a spring-tine rake or a powered scarifier. Once this is done, you can resow any bare patches with a matching grass seed mix.

A NEW LAWN

Laying turf is the quickest way to create a new lawn, but seed is cheaper. Whatever you choose, the ground needs to be prepared and levelled first. If you opt for seed, choose a good-quality mixture and sow according to the instructions. You may need to protect the seed from birds, even if it has been treated with bird deterrent.

LAYING TURF

YOU WILL NEED
Garden rake
Turf
Pegs and string
Plank
Knife

Autumn is the ideal time to lay turf, but it can be laid at any time of year as long as the ground is not frozen or very dry. Choose a supplier who offers specific types of grass for different uses and allows you to see samples before ordering. Fresh turf is essential; if it has been recently harvested it will be a fresh green colour – avoid any that smells rotten or is starting to go yellow.

For ease of laying and handling, the turf should be cut so that it is of an even thickness, and it should hold together. Turf will keep rolled up for a day or two after cutting if the weather is cool and the soil is kept moist. Otherwise, it needs to be unrolled on a patio in a lightly shaded place and kept watered. When laying a large lawn, it helps to put down planks over the newly laid turf and to work from these.

1 Mark out the shape of the lawn with pegs and string. It is easier to lay a large square or rectangle of turf and to cut the lawn into its final shape later.

2 Gently firm the soil with the back of your heels. Start in one corner and work in a line across the plot.

3 Unroll the first turf strip against a straight edge. Position the second roll so that the end is just overlapping the end of the first roll. Firmly press down the overlapping edges. Complete the row, leaving any overhanging edges to be dealt with later on.

4 For second and subsequent rows, stagger the joints (as you would bricks in a wall) by overlapping the boundary of the lawn; the extra can be trimmed off later. Overlap the edges of the turf rolls, pressing down hard; this allows for any soil shrinkage.

5 After laying the lawn, soak it until the soil underneath is wet. Water daily if the weather is dry. After a couple of weeks, trim the overhanging lawn edges, using a sharp spade or half-moon cutter, then mow with the mower on its highest setting.

GARDEN TOOLS

The right tools make gardening tasks much easier, quicker and safer. You will use the basic, simple tools for digging, weeding, planting, watering and pruning as long as you are gardening, so buy good-quality tools that will last. It is less necessary to buy some of the larger power tools.

▽ HAND TOOLS

Good-quality hand tools will last a lifetime, so it is worth buying those you will use constantly straightaway – and looking after them. Stainless steel can be wiped clean and cuts through soil easily.

The tools you need and use while taming a wilderness or putting in new garden features aren't necessarily going to be useful in the long-term. So, particularly with power tools, you need to assess how much you are going to use them in the future to decide whether to buy or hire them. It is not just a question of money – most power tools are awkward to store, and need regular maintenance. As a rule of thumb, if you will use a tool more than twice a year, it is worth buying; otherwise hiring is a better option.

TOOLS TO HIRE

If you have a large garden, it is often a good idea to rent a shredder, power scarifier and brushcutter once a year to help with seasonal chores. Always make sure you know how to work the tool and see it working before hiring it. You should also be supplied with the right safety gear.

TOOLS TO BUY

Hand tools worth buying early on are a garden trowel, hand fork, secateurs, garden shears, spade, fork, Dutch hoe, soil rake, lawn rake, broom, wheelbarrow and a couple of watering cans. Power tools to buy include a mower, hedge trimmer and, possibly, a shredder. Petrol versions of power tools cost more than electric ones, but last longer. Always use a residual current device (RCD) and check the cable for wear frequently.

Dutch hoe

Half-moon cutter

Hole auger

Spade

Fork

Spring-tine rake

Hand trowel and fork

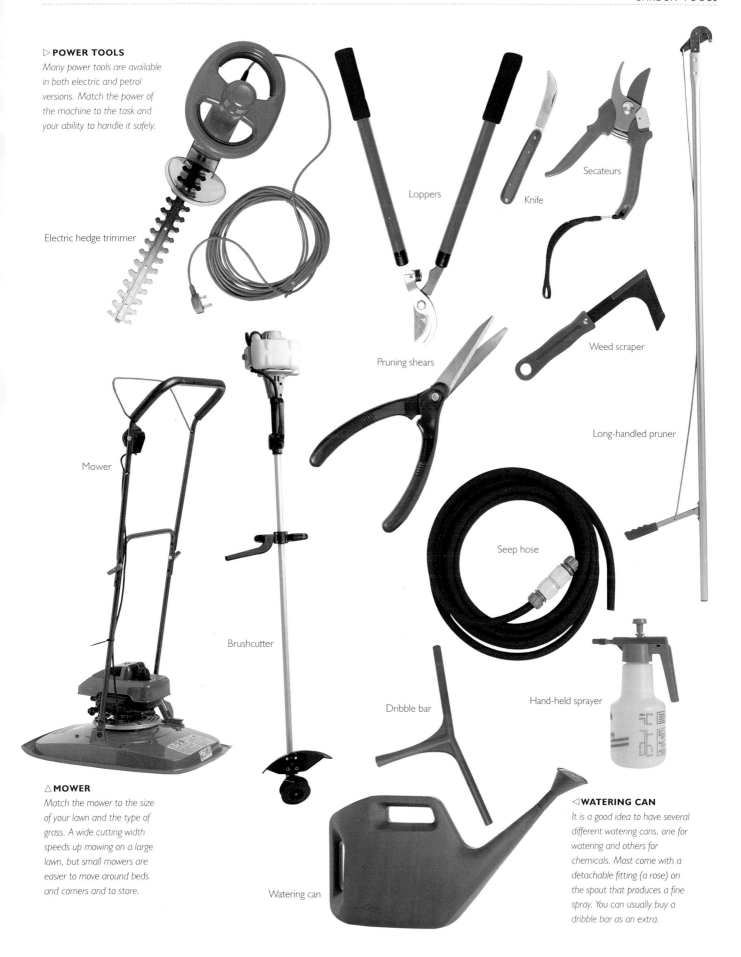

▷ **POWER TOOLS**

Many power tools are available in both electric and petrol versions. Match the power of the machine to the task and your ability to handle it safely.

Electric hedge trimmer

Loppers

Knife

Secateurs

Pruning shears

Weed scraper

Long-handled pruner

Mower

Seep hose

Brushcutter

Dribble bar

Hand-held sprayer

△ **MOWER**

Match the mower to the size of your lawn and the type of grass. A wide cutting width speeds up mowing on a large lawn, but small mowers are easier to move around beds and corners and to store.

Watering can

◁ **WATERING CAN**

It is a good idea to have several different watering cans, one for watering and others for chemicals. Most come with a detachable fitting (a rose) on the spout that produces a fine spray. You can usually buy a dribble bar as an extra.

219

INDEX

ACKNOWLEDGMENTS

If the publishers have unwittingly infringed copyright in any illustration reproduced, they would pay an appropriate fee on being satisfied to the owner's title.

t = top; b = bottom; l = left; r = right; c = centre

1 Marcus Harpur; 2–3 Claire Davies/ Garden Picture Library, 3 Jerry Harpur; 4 S. & O. Mathews; 6b S. & O. Mathews; 7t Andrew Lawson (Designer: Penelope Hobhouse), 7b Gary Rogers; 8 Juliette Wade; 9t Jerry Harpur (Plettenberg Bay, SA), 9b Jerry Harpur; 10–11 Steve Wooster; 12 Jerry Harpur; 13t Marcus Harpur (Park Farm, Chelmsford, Essex), 13b John Glover/ Garden Picture Library; 14 Liz Dobbs, 14–15 Marcus Harpur (Designer: Beth Chatto); 16 Sunniva Harte, 17t Mel Watson/ Garden Picture Library, 17b Juliette Wade; 18 John Glover, 19 Derek St. Romaine; 20 Andrew Lawson, 21 Andrew Lawson; 22 Georgia Glynn-Smith/ Garden Picture Library; 22–23 Catriona Tudor Erler, 23 Anne Hyde; 24 Jerry Harpur (Hollington Nursery, Newbury, Bucks.), 25 Clive Nichols (Designer: Sue Berger); 26t Juliette Wade (Warwick House, Hampshire), 26b Andrew Lawson, 27 Howard Rice/ Garden Picture Library; 28 Clive Nichols (Designer: Jill Billington), 29 Marianne Majerus; 30tl Derek St. Romaine, 30tr Perdereau, 30b Anne Hyde, 31t Anne Hyde, 31b Derek St. Romaine; 32 Andrea Jones/ Garden Picture Library, 32–33 Jerry Harpur (Xavier Guerrand-Hermes, Marrakech), 33 Jonathan Buckley (Rommany Road, Gypsy Hill), 34 Jerry Harpur (Designer: Jason Payne, London), 35l Jerry Harpur (Designer: Bob Flowerdew), 35r Jerry Harpur (Designer: Tim du Val, New York); 36 Mayer/ le Scanff (Garden Picture Library), 37l S. & O. Mathews, 37r Philippe Bonduel/ Garden Picture Library; 38 Liz Dobbs; 41 Liz Dobbs; 42 Clive Nichols (Clive and Jane Nichols), 42–43 Anne Hyde; 44l Jerry Harpur, 44r Perdereau (Le Clos du Coudray), 45 Marianne Majerus (Designer: Will Giles); 46t Lynne Brotchie/ Garden Picture Library, 46b S. & O. Mathews (Hillbarn House), 47 Juliette Wade (Rofford Manor, Oxon.); 48 Friedrich Strauss/ Garden Picture Library, 48–49 Clive Nichols (Designer: Anthony Noel), 49 John Glover/ Garden Picture Library; 50t Sunniva Harte, 50b Clive Nichols (Chenies Manor, Bucks), 51 Marion Nickig; 52 John Glover/ Garden Picture Library, 53 Anne Hyde; 54l Clive Nichols, 54r Mark Bolton; 55 Perdereau (Mussy sur Dun, Saone et Loire); 56 John Glover, 57t Perdereau, 57b Marcus Harpur (Park Farm, Chelmsford, Essex); 58 Howard Rice/ Garden Picture Library, 59l Andrew Lawson, 59r Andrew Lawson; 60 Jerry Harpur (House of Pitmuies, Guthrie by Forfar, Scotland), 61t Perdereau, 61b Jerry Harpur (Designer: John Plummer); 62 S. & O. Mathews, 63 John Glover (Designer: Sue Fischer); 64 Sunniva Harte (Goodman-Portland), 64–65 Andrew Lawson (Designer: Mirabel Osler), 65 Juliette Wade (Old House, Oxon.); 66 Jerry Harpur (Designer: Fiona Lawrenson), 67t Jerry Harpur (Ron Simple), 67b John Glover; 68t S. & O. Mathews, 68b Andrew Lawson (Eastgrove Cottage, Hereford), 69t Jerry Harpur (Designer: Claus Scheinert), 69b Marcus Harpur; 70 Jerry Harpur, 71t Marianne Majerus (Turn End), 71b S. & O. Mathews (Rosa Fruhlingsgold); 72 Andrew Lawson, 73t Jonathan Buckly, 73b Perdereau; 74 Catriona Tudor Erler, 75l Jerry Harpur (Designer: Simon Fraser), 75r Marianne Majerus (Designer: Jon Baillie); 76–77 Colin Philp (Design: Wood Giangrande), 77 Jerry Harpur (Designer: Colin & Jacqui Small); 78 Jonathan Buckley (Designer/owner: Bryan D'Ahlberg), 79l Perdereau, 79r Juliette Wade; 80 Andrew Lawson, 81 Derek St. Romaine; 82 Design: Wood Giangrande, 83t Jerry Harpur (Designer: Beth Chatto), 83b Jerry Harpur (Designer: Francesca Watson, Cape Town); 84 Jerry Harpur (Designer: Claus Scheinert), 84–85 Jerry Harpur (Designer: Andrew Weaving),

85c S. & O. Mathews, 85r Jerry Harpur; 86 Perdereau, 86–87 Jonathan Buckley (Forant Hut, Dorset); 87t S. & O. Mathews, 87b Gary Rogers; 88l Juliette Wade (B. Guinness), 88r Clive Nichols (Designer: Sarah Eberle, Fisher Price), 89 Juliette Wade; 90 Andrew Lawson, 91l JulietteWade, 91r Perdereau; 92 Jerry Pavia/ Garden Picture Library, 92–93 Jerry Harpur (Designer: Beth Chatto), 93 Jerry Harpur; 94 Howard Rice/ Garden Picture Library, 94–95 S. & O. Mathews (Designer: Beth Chatto), 95 Design: Wood Giangrande; 96 Michele Lamontagne/ Garden Picture Library, 97t Nicola Browne (The Garden House), 97b Jerry Harpur (Garden in the Woods, Massachusetts); 98l Jerry Harpur, 98r Marcus Harpur (Designer: Beth Chatto), 99l Mark Bolton, 99r Michele Lamontagne/ Garden Picture Library; 100 Jerry Harpur (Robert Watson, NZ), 100–101 Jerry Harpur ('Brenthurst', Johannesburg), 101 S. & O. Mathews; 102t John Glover, 102b Sunniva Harte/ Garden Picture Library, 103l Clive Nichols (The White House, Elizabeth Woodhouse), 103r Sunniva Harte (Corner Cottage); 104 Jerry Harpur (Designer: Edwina von Gal, NYC), 104–105 Nicola Browne (Designer: Naila Green), 105 Mark Bolton; 106 S. & O. Mathews, 106–107 Marianne Majerus (Designer: Martin Gibbons), 107 Catriona Tudor Erler (Freymiller Garden, Rancho Santa Fe, CA); 108t Andrew Lawson, 108b S. & O. Mathews, 109t S. & O. Mathews, 109b Perdereau; 110 Gary Rogers, 111 Geoff Dann/ Garden Picture Library, 111r Mark Bolton/ Garden Picture Library; 112t Perdereau, 112b Marijke Heuff/ Garden Picture Library, 113l Nicola Browne (Designer: Bosvigo), 113r Jerry Harpur (Clare College, Cambridge); 114t Howard Rice/ Garden Picture Library, 114b Brigitte Thomas/ Garden Picture Library, 115t Brigitte Thomas/ Garden Picture Library, 115b John Glover/ Garden Picture Library; 116t Brian Glover/ Garden Picture Library, 116b Michele Lamontagne/ Garden Picture Library, 117 John Glover/ Garden Picture Library; 118 Mayer le Scanff/ Garden Picture Library, 118t J.S. Sira/ Garden Picture Library, 119t J.S. Sira/ Garden Picture Library; 119b J.S. Sira/ Garden Picture Library; 120l Brigitte Thomas/ Garden Picture Library, 120r Jerry Harpur (Joe Eck & Wayne Winterrowd, Vermont), 121l Ron Evans/ Garden Picture Library, 121r Jerry Harpur (Terry Welch, Seattle); 122l Didier Willery/ Garden Picture Library, 122r Neil Holmes/ Garden Picture Library, 123 Anne Hyde; 124 Brigitte Thomas/ Garden Picture Library, 125 Juliette Wade/ Garden Picture Library; 126l Marianne Majerus (Designer: Penny Snell), 126r Perdereau, 127t Juliette Wade, 127b Sunniva Harte; 128t Kit Young/ Garden Picture Library, 128b Kate Zari/ Garden Picture Library, 128–129 Michele Lamontagne/ Garden Picture Library, 129 Jerry Harpur ('Boccanegra', Italy); 130 Eric Crichton/ Garden Picture Library, 131 Mayer/ le Scanff (Le Bagoi); 132 Jerry Harpur, 132–133 Andrew Lawson, 133t S. & O. Mathews, 133b Howard Rice/ Garden Picture Library; 134t Nicola Browne (Le Manoir aux Quat'Saisons), 134b John Glover; 135l Andrew Lawson, 135r Jerry Harpur; 136t S. & O. Mathews, 136b Gary Rogers, 137 Gary Rogers; 138t Mark Bolton, 138b John Glover/ Garden Picture Library, 139l Gary Rogers, 139r Gary Rogers; 140 Jonathan Buckley (Deirdre Spencer), 141 John Glover (Designer: Fiona Lawrenson), 142t Jerry Harpur (Designer: Heide Baldwin, Santa Barbara, CA), 142b Peter Anderson, 143 Anne Hyde; 144 Anne Hyde, 144–145 Perdereau, 145 Juliette Wade; 146l Clive Nichols (Designer: Lucy Gent), 146r Ron Sutherland/ Garden Picture Library, 147t Ron Sutherland/ Garden Picture Library, 147b Steven Wooster/ Garden Picture Library; 148l Ron Sutherland/ Garden Picture Library, 148r Andrew Lawson, 149 Jerry Pavia/ Garden Picture Library; 150 Sunniva

Harte, 151 Juliette Wade; 152 S. & O. Mathews, 153t Jerry Harpur (Rofford Manor, Designer: Michael Balston), 153b Liz Dobbs; 154–155 Marijke Heuff/ Garden Picture Library, 155 Ron Sutherland/ Garden Picture Library, 156t Juliette Wade/ Garden Picture Library, 156b J.S. Sira/ Garden Picture Library, 157 Perdereau; 158 S. & O. Mathews, 159l Juliette Wade (Woodpeckers, Warks.), 159r Marion Nickig; 160 Marijke Heuff/ Garden Picture Library (The Priona Gardens), 161t Juliette Wade/ Garden Picture Library, 161b Gary Rogers/ Garden Picture Library; 162 John Miller/ Garden Picture Library, 163l Juliette Wade/ Garden Picture Library, 163r Paul Windson/ Garden Picture Library, 164 Brigitte Thomas/ Garden Picture Library, 164–165 Friedrich Strauss/ Garden Picture Library, 165 Howard Rice/ Garden Picture Library; 166t Jerry Harpur (Hanging Dog Nursery, Albion Garden, CA), 166b David Askham/ Garden Picture Library, 167 Jerry Harpur (Stone House Cottage); 168t Andrew Lawson (Designer: Andy Rees), 168b Marianne Majerus, 168r Nicola Browne, 169l John Glover, 169r Marianne Majerus; 172l Jerry Harpur (Designer: Julia Scott), 172r Jerry Harpur (Designer: George Cooper), 173t Jerry Harpur (Old Rectory, Sudborough), 173b Jerry Harpur (Barnsley House, Cirencester); 174 Roger Foley (Taliafero-Cole Garden, Colonial Williamsburg), 175t Jerry Harpur (Designer: Bruce Kelly, NY), 175b Roger Foley (Blair Herb Garden, Colonial Williamsburg); 176–177 Jerry Harpur ('Chiffchaffs', Bourton, Dorset), 177t Andrew Lawson, 177b Design: Geoffrey Wood; 178 Jerry Harpur (Bob Flowerdew), 178–179 Jerry Harpur (Old Rectory, Sudborough), 179 Jerry Harpur (Barton Court); 180 Perdereau, 181t Jerry Harpur (Great Dixter, Northiam, Sussex), 181b Jerry Harpur (Savill Garden, Windsor); 182t Jerry Harpur (Designer: Oehme & van Sweden Associates, Washinton DC), 182b Marcus Harpur, 183 Roger Foley (Designer: Oehme & van Sweden Associates, Gratz Garden); 184l John Ferro Sims/ Garden Picture Library, 184r John Ferro Sims/ Garden Picture Library (La Foce, Tuscany), 185l John Ferro Sims/ Garden Picture Library (Villa Gamberaia, Tuscany), 185r Henk Dijkman/ Garden Picture Library; 186l Jerry Harpur (Ryoan-Ji Temple, Kyoto), 186r Jerry Harpur (Japanese Stroll Garden, Long Island, NY), 187l Sunniva Harte (Japanese Garden, Portland), 187r Sunniva Harte (Japanese Garden, Portland); 188l Simon Kenny/ Belle/ Arcaid (Designer: Graeme Grenlagh, Stylist: Nadine Bush), 188r Jerry Harpur (Designer: Simon Fraser), 189t Juliette Wade (Osler Road, Oxford), 189b Jerry Harpur (Designer: Tom Hobbs, Vancouver, BC); 190t John Glover (Designer: Jonathan Baillie), 190b Jerry Harpur (Designer: Jeff Mendosa, NY), 191t Jerry Harpur (Designer: Robert Watson, NZ), 191b Jerry Harpur (Sir Peter & Lady Finley, Sydney, NSW); 192 Jerry Harpur (Tom Carruth & John Furman, Altadena, CA), 193l Jerry Harpur (Thomas Church, San Francisco, CA), 193r Jerry Harpur (Tom Carruth & John Furman, LA); 195t Jerry Harpur (Keith Kirsten, Johannesburg), 195b Jerry Harpur (Bobbi Hicks, NSW), 195l Jerry Harpur (Designer: Jason Payne), 196–197 S. & O. Mathews, 198l Anthony Cooper/ A-Z Botanical Collection, 198r Houses and Interiors, 199t Harry Smith; 199b Houses & Interiors